MW01602319

# Complete Guide to the Use and Maintenance of Hand and Power Tools

**Also by the Author**

*Workbench Guide to Tape Recorder Servicing*
Parker Publishing Company, Inc. © 1977

# Complete Guide to the Use and Maintenance of Hand and Power Tools

G. Howard Poteet

Parker Publishing Company, Inc. West Nyack, New York

PARKER PUBLISHING COMPANY, INC.

West Nyack, N.Y.



**Library of Congress Cataloging in Publication Data**

Poteet, G. Howard.
Complete guide to the use and maintenance of hand and power tools.

Includes index.
1. Tools--Handbooks, manuals, etc. 2. Power tools--Handbooks, manuals, etc. I. Title.
TJ1195.P67 621.9 78-7972
ISBN 0-13-161133-X

**Printed in the United States of America**

# How This Book Will Help You

This book is for everyone who works with tools. It will show you how to skillfully select, use, and maintain any hand or power tool.

Want to get the most for your money? You'll see how you can pinpoint precisely what tools you need for the kinds of work you want to do. Then you'll find out exactly how to choose a quality tool that fits your needs. You'll learn how to tell a good tool from a shoddy one even if they both appear identical at first glance. For instance, if you need to know why one table saw is better than another, turn to Chapter Two and you'll find the nine key points to check before making your selection.

You'll see clearly, through step by step instructions, how to use any tool effectively so you can complete a job professionally. For example, want to know how to drive a nail straight—without its bending? In Chapter Five, you'll find a useful shop tip that many old-time carpenters use, but never tell anybody about! Need to turn a brass knob to replace one that has been lost? Simply follow the instructions in Chapter Three. Correct uses for all tools are so clearly described and illustrated that you can't possibly make a mistake. In addition, you'll learn how to use any tool *safely*!

In this practical book, you'll find ways to service and maintain any hand or power tool. Keep your equipment in tiptop shape by following the well organized instructions and this book will pay for itself. As an example, do you know that you can double the life of chisels simply by storing them correctly? Or that there are four ways to correct the slow and erratic motor speed of your drill press? Valuable hints, suggestions, and instructions are found on every page of this text.

Have you ever wondered just how good your skills are? Included in the book is a series of **Skillbuilders**—brief tests to show you how to equal or exceed the skill of other advanced amateurs, professionals, and experienced craftsmen in sawing, nailing, drilling, and other tasks.

Once you see how your skills compare with the skills of others, turn to the chapters dealing with specific tools to find out quickly and precisely the ways to handle unfamiliar equipment more efficiently.

You'll even find a guide that helps you select tools for your own workshop. The **Shopbuilders**—brief guides to tool selection—specify exactly which tools you should get in developing your shop, from a simple set of tools in a wooden box to a full-fledged metal-and-wood shop that can turn out projects of professional caliber. Whether you want to buy a screwdriver or a lathe, this section will give you useful and valuable advice.

Many practical charts and tables are included throughout the book. You'll find one showing you the types and sizes of nails; another lists drill bit sizes. In addition, dozens of illustrations show you the differences between types of saws and other tools, in addition to showing you exactly how to use tools effectively and safely.

This book is practical and comprehensive. It covers hand tools from hacksaws to keyhole saws, hand power tools from sabre saws to drills, and heavy equipment from lathes to radial saws. You don't need to be a mechanical engineer to understand how to use and maintain this equipment. Simply follow the directions in this book. It covers ways to work with wood and metal and shows how to select and use the best tool for the job. No other book at any price gives as complete and detailed a description of every facet of tool use.

For an example of how to use the information in this book to guide you, examine this chart. Since all power tools use the same type of electric motor, this chart is useful when something goes wrong.

### What to Do if The Motor Doesn't Work

1. If the motor doesn't start:
   a. push RESET button
   b. reset circuit breaker
   c. check fuses, plug, possible broken connections
   d. increase the size of the extension cord
   e. check line voltage
   f. adjust and lubricate bearings

   g. renew sleeves and center rotor
   h. rewind motor (or replace if too expensive)
2. If the motor overheats:
   a. reduce the load
   b. check for broken connections or short circuits
   c. replace worn bearings
   d. loosen bearings (or lubricate)
   e. tighten pulley
   f. clean dirt from motor housing and armature windings
3. If the motor vibrates too much:
   a. balance rotor
   b. replace bearing sleeve
   c. tighten bolts
   d. replace pulley
   e. replace belts
4. If the motor sparks too much when starting:
   a. clean commutator
   b. renew brushes
   c. check for shorted rotor winding
   d. lighten load
   e. check for open rotor or stator coil
   f. check for poor ground or connections.
5. If the motor sparks too much at normal speed:
   a. replace worn brushes
   b. clean or replace governing device
6. If the motor runs at excessive speed:
   a. replace or adjust governing mechanism
7. If the motor runs at too slow a speed:
   a. reduce load
   b. clean commutator
   c. replace or adjust brushes
   d. check voltage connections
   e. increase size of extension cord (wire size—not length)
8. If the motor hums but won't start:
   a. replace brushes
   b. lubricate sticking winding switch

c. lighten load
d. replace defective starting capacitor
e. replace open rotor or stator coil
f. check voltage and connections
g. check for frozen shaft

9. If the motor will not start with the rotor in a certain position:
   a. check for open rotor or stator coil
   b. check connections
10. If the motor accelerates slowly:
   a. clean commutator
   b. clean or replace brushes
   c. lighten load
   d. check voltage and connections

You'll find yourself turning to this book time and time again to find out how to shape wood more rapidly, how to sharpen your metal files more easily, and how to use your circular saw more safely. You'll learn new uses for tools you already own and find out how to select and use new tools as you expand your workshop. This book will show you how to get the most out of every tool that you use.

**G. Howard Poteet**

# Contents

**Chapter 10 - Sprayers and Other Painting Tools (cont.)**

## Chapter 12 - Making Your Workshop Safe (cont.)

# List of Illustrations

| Figure | | Page |
|---|---|---|

| Figure | | Page |
|---|---|---|

| Figure | | Page |
|---|---|---|

# Complete Guide to the Use and Maintenance of Hand and Power Tools

# 1

# Ways to Use Rules and Other Measuring Devices

## Part A: Woodworking

Success in completing any woodworking project depends upon accuracy in measurement, which in turn depends upon the quality of your instruments and your skills in using them.

### How to Use Rulers, Sticks and Tape

You will measure many projects with only a ruler or a tape. Rulers vary from 6″ to 12″ and yardsticks, of course, measure 36″ or 3′. Gradations range from the longest lines which mark inches, to the next longest marks for half-inches, to marks for quarter-inches and sometimes eighths-of-an-inch. Some rules even indicate $^{1}/_{16}$″, $^{1}/_{32}$″, and $^{1}/_{64}$″.

Longer rulers are folding or are made of metal or cloth tape. Folding rulers usually range from 2′ to 6′ in length, but are not highly accurate. Steel tapes, made with a curved midsection for rigidity, are fairly accurate although they sag when extended over a long distance and must be supported by other means. (Figures 1.1, 1.2, and 1.3)

To obtain the best results in measuring with a ruler, use the thinnest ruler you can find or hold the ruler on its edge against the surface being measured. By thus eliminating parallax (an inaccuracy caused by a change in the angle of view), you will obtain a more accurate reading.

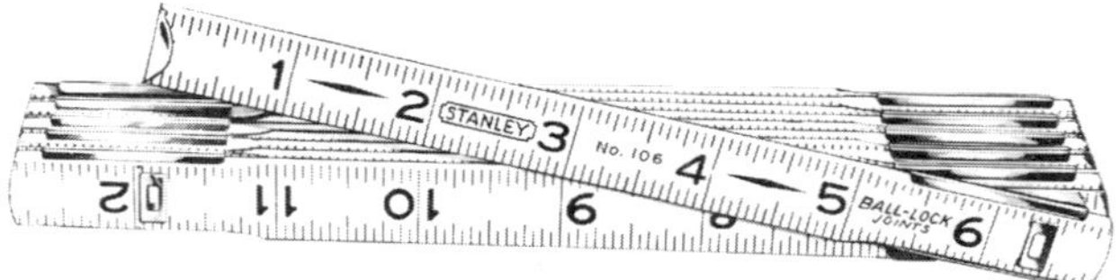


1.1 A Folding Rule
Courtesy: Stanley Tools

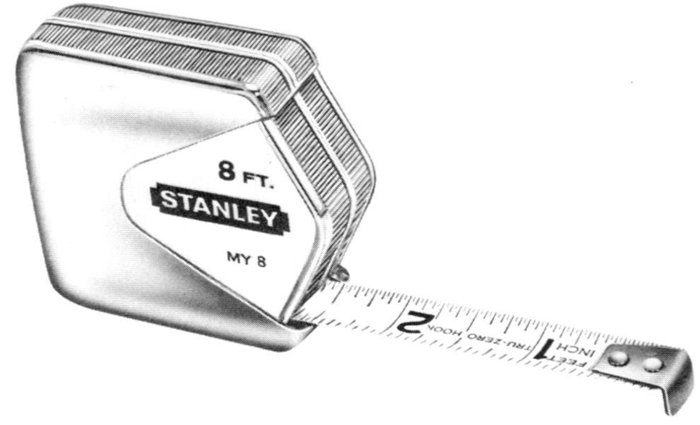


1.2 A Handy 8′ Tape
Courtesy: Stanley Tools

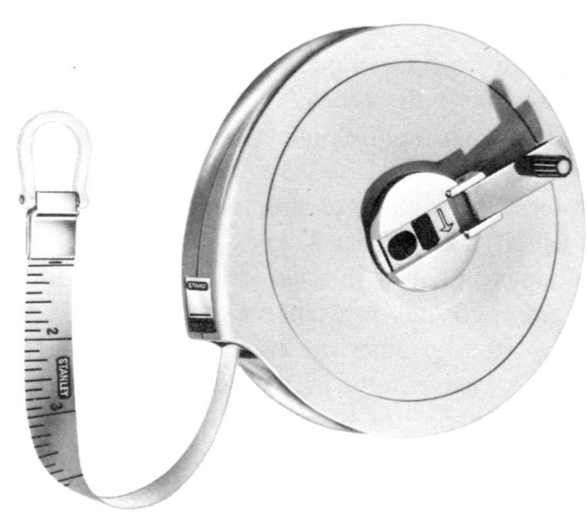


1.3 A 50′ Tape
Courtesy: Stanley Tools

Measuring with a tape may require an assistant. Note that a hook or eye at the end of the tape is almost always part of the first measured inch. Some tapes include a measurement on the tape holder so that you can make inside as well as outside measurements of boxes and similar objects. Measure large objects with rulers and tapes. (Figures 1.4, 1.5, and 1.6)

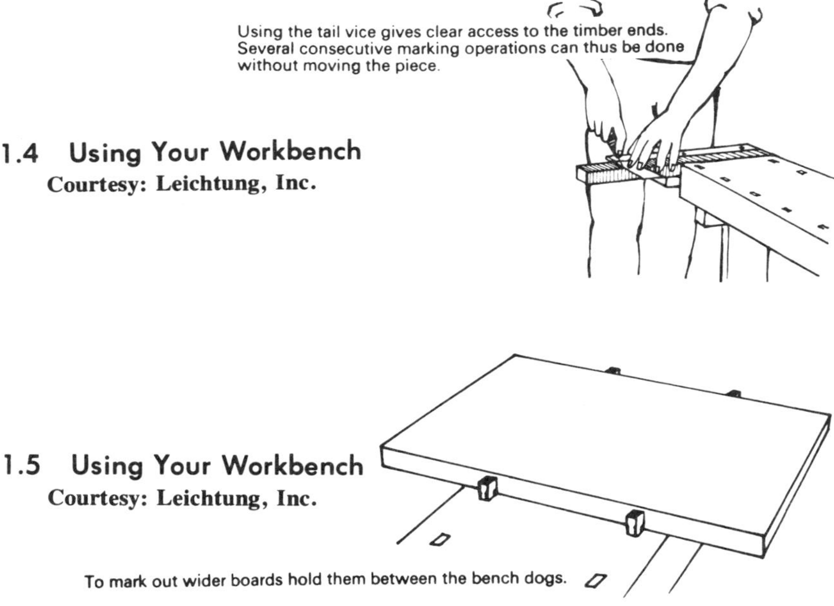


**1.4 Using Your Workbench**
**Courtesy: Leichtung, Inc.**

**1.5 Using Your Workbench**
**Courtesy: Leichtung, Inc.**

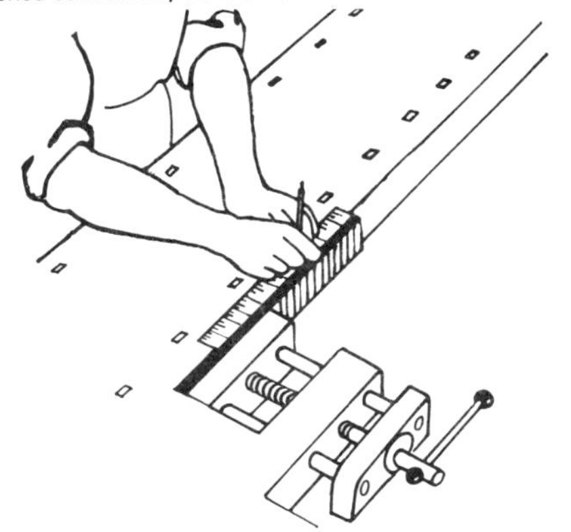


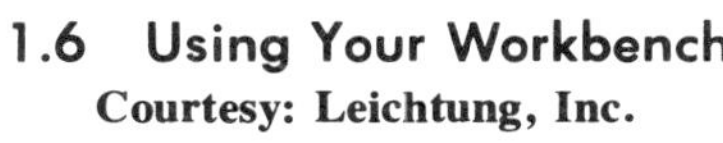

**1.6 Using Your Workbench**
**Courtesy: Leichtung, Inc.**

## Levels, Squares, and Protractors and Their Use

**Levels** are used to find out whether or not surfaces are true. A glass tube is used, partly filled with alcohol or chloroform and mounted in a metal or wooden frame. Leveling is achieved when this bubble is centered between the lines on the tool. Always watch the bubble in the bottom glass vial if there is a vertical or horizontal pair. Shim up or move the object until the bubble appears in the exact center of the glass tube. (Figures 1.7 and 1.8)

**1.7 A Level**
**Courtesy: Stanley Tools**

**1.8 Leveling Accurately**
**Courtesy: Stanley Tools**

Adjustments can be made on many levels by turning them end for end on a known true surface to see if the bubbles match positions. Usually, an adjustment can be made by loosening a screw and moving the bubble holders slightly. This seldom needs to be done unless the level has been roughly treated or dropped. On rare occasions, you may need to replace a broken bubble vial. This is done in the same manner.

For highly accurate work, precision levels are calibrated so that you can read minutes and degrees for adjustments in differences between surfaces. In the average workshop, however, such accuracy is seldom needed.

**Steel squares** are generally used for making sure that surfaces are at right angles to each other. These squares range in size from 8″ by 12″ to 18″ by 24″ and are used by placing them against a surface to see if space exists between the square and the surface of the work. If you shine a light behind them, it makes the job of seeing the difference much easier.

A **try square** usually has a wooden handle and a metal blade on which inches and fractions of an inch are marked. It is used to mark and check lines and surfaces which must be at right angles to each other. (Figure 1.9)

A **sliding bevel T-square** is a try square that is adjustable for laying out angles other than right angles. It may be set by checking it against a protractor or drafting triangle or by placing it against intersecting lines on a square. It is frequently used to check the angle of a chamfer or bevel by placing it against the surface of the project and moving it along that surface. (Figure 1.10)

**1.9 A Try Square**
**Courtesy: Stanley Tools**

**1.10 A Sliding Bevel T-Square**
**Courtesy: Stanley Tools**

1.11 A Combination Square
Courtesy: Stanley Tools

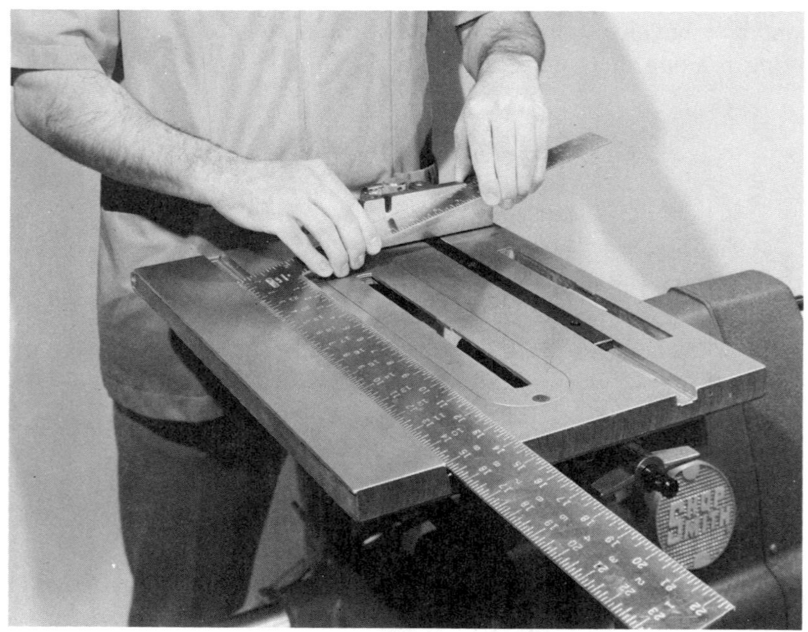

1.12 A Framing Square in Use

A **combination square** has three movable heads: the center head, the protractor head and a square head. The square head may be adjusted to any position along the square to serve as a depth or height gauge or a scribing gauge. A spirit level in the head can be checked to see if surfaces are level. The center head, a V-shaped object, slides along the blade with the center of the "V" at the top edge of the blade. This function makes it useful in finding the exact center of dowels and similar objects. The protractor head, or bevel protractor (as it is sometimes called), can be attached to the scale and locked at any angle. (Figure 1.11)

### Your Framing Square and How to Get the Most Out of It

Your carpenter's **framing square** can be used for more than just finding out if a project is shaped squarely. Tables on the square show lots of information. A rafter table shows correct proportions for different sized rafters. An essex table gives the board feet of different lengths of 1″ boards. The octagon table shows the necessary measurements to lay out an eight-sided figure. The brace table shows the required length of braces and the hundredths table indicates decimal divisions of an inch. (Figure 1.12)

### Plumb Bobs, Chalk Lines, and Other Assorted Measuring Devices and Methods of Using Them Effectively

A **plumb bob** is a pointed weight (from 6 to 24 ounces) suspended from a cord to determine a vertical line. Most plumb bobs have detachable tips so that a damaged one can be replaced—otherwise, the instrument is inaccurate. Use a plumb bob whenever you are erecting a vertical upright by attaching it above the object that you need to check. Wait until the bob stops moving and then sight at a distance at eye level.

**Chalk lines** are used to make straight lines over long distances (6′ and more). Coat the line with chalk—usually available in a light blue colored half-sphere for easy handling. Hold the chalk in one hand and pull the cord over it with the other. Then, attach one end of the cord to a nail or similar object, and stretch the cord tight, holding it to the second point by hand.

When the cord is stretched taut, snap it against the surface as if you were plucking a bow string. The chalk will transfer to the surface in a sharp, clean line.

Although metric units are not yet in widespread use, they are becoming more and more common. In time, fractional measurements will be replaced by metric measurements. The chart in Figure 1.13

may be used to convert measurements in fractions into their metric equivalents and vice versa.

| INCHES | | MM |
|---|---|---|
| FRACT. | DECIMALS | |
| | .00004 | .001 |
| | .00039 | .01 |
| | .00079 | .02 |
| | .001 | .025 |
| | .00118 | .03 |
| | .00157 | .04 |
| | .00197 | .05 |
| | .002 | .051 |
| | .00236 | .06 |
| | .00276 | .07 |
| | .003 | .0762 |
| | .00315 | .08 |
| | .00354 | .09 |
| | .00394 | .1 |
| | .004 | .1016 |
| | .005 | .1270 |
| | .006 | .1524 |
| | .007 | .1778 |
| | .00787 | .2 |
| | .008 | .2032 |
| | .009 | .2286 |
| | .00984 | .25 |
| | .01 | .254 |
| | .01181 | .3 |
| 1/64 | .01563 | .3969 |
| | .01575 | .4 |
| | .01969 | .5 |
| | .02 | .508 |
| | .02362 | .6 |
| | .025 | .635 |
| | .02756 | .7 |
| | .0295 | .75 |
| | .03 | .762 |
| 1/32 | .03125 | .7938 |
| | .0315 | .8 |
| | .03543 | .9 |
| | .03937 | 1 |
| | .04 | 1.016 |
| 3/64 | .04687 | 1.191 |
| | .04724 | 1.2 |
| | .05 | 1.27 |
| | .05512 | 1.4 |
| | .05906 | 1.5 |
| | .06 | 1.524 |
| 1/16 | .06250 | 1.5875 |
| | .06299 | 1.6 |
| | .06693 | 1.7 |
| | .07 | 1.778 |
| | .07087 | 1.8 |
| | .075 | 1.905 |
| 5/64 | .07813 | 1.9844 |
| | .07874 | 2 |
| | .08 | 2.032 |
| | .08661 | 2.2 |
| | .09 | 2.286 |
| | .09055 | 2.3 |
| 3/32 | .09375 | 2.3812 |
| | .09843 | 2.5 |
| | .1 | 2.54 |
| | .10236 | 2.6 |
| 7/64 | .10937 | 2.7781 |
| | .11811 | 3 |
| 1/8 | .1250 | 3.175 |

| INCHES | | MM |
|---|---|---|
| FRACT. | DECIMALS | |
| | .13780 | 3.5 |
| 9/64 | .14063 | 3.5719 |
| | .150 | 3.810 |
| 5/32 | .15625 | 3.9688 |
| | .15748 | 4 |
| 11/64 | .17188 | 4.3656 |
| | .1750 | 4.445 |
| | .17717 | 4.5 |
| 3/16 | .18750 | 4.7625 |
| | .19685 | 5 |
| | .20 | 5.08 |
| 13/64 | .20313 | 5.1594 |
| | .21654 | 5.5 |
| 7.32 | .21875 | 5.5562 |
| | .2250 | 5.715 |
| 15/64 | .23438 | 5.9531 |
| | .23622 | 6 |
| 1/4 | .250 | 6.35 |
| | .25591 | 6.5 |
| 17/64 | .26563 | 6.7469 |
| | .275 | 6.985 |
| | .27559 | 7 |
| 9/32 | .28125 | 7.1438 |
| | .29528 | 7.5 |
| 19/64 | .29688 | 7.5406 |
| | .30 | 7.62 |
| 5/16 | .3125 | 7.9375 |
| | .31496 | 8 |
| 21/64 | .32813 | 8.3344 |
| | .33465 | 8.5 |
| 11/32 | .34375 | 8.7312 |
| | .350 | 8.89 |
| | .35433 | 9 |
| 23/64 | .35938 | 9.1281 |
| | .37402 | 9.5 |
| 3/8 | .375 | 9.525 |
| 25/64 | .39063 | 9.9219 |
| | .39370 | 10 |
| | .400 | 10.16 |
| 13/32 | .40625 | 10.3188 |
| | .41339 | 10.5 |
| 27/64 | .42188 | 10.7156 |
| | .43307 | 11 |
| 7/16 | .43750 | 11.1125 |
| | .450 | 11.430 |
| | .45276 | 11.5 |
| 29/64 | .45313 | 11.5094 |
| 15/32 | .46875 | 11.9062 |
| | .47244 | 12 |
| 31/64 | .48438 | 12.3031 |
| | .49213 | 12.5 |
| 1/2 | .50 | 12.7 |
| | .51181 | 13 |
| 33/64 | .51563 | 13.0969 |
| 17/32 | .53125 | 13.4938 |
| | .53150 | 13.5 |
| 35/64 | .54688 | 13.8906 |
| | .550 | 13.970 |
| | .55118 | 14 |
| 9/16 | .56250 | 14.2875 |
| | .57087 | 14.5 |
| 37/64 | .57813 | 14.6844 |
| | .59055 | 15 |

| INCHES | | MM |
|---|---|---|
| FRACT. | DECIMALS | |
| 19/32 | .59375 | 15.0812 |
| | .600 | 15.24 |
| 39/64 | .60938 | 15.4781 |
| | .61024 | 15.5 |
| 5/8 | .6250 | 15.875 |
| | .62992 | 16 |
| 41/64 | .64063 | 16.2719 |
| | .64961 | 16.5 |
| | .650 | 16.51 |
| 21/32 | .65625 | 16.6688 |
| | .66929 | 17 |
| 43/64 | .67188 | 17.0656 |
| 11/16 | .68750 | 17.4625 |
| | .68898 | 17.5 |
| | .700 | 17.78 |
| 45/64 | .70313 | 17.8594 |
| | .70866 | 18 |
| 23/32 | .71875 | 18.2562 |
| | .72835 | 18.5 |
| 47/64 | .73438 | 18.6531 |
| | .74803 | 19 |
| 3/4 | .750 | 19.050 |
| 49/64 | .76563 | 19.4469 |
| | .76772 | 19.5 |
| 25/32 | .78125 | 19.8438 |
| | .78740 | 20 |
| 51/64 | .79688 | 20.2406 |
| | .800 | 20.320 |
| | .80709 | 20.5 |
| 13/16 | .81250 | 20.6375 |
| | .82677 | 21 |
| 53/64 | .82813 | 21.0344 |
| 27/32 | .84375 | 21.4312 |
| | .84646 | 21.5 |
| | .850 | 21.590 |
| 55/64 | .85938 | 21.8281 |
| | .86614 | 22 |
| 7/8 | .875 | 22.225 |
| | .88583 | 22.5 |
| 57/64 | .89063 | 22.6219 |
| | .900 | 22.860 |
| | .90551 | 23 |
| 29/32 | .90625 | 23.0188 |
| 59/64 | .92188 | 23.4156 |
| | .92520 | 23.5 |
| 15/16 | .93750 | 23.8125 |
| | .94488 | 24 |
| | .950 | 24.130 |
| 61/64 | .95313 | 24.2094 |
| | .96457 | 24.5 |
| 31/32 | .96875 | 24.6062 |
| | .98425 | 25 |
| 63/64 | .98438 | 25.0031 |
| 1 | 1.00000 | 25.4 |
| | 1.06299 | 27 |
| | 1.10240 | 28 |
| | 1.18110 | 30 |
| 1 ¼ | 1.250 | 31.75 |
| | 1.29921 | 33 |
| | 1.3780 | 35 |
| | 1.41732 | 36 |
| 1 ½ | 1.500 | 38.1 |
| | 1.53543 | 39 |

| INCHES | | MM |
|---|---|---|
| FRACT. | DECIMALS | |
| | 1.57480 | 40 |
| | 1.65354 | 42 |
| 1 ¾ | 1.750 | 44.45 |
| | 1.77170 | 45 |
| | 1.88976 | 48 |
| | 1.96850 | 50 |
| 2 | 2.000 | 50.8 |
| | 2.04724 | 52 |
| | 2.16540 | 55 |
| | 2.20472 | 56 |
| 2 ¼ | 2.250 | 57.15 |
| | 2.36220 | 60 |
| 2 ½ | 2.500 | 63.5 |
| | 2.51968 | 64 |
| 2 ¾ | 2.750 | 69.85 |
| | 2.83464 | 72 |
| | 2.95280 | 75 |
| 3 | 3.000 | 76.2 |
| | 3.14960 | 80 |
| 3 ½ | 3.500 | 88.9 |
| | 3.54330 | 90 |
| | 3.9370 | 100 |
| 4 | 4.000 | 101.6 |
| | 4.33070 | 110 |
| 4 ½ | 4.500 | 114.3 |
| | 4.72440 | 120 |
| 5 | 5.000 | 127 |
| | 5.51180 | 140 |
| | 5.90550 | 150 |
| 6 | 6.000 | 152.4 |
| | 6.29920 | 160 |
| | 7.08660 | 180 |
| | 7.8740 | 200 |
| 8 | 8.000 | 203.2 |
| | 8.66140 | 220 |
| | 9.44880 | 240 |
| | 9.84250 | 250 |
| 10 | 10.000 | 254 |
| | 10.23620 | 260 |
| | 11.02360 | 280 |
| | 11.8110 | 300 |
| 1 Foot | 12.000 | 304.8 |
| | 12.59840 | 320 |
| | 13.38580 | 340 |
| | 13.77950 | 350 |
| | 14.17320 | 360 |
| | 14.96060 | 380 |
| | 15.7480 | 400 |
| 16 | 16.000 | 406.4 |
| | 17.71650 | 450 |
| | 19.6850 | 500 |
| 20 | 20.000 | 508 |
| | 23.6220 | 600 |
| 2 Feet | 24.000 | 609.6 |
| 3 Feet | 36.000 | 914.4 |
| | 39.370 | 1 Meter |
| 4 Feet | 48.000 | 1.219.2 |
| 5 Feet | 60.000 | 1.524 |
| 6 Feet | 72.000 | 1.828.8 |
| | 78.740 | 2 Meters |
| 8 Feet | 96.000 | 2.438.4 |
| | 118.110 | 3 Meters |
| | 196.850 | 5 Meters |

**1.13 Fractions, Decimals and Millimeters: A Chart**

**Courtesy: Garrett Wade**

# Part B: Metalworking

In addition to using the preceding instruments in measuring metal, you will want to use the precise instruments called calipers and micrometers. While these devices are sometimes used in woodworking, their main use is in the metal shop where very close tolerances or measurements are more important.

### Calipers and Ways to Use Them Correctly

Precise measurements on small objects are made with calipers. They are adjusted by pushing or pulling the legs of the instrument open or closed. Fine adjustments are made by tapping the legs open or the joint holding them closed. Outside calipers have legs which are curved inwards; inside calipers have legs which are curved outwards. (Figure 1.14)

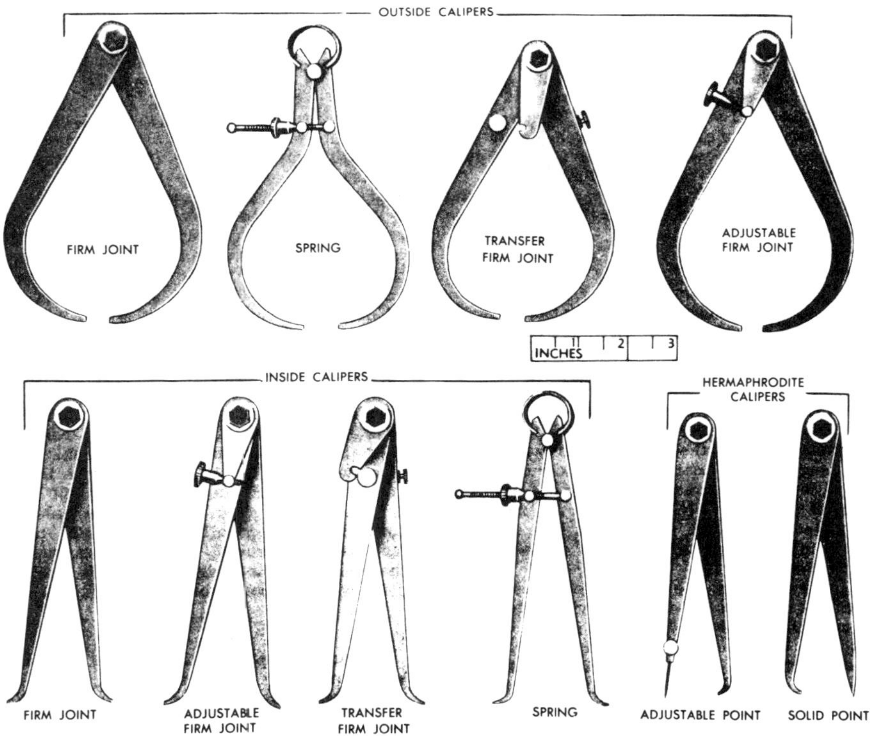


1.14 Types of Calipers

There are a variety of types. **Spring-jointed calipers** are adjusted with a screw instead of pushing and pulling. **Odd-leg calipers** or **hermaphrodite calipers** combine an inside leg and an outside leg and are used to locate such things as the center of a shaft. **Transfer calipers** are used to measure grooves. **Slide calipers** or **caliper squares** use a ruler or scale which slides inside an object and gives direct readings of caliper settings—an impossibility with other types of calipers.

A **Vernier caliper** consists of an L-shaped member which slides with a scale and a sliding jaw. This caliper gives the most accurate measurement of all calipers. It can be used for internal and external measurements. However, you must know how to read the Vernier scale, and that is explained below.

For simple, yet accurate measurements, set the legs wider than the work and adjust to coincide with the inside or outside dimensions of the project. Then, transfer this dimension to a scale or machine the work until it matches. Obviously, do not attempt to make measurements on work which is moving in a lathe or other device; it's far too dangerous.

Use these simple methods to make measurements with the selected types of calipers:

1. *To measure the outside surface*, adjust the legs until you feel a slight drag.

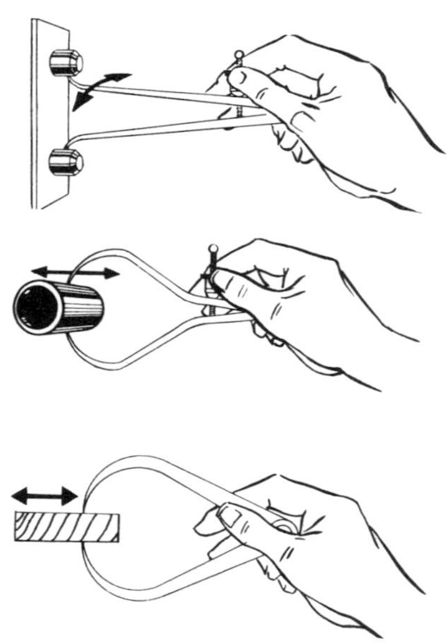

**1.15 Measuring With Calipers**

2. *To measure the distance between two surfaces*, touch one leg to one surface, increase the setting and move the leg until you feel a slight drag which indicates that the leg is touching the other surface.

3. *To measure the diameter of a hole*, touch one leg against the side of the hole and move the other leg in and out of the hole while adjusting it until you feel it touch firmly against the other side.

4. *To measure hard-to-reach spots*, use a transfer firm joint caliper to obtain the right feel and then lock the joint. Loosen the binding joint nut, open the caliper, remove it and tighten the binding nut which will return the caliper to its original setting. (Figure 1.15)

Maintenance of your calipers is simple. Do not use these measuring tools for any purpose except that for which they are intended. Keep them clean and free from rust, but avoid oiling them. Otherwise, you will find it difficult to keep them tight enough at the joints to make accurate measurements.

### Precise Measurements with Micrometers and How to Make Them

**Micrometers** are called mikes by most craftsmen and are used to make precise measurements to one thousandth of an inch, written as the decimal *.001*. There are three basic types: the outside micrometer caliper, the inside micrometer and the depth micrometer.

There is a bit of a trick to reading a micrometer, but you will easily master it. The size of a micrometer indicates the largest size it will measure; however, it only measures a distance within one inch smaller than that size. That is, a 2″ micrometer will only measure between 1″ and 2″.

To make a measurement, first find a size that will roughly fit the object you wish to measure. Then, notice that there are two scales: a sleeve scale and a thimble scale (Figures 1.16 and 1.17). When you turn the spindle, you move .025″ or 1/40″. Thus, the one inch line on the sleeve is marked or divided into forty parts. Every fourth mark is numbered 1, 2, 3, 4 and so on. When the spindle stops between these graduated lines, you use the scale on the thimble which is divided into 25 equal parts for each turn. Every fifth line on this thimble scale is marked 5, 10, 15 and so on. Count these units on the thimble scale and add them to the reading on the sleeve scale.

Thus, to find a reading to three decimal places—which is the most common reading—follow these steps:

1. Read the sleeve scale by noting the number and adding 25 for each full line after it.

2. To measure in between these lines, add the number on the thimble to it.

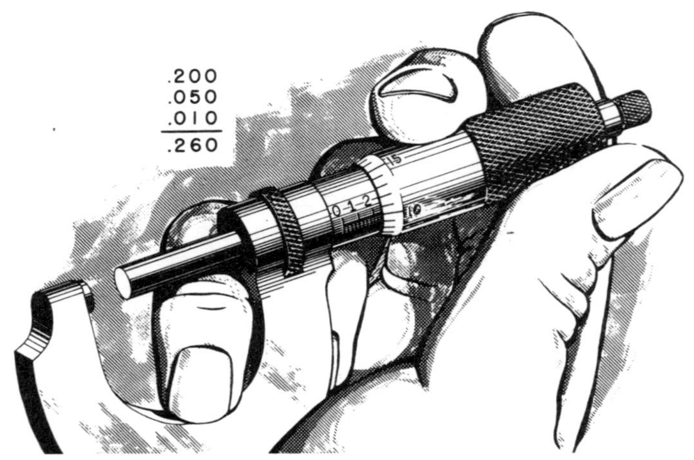


1.16 Reading a Micrometer Caliper

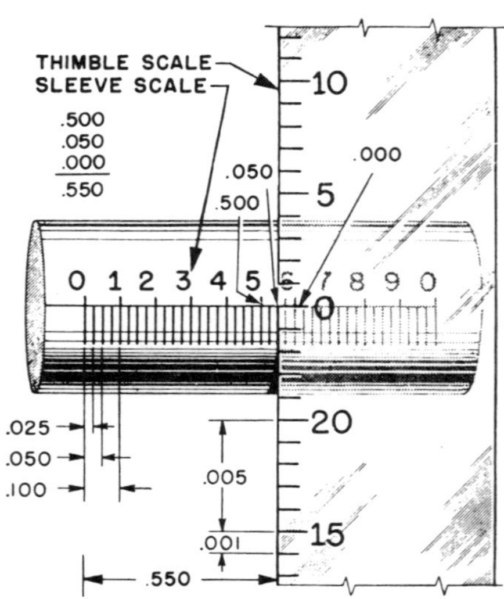


1.17 Enlarged Sleeve and Thimble Scales

If you wish to measure to four decimal places, estimate the distance in tenths between the gradations on the thimble scale. Each gradation equals one ten-thousandth of an inch (.0001).

To be even more accurate, a Vernier scale will measure to one ten-thousandth of an inch so that you do not need to guess. Look for the Vernier scale line which matches or coincides with a line on the thimble scale and read that number.

Inside micrometer calipers are read the same way, except that the figures are in *reverse*. This is because you are moving the micrometer in the opposite direction when you find an inside measurement. (Figure 1.18)

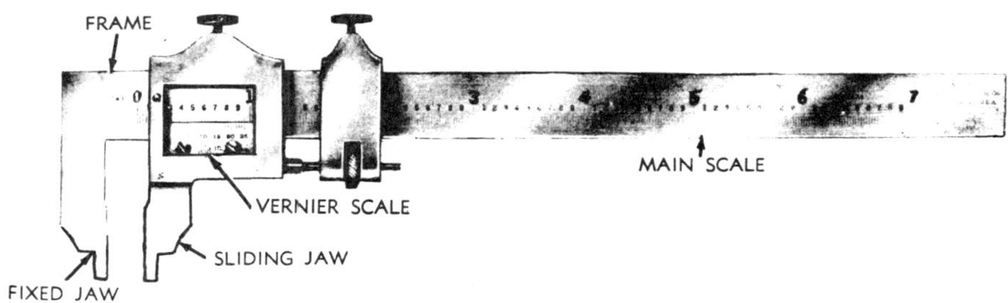


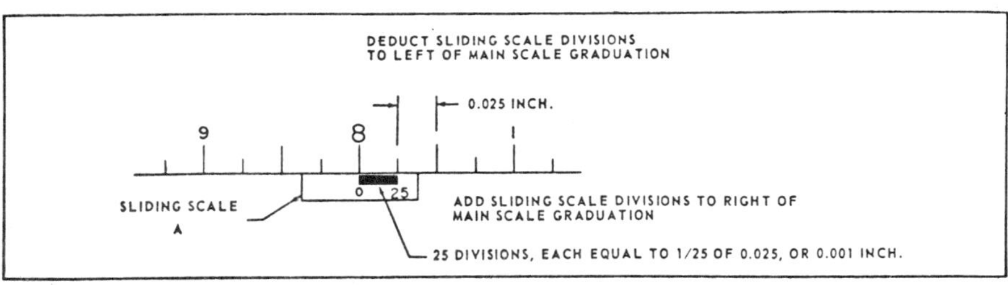


**1.18 A Vernier Caliper**

## Ways to Use Marking Gauges and Bevel Gauges

Gauges are measuring devices that are useful in many situations. A **surface gauge** is used to scribe lines as a means of transferring measurements from one surface to another. A scriber is attached to a spindle ranging from 4″ to 18″ long which, in turn, is mounted on a base. This spindle is adjustable and the scriber is adjustable on the spindle.

To use the surface gauge, set it on a level surface and adjust the spindle and the scriber to get the scriber point at the precise point you wish. You must make any measurements with a square, in order to ensure accuracy.

A **surface plate** provides a true plane surface. It is usually a steel plate, ribbed on one side and reinforced on the reverse. Test the surface by moving the surface plate over it to see if there is any unevenness which will be indicated by the feel; the plate will rock or move unevenly. If your work requires great precision, coat the surface of the plate with bearing blue or Prussian Blue (available at most hardware stores). Move the plate across the surface of the project and the high points will be colored blue; low points will not.

Most of the time you will find that a straight edge will give you an adequate measurement. Hold the straight edge on the surface and sight at eye level to see if there is any space between it and the surface. If necessary, you can measure this difference with a feeler gauge (a device with a combination of blades of different measured thickness).

**Thread gauges** are useful in finding out the number of threads and the pitch of any screw, bolt or nut. Although most craftsmen seldom have use for this device, it looks and measures like a feeler gauge except that its blades are serrated. The size is marked on each blade. To use it, insert the serrated blades one by one into the threads that you are measuring until you find a perfect fit.

**Wire gauges** are used to measure the diameter of wires. Insert wire into a hole that fits snugly and read the size off the gauge. The larger the gauge number, the smaller the diameter of the wire. (Figure 1.19)

**Telescoping gauges** measure the inside diameter of holes. Sets range from 5/16″ to ½″ and 3½″ to 6″. Grasp this T-shaped tool by the shaft, and compress the crossarms so that they telescope into each other. Insert the gauge into a hole, allow the arms to expand and tighten the locknut on the handle to lock them in place. Then, withdraw and measure.

**Small hole gauges** measuring distances of ⅛″ to ½″ are usually found in sets of four with handles having a split ball mounted on the end. Insert this into the hole and, by turning the handle, expand the gauge until you get a snug fit. Withdraw and measure. An even simpler method, although not as accurate, is to roll a ball of putty or clay and insert it into the hole until it takes the same shape and size of the hole. Remove and measure.

**Marking gauges**, made of wood or metal, have a movable head on a beam that you can tighten with a thumbscrew at any point. The beam has a pin which sticks out 1/16″ and does the marking. Measure separately. Do not use the measurements on the gauge itself; they are usually inaccurate. Tighten the head and, keeping it against the edge of the project, move it along so that the scribing point scratches or cuts a line.

Dividers or compasses are used to transfer measurements and to scribe circles. Place one leg of the divider at the center of the circle and adjust the other leg to the outside edge of the desired circle. Twirl the leg around by rotating the handle between your thumb and forefinger.

| Gage No. | Birmingham wire gage (B.W.G.) or Stubs iron wire gage, for iron wires, hot and cold rolled sheet steel | American wire gage, or Brown & Sharpe (for non-ferrous sheet and wire) | U.S. Standard gage for sheet and plate iron and steel | Steel wire gage, or the W & M (Washburn & Moen) for steel wire |
|---|---|---|---|---|
| 0 | .340 | .3249 | .3125 | .3065 |
| 1 | .300 | .2893 | .2812 | .2830 |
| 2 | .284 | .2576 | .2656 | .2625 |
| 3 | .259 | .2294 | .2500 | .2437 |
| 4 | .238 | .2043 | .2343 | .2253 |
| 5 | .220 | .1819 | .2187 | .2070 |
| 6 | .203 | .1620 | .2031 | .1920 |
| 7 | .180 | .1443 | .1876 | .1770 |
| 8 | .165 | .1285 | .1718 | .1620 |
| 9 | .148 | .1144 | .1562 | .1483 |
| 10 | .134 | .1019 | .1406 | .1350 |
| 11 | .120 | .0907 | .1250 | .1205 |
| 12 | .109 | .0808 | .1093 | .1055 |
| 13 | .095 | .0719 | .0937 | .0915 |
| 14 | .083 | .0640 | .0781 | .0800 |
| 15 | .072 | .0570 | .0703 | .0720 |
| 16 | .065 | .0508 | .0625 | .0625 |
| 17 | .058 | .0452 | .0562 | .0540 |
| 18 | .049 | .0403 | .0500 | .0475 |
| 19 | .042 | .0359 | .0437 | .0410 |
| 20 | .035 | .0319 | .0375 | .0348 |
| 21 | .032 | .0284 | .0343 | .0317 |
| 22 | .028 | .0253 | .0312 | .0286 |
| 23 | .025 | .0225 | .0281 | .0258 |
| 24 | .022 | .0201 | .0250 | .0230 |
| 25 | .020 | .0179 | .0218 | .0204 |
| 26 | .018 | .0159 | .0187 | .0181 |
| 27 | .016 | .0142 | .0171 | .0173 |
| 28 | .014 | .0126 | .0156 | .0162 |
| 29 | .013 | .0112 | .0140 | .0150 |
| 30 | .012 | .0100 | .0125 | .0140 |
| 31 | .010 | .0089 | .0109 | .0132 |
| 32 | .009 | .0079 | .0101 | .0128 |
| 33 | .008 | .0071 | .0093 | .0118 |
| 34 | .007 | .0063 | .0085 | .0104 |
| 35 | .005 | .0056 | .0078 | .0095 |
| 36 | .004 | .0050 | .0070 | .0090 |

**1.19 Gauges of Wire and Sheet Metal**

## SHOPBUILDER #1

Selections of woodworking measuring tools—(Choose according to your needs/Build your shop step-by-step)

BASIC TOOLS: (All fractional *and* metric measurements)

a. 12″ ruler
b. 36″ yardstick
c. steel or mylar power tape reel
d. 9″ level

AMATEUR TOOLS: (Include tool list above)

e. folding wood extension rule (6′ or 2 meters)
f. 50′ reel tape
g. 48″ extruded magnesium level
h. steel rafter square (24″ x 16½″)
i. try square (8″)

ADVANCED AMATEUR TOOLS: (Include tool lists above)

j. combination square
k. pocket level
l. drill gauge
m. protractor

PROFESSIONAL: (Include tool lists above)

n. double point scriber
o. marking gauge
p. plumb bob

PROFESSIONAL CRAFTSMAN: (Include tool lists above)

q. non-calibrated transfer calipers (outside)
r. non-calibrated transfer calipers (inside)
s. sliding T-bevel square
t. screw pitch gauge

## SKILLBUILDER #1

**Use these tests to determine the level of your skill: MICROMETER READING**

| | |
|---|---|
| **ADVANCED AMATEUR:** | Read a micrometer caliper accurately graduated in thousandths-of-an-inch in one minute without referring to the text. (You may use paper for figuring if needed.) |
| **PROFESSIONAL:**<br>*Do the above plus* | Read a micrometer caliper accurately graduated in ten-thousandths-of-an-inch in 45 seconds without referring to the text and without figuring on paper. |
| **SKILLED CRAFTSMAN:**<br>*Do the above plus* | Read a Vernier micrometer caliper accurately graduated in two-thousandths of a millimeter in 30 seconds without referring to the text or figuring on paper. |

# 2

# Using Saws and Other Cutting Tools

## Part A: Woodworking

After measurements are made, the next important step in any project is in cutting the material to proper shape and size. Usually this is done with some type of saw.

### Why Different Saws Are Needed for Various Materials

A saw is simply a steel blade with teeth. It has a handle and a toe or point which is the part of the blade at the opposite end from the handle. The part nearest the handle is called the heel. Teeth run along the edge of the blade and are alternately bent to cut grooves or a kerf.

The number of teeth per inch, the shape and size of the teeth, and the amount of set or bending vary according to the use for which the saw is intended. This is measured by points—the number of teeth per inch plus one. This number is usually stamped near the handle.

There are two basic types of saws: the **crosscut** and **ripsaw.** Crosscut saws are used for cutting across the grain. The teeth are shaped like the point of a dagger—sharp on both sides. Ripsaws, with points sharpened on one side (like a chisel), cut with the grain. (Figure 2.1)

### Selecting the Right Saw for the Right Type of Cut

There are special types of crosscut saws that you will use a great deal in woodworking. A **backsaw** is a special type of crosscut saw which is used in making picture frames and similar work where a straight angle cut is necessary. A smaller or thinner version of the backsaw is a **dovetail saw**. A **coping saw** is a thin-bladed saw in a holder that permits it to cut back upon itself. (Figures 2.2 and 2.3)

A specialized version of the ripsaw is the **compass saw** or keyhole saw which has a long, narrowing blade. Usually, you bore a hole large enough to insert the saw before beginning to cut. (Figure 2.4)

**2.1 A Ripsaw**
**Courtesy: Stanley Tools**

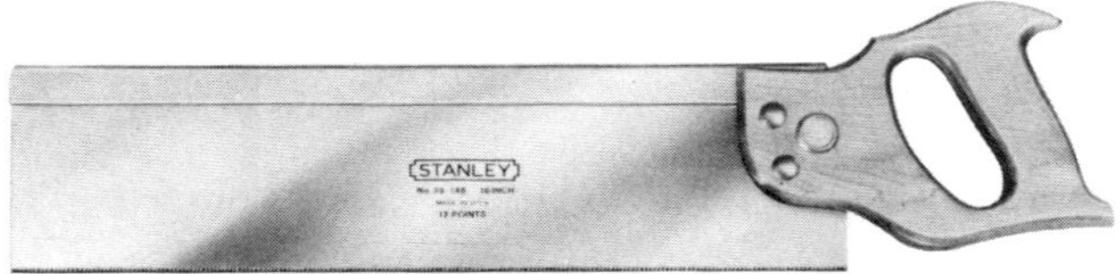


**2.2 A Backsaw**
**Courtesy: Stanley Tools**

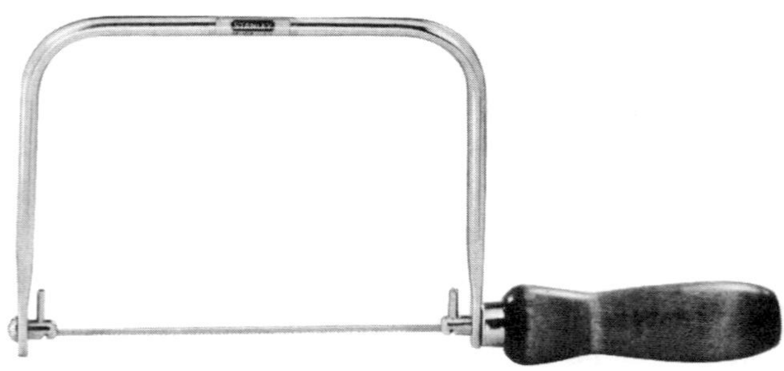

**2.3 A Coping Saw**
**Courtesy: Stanley Tools**

**2.4 A Compass Saw**
**Courtesy: Stanley Tools**

## Ways to Cut Material Safely

Use a crosscut saw to cut across the grain of a piece of wood by placing the board on a sawhorse. Holding the saw in your right hand, extend your forefinger along the edge of the handle. Grasp the board with your left hand so that you can guide the middle of the saw blade

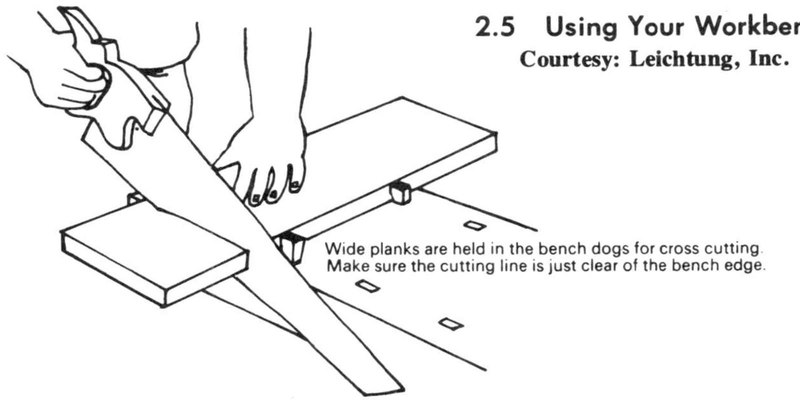


**2.5 Using Your Workbench**
**Courtesy: Leichtung, Inc.**

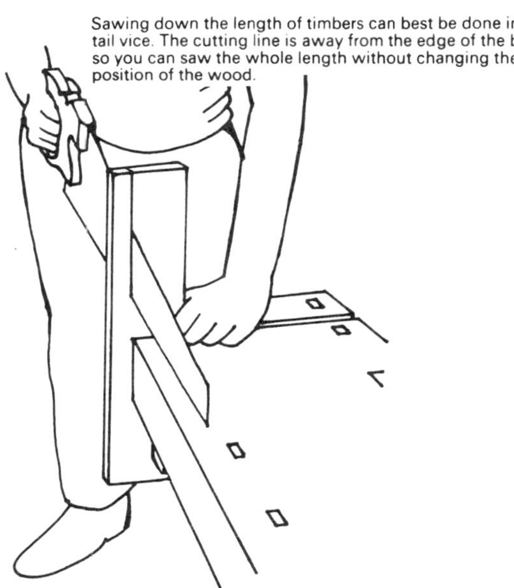


**2.6 Using Your Workbench**
**Courtesy: Leichtung, Inc.**

with your thumb (being careful to avoid the teeth). Place the heel of the saw on the mark, making sure that the saw is at a 45 degree angle to the surface of the wood and that it is at right angles with the board. Then, pull toward you to make the cut. Take short strokes and then increase their length. Keep your arm at your side, not out in front of you as you make the strokes. Move your left hand farther away after the saw is started. Watch the line and at the end of the cut, move slowly. Stop sawing before you've cut all the way through and reverse the board, sawing from the opposite direction until the two cuts meet. For safety's sake in cutting small pieces of wood, use a vise. (Figures 2.5 and 2.6)

### How to Sharpen Your Handsaws

It is best to have your handsaws sharpened by someone specializing in it. However, you can do the job yourself with a few specialized tools.

There are three steps to sharpening any saw:

1. *Jointing*. This step is not always needed. If the teeth are misshapen, use a saw jointer. Open it, slip it over the blade and run it back and forth over the teeth so that the high teeth are cut down to the size of the others.

2. *Setting*. Bend the teeth alternately so that grooves are cut wider than the width of the saw blade. This does not have to be done every time the saw is sharpened. Adjust the saw set to the number of teeth per inch and squeeze or hit with a mallet according to the model. The distance the teeth are set is usually one-half their height and one-half their thickness. (Figure 2.7)

3. *Sharpening*. After the teeth are set sharpen them with a file, holding the saw in a vise or with a filing clamp. Keep the handle to the

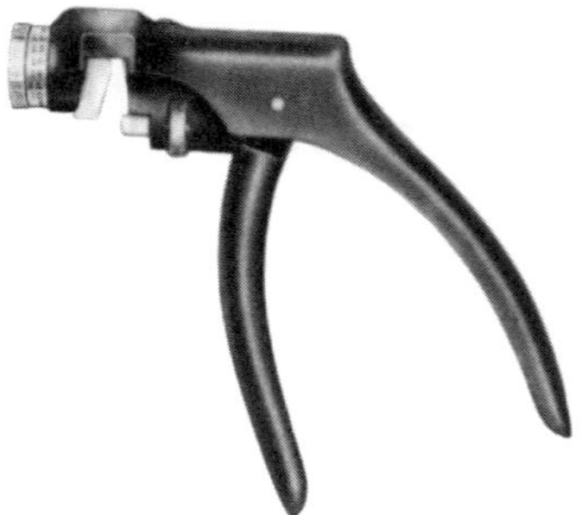

**2.7 A Saw Set**
**Courtesy: Leichtung, Inc.**

right. Using one or two forward strokes, hold the file at a 90 degree angle to the blade for ripsaws and a 45 degree angle to the blade for crosscut saws. File the teeth facing you and then reverse the saw and file the other teeth. Lay the saw flat and touch the file gently to both sides of the teeth to remove burrs.

When you've finished, you can expect the saw to be sharp for about 40 hours of sawing.

## How to Select Any Portable Power Tool (drill, circular saw, sander, sabre saw)

| General Features | Yes or No? (Two *No* answers mean the tool is unacceptable) |
|---|---|
| Is the motor large enough to drive the tool safely and efficiently? (1/3 hp is usually the minimum) | |
| Does the tool require variable drive speeds to work safely and efficiently? Does the tool supply them? | |
| Can accessories be obtained easily? Is it simple to install them? Are additional tools needed to do so? | |
| Is the tool well-constructed? (Is it rustproofed? Lubricated for life?) Is it made by a well-known manufacturer? | |

| | |
|---|---|
| Are the controls clearly labeled and readily accessible? | |
| Does the tool seem safe? Is it double insulated or grounded by a three-wire cord? | |
| Is the tool complete or must you purchase additional accessories to be able to put it to use? | |
| Is its capacity sufficient for your use? (Will it cut thick pieces or wood, bore holes large enough or sand large surfaces quickly and efficiently?) | |
| Is it easy to get service or replacement parts? (Does it take standard sized blades?) | |
| Can you do accurate work with the tool? (Are scales, markings and similar gauges accurate?) | |

### Portable Power Saws and How to Use Them

Portable power saws consist of saws which use a circular blade and those which use a straight blade.

**Circular saws** are motor driven tools which can range in size from 1/6 hp and a 4″ blade up to 1½ hp and a 14″ blade and larger. Hand power saws are run by pressing a trigger in the handle of the saw. Choose a saw with a motor rating of at least 1 hp and a minimum blade diameter of 6½″.

For crosscutting, draw a line and align with it the guide mark on the front of the blade. Start the saw and make the cut as explained below. For ripsawing, most saws have a rip guide which can be adjusted to guide the saw straight.

Check your circular saw carefully before pressing the start button. Rest the front shoe on the project. Press the trigger firmly but smoothly. Squeeze, don't pull. Let the blade reach full speed before starting your cut. Avoid forcing the saw; let it do its own work. If it should stall, release the trigger and pull the saw back an inch or so. Restart the saw and let the blade reach full speed. Then continue cutting.

Keep the weight of the saw on the stationary portion of the work. If you place the work *between* sawhorses, for example, the weight will bind the blade. For best and safest efforts, use C-clamps to keep the wood rigid. Furthermore, if you use wedges to keep the saw cut open when you are ripping a long piece of wood, you will avoid binding the blade.

Adjust your saw for different depths of cutting only with the saw *unplugged*. Loosen the wing nut at the rear of the sawdust chute at the back of the shoe. Pull the base plate down until the blade protrudes sufficiently. Usually, the top edge of the blade should be no more than ¼" to ½" above the top of the wood. Be sure that the wing nut is tightened by hand.

Bevel cuts may be made by loosening the wing nut at the *front* of the shoe and tilting the saw to the desired angle. Do this only after you have unplugged the saw. Then, retighten the wing nut as tight as you can by hand. Do not attempt to use pliers or other tools to tighten it further.

To change blades, place a large bolt or rod (a 20 penny nail is fine) through the teeth of the blade underneath the shoe to keep the blade from moving. Use a wrench to turn the hex bolt holding the blade in a *counterclockwise* direction. Remove the old blade and insert the new one. Be sure that the teeth are pointed in the correct direction. The correct rotation is usually marked on the blade itself. The teeth should point upwards toward the front of the saw when you are looking at it from the top. Keeping the blade from moving, tighten.

The safety clutch can be adjusted, but again, be certain that the saw is unplugged. This clutch permits the blade to slip if it begins to bind in the cut. If, however, the blade slips while normal cutting is taking place, you can tighten the bolt slightly. Beware that tightening the bolt too much will stop the clutch action altogether. For proper adjustment, assemble the blade flange, the blade, the "D" washer, the star spring and the bolt—in that order—and then tighten the bolt by hand until the parts are firm. Then, holding the blade by hand, give the bolt a ¼ turn with the wrench. This is usually adequate to maintain good clutch action.

Be certain that the saw is unplugged whenever you work on any part of it. Some workers keep the plug in their left hand as they work on the saw. It may get in the way sometimes, but the minor inconvenience is nothing compared to the peace of mind you'll have knowing that the saw was not accidentally connected to a power source by someone else.

Maintenance consists mainly of keeping the saw as clean as possible. Sawdust may cause the lower guard to bind if it is not kept clean and the motor may overheat if the inlet and outlet air passages become clogged. Brush or blow them out with the saw—as always—*unplugged*. Get in the habit of never putting the saw away without cleaning it and it will last much longer.

The **sabre saw** is a power driven jigsaw which lets you cut straight and curved lines in wood and metal. It is a lightweight machine which is not intended for fast cutting. Select a model with a motor rating of at least ⅓ hp. (Figure 2.8)

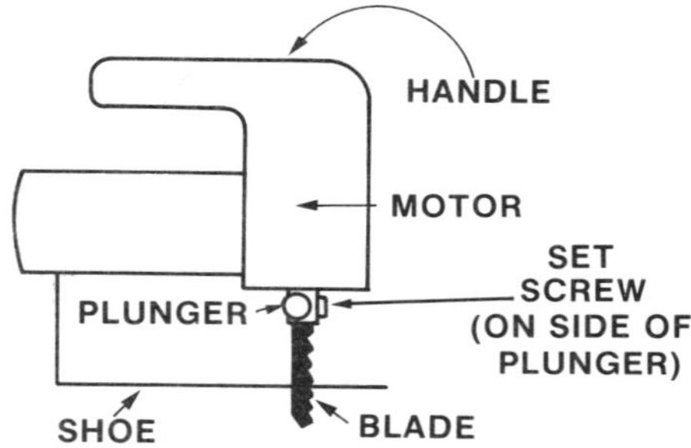


**2.8 A Sabre Saw**

For most cutting, grasp the handle firmly, placing the front shoe on the edge of the work while lining up the blade with the line you wish to cut. Turn the switch on, let the blade run for a second or two and then slowly but firmly guide the tool into the material. Most workers press down securely on the handle to keep the saw from vibrating and wandering off track. Do not, however, force the tool.

To make straight long cuts, use the rip guide attachment (if the width of the material permits) or attach a board with C-clamps to guide the shoe. Do not remove the saw from the cut without shutting off the motor.

Another method of cutting with the sabre saw is called the **plunge cut**. Although it is safer to drill a hole first and then insert the saw (to cut through walls, for example), it is possible to cut into a wall by grasping the saw handle with the front of the saw facing you. In this method, tilt the back of the saw into the air away from you. Hold the saw firmly and turn on the power. Tilt the back of the saw downward until the blade touches the point where you wish the cut to begin. Continue tilting the saw downward until the blade cuts through. Obviously, you need to watch for wiring and pipes concealed in the wall. (Figure 2.9)

**2.9 Plunge Cutting**
**Courtesy: Remington Arms Co., Inc.**

To make **bevel cuts**, first unplug the saw. Then loosen the pivot screw which is locked in a slot the shape of an arc. Adjust the shoe to the desired angle which is usually marked in degrees stamped above the slot. Tighten firmly by hand and then plug in the saw for use.

There are numerous blades which you can use in your sabre saw ranging from woodcutting blades made of high carbon steel, to metal blades of high speed steel, to tungsten carbide blades which will cut through ceramic tile, plastic laminates, slate flooring, quarry tile flooring and asbestos cement. Blades are available in the form of a knife blade, a scroll cutter shaped like a saw-edged drill bit, and a rasp and file.

All sabre saws use standard ¼″ shank blades. To install any blade, first be sure the saw is unplugged. Then, loosen the set screw or screws on each side of the plunger until they clear the blade slot. Next, insert the blade as far as it will go, keeping the blade teeth facing downwards and to the front of the saw. If there are two screws, tighten one until it touches the blade and then tighten the other securely. If there is only one screw, tighten it. You should check these screws periodically to see that they are secure.

A **reciprocal saw** looks like a heavy-duty sabre saw with the blade sticking out in front instead of under the housing. It is used to cut everything from 6″ fence posts to the thinnest plastic sheets. You will find it useful in cutting large cables, pipes and metals of all sorts. With carbide-tipped blades you can even cut bricks. Apply candle wax lightly to your blades to improve them. (Figure 2.10)

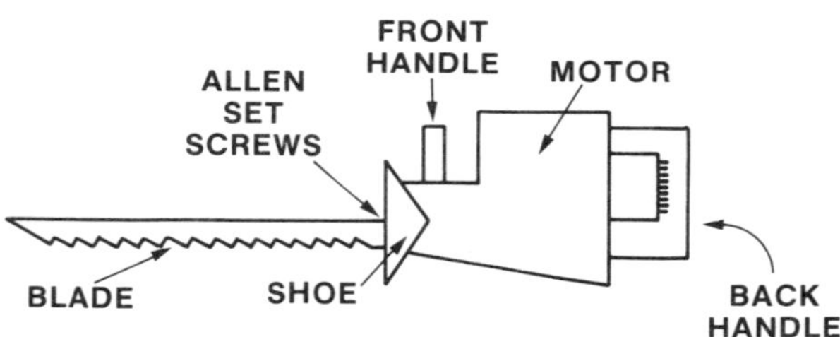


**2.10 A Reciprocal Saw**

For most cutting, leave the shoe in the 90 degree position and hold it against the work firmly. To avoid vibration, clamp the work down with C-clamps. For example, thin metal must be clamped between sheets of plywood or the vibration will make it almost impossible to cut. For **perpendicular flush cutting**, hold the saw upright with the shoe flush against the wall or similar object. For **parallel flush cutting** (cutting from left to right flush with the bottom of the tool), you will have to use a separate blade which is designed to fit at right angles to the standard blade. On some models, the guide plate must be removed and turned over with the open end facing the bottom of the saw in order to receive this type of blade. To insert, you must remove the standard blade and then insert the new blade directing the teeth to the right or left of the saw instead of facing down. Insert the special flathead screw through the large hole in the blade and tighten. Note that these special blades are installed on the side of the plunger.

Regular blades with a ¼″ or ½″ shank are inserted by first loosening the two Allen set screws until both clear the blade slots. Be sure the saw is unplugged after running briefly to put the screws in a spot where you can reach them. Insert the blade as far as it goes with the teeth facing any direction you wish. Tighten the screw bearing on the *edge* of the blade until it touches the blade. Next, tighten the other screw bearing on the *side* of the blade. Then tighten the first screw bearing on the edge of the blade.

For bevel cutting loosen the screws in the slotted arcs on the side of the shoe (making sure that the saw is unplugged first), and adjust the shoe to the desired angle and retighten. On models that have an adjustable shoe, you can loosen these same screws and reposition the shoe, thereby exposing an unused section of the blade to achieve maximum life. Be sure to retighten securely. Do not, however, position the shoe at an extreme 45 degree angle or the blade will cut into the saw.

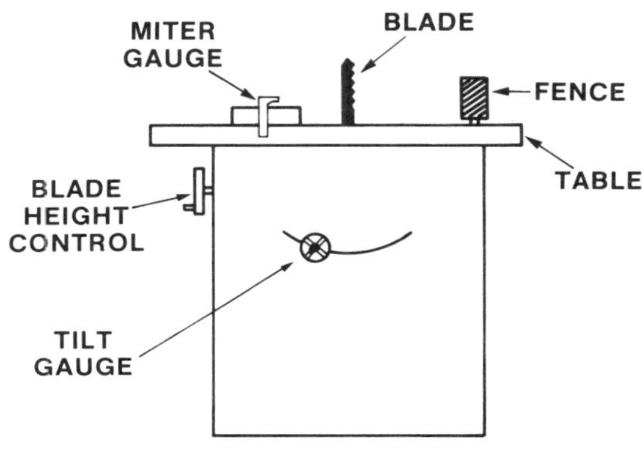


2.11 A Circular Saw

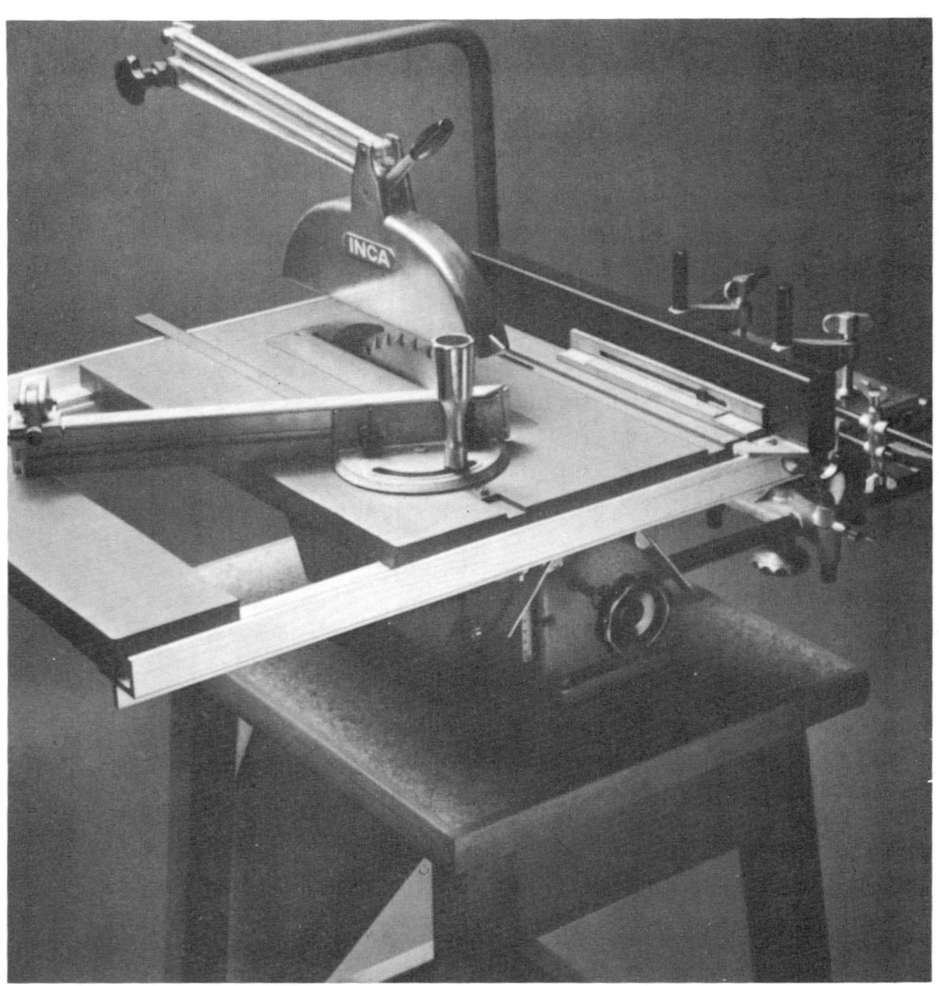


2.12 A Cabinetmaker's Saw
Courtesy: Garrett Wade

Plunge cutting is a useful method for cutting into a wall without first boring a hole and then inserting the saw. Grasp the handle with the saw facing the work and then tilt the front of the saw downwards. Start the saw, placing the front edge of the shoe on the work and resting the heel of the shoe on a wood block nailed to the work. Continue tilting the saw downwards until the blade cuts through. Beware of concealed wiring or pipes if you are cutting through a wall. Furthermore, since there is a risk of breaking the saw blade, this procedure is best limited to work not thicker than ⅝″. (Figures 2.11 and 2.12)

## How to Select Your Table Saw

| General Features | Yes or No? (Two *No* answers mean the tool is unacceptable |
|---|---|
| Is there sufficient power? (At least ½ hp) | |
| Is the blade large enough? (At least 8″) | |
| What is the depth of cut? (3″ is the minimum) | |
| What is the maximum distance from the blade to the fence? (36″ is needed) | |
| What is the distance from the front of the table to the blade? (5″ is good) Are extensions available? | |
| Is the table large enough? (8″ sq. is the minimum) Extensions available? | |

| | |
|---|---|
| Does the blade or the table tilt (preferably the blade) 0–45 degrees? | |
| Is the fence square and self-locking? | |
| Is there a miter gauge included? (Accurate adjustment from 0–60 degrees?) | |

## How to Service and Repair Your Circular Table Saw

1. If the speed seems slow and erratic:
   a. check to see if the pulley is loose (tighten)
   b. see if saw blade is attached correctly
   c. clean and lubricate motor (replace brushes if needed)
   d. check to see if speed indicator is operable (if applicable)
2. If the saw blade is out of alignment:
   a. adjust and correct with normal procedures (move tilt gauge)
   b. inspect the arbor supports and trunnions (part on which it pivots) for wear or damage (repair or replace)*
   c. check blade for damage
3. If the table is out of line:
   a. adjust and correct by moving the tilt gauge
   b. inspect trunnions and repair or replace*
   c. regrind table*
4. If the tilt gauge controls stick:
   a. clean and lubricate
   b. check for damage and replace (if parts are available)*

---

*means this operation is very expensive

5. **If the blade vibrates:**
   a. **tighten blade and other components**
   b. **examine for loose spindle and worn bearings (replace if available)***
6. **If the saw is noisy:**
   a. **tighten blade and other components**
   b. **lubricate sparingly (use #10 machine oil)**
   c. **check for loose or damaged bearings**

### Using Table Saws, Jigsaws, and Bandsaws

Use your table saw for accurate cuts of wood projects of all kinds. Before switching on the motor, examine the blade to see that the teeth are facing towards you and that the arbor nut (which holds the blade onto the arbor) is tight. Make sure that the blade is set at the correct angle and that the saw guards are in position.

Adjust the blade, if necessary, so that it will be no more than ¼″ to ½″ higher than the wood you are sawing. Set the fence to within ⅛″ of the correct distance by hand, then adjust to precisely the point you wish and lock it into place.

Turn the saw on and let it run for 5 seconds or more to reach its optimum speed. With your hands, hold the work on the miter gauge so that one hand is on the gauge, guiding it, and the other is pressing the miter gauge forward. Keep your body out of the line of the saw. Do not put your hands on the wood or get them close to the saw blade. Do not force the wood into the blade; let the blade do the work. When the cut is complete, return the work and the miter gauge back to the starting point. Turn the switch off and only after the motor has stopped, remove the wood. (Figure 2.13)

Make miter cuts by adjusting the miter gauge to the required angle. The blade will make the wood creep or move, so grip the wood and gauge tightly, keeping your fingers well away from the blade. Make the cut as described above.

Rip cuts are made without the miter gauge. Feed the work through after adjusting the fence to the required distance. Use a stick to push the work through with one hand while holding the work down with the other—well out of the way of the saw blade. If the work is very long

---

*means this operation is very expensive

(more than 3′), arrange a support or holder for it as it emerges from the blade.

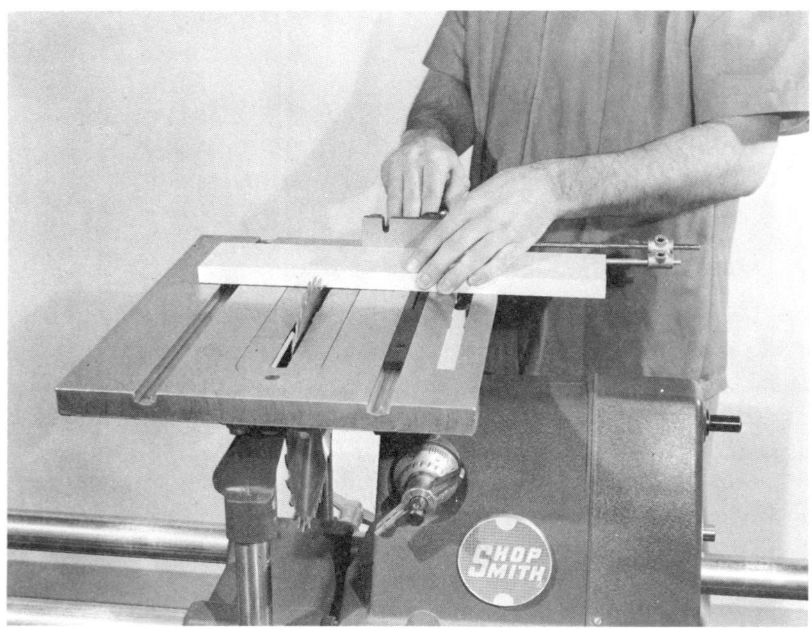


2.13 Using the Miter Gauge (Guards removed for photo)
Courtesy: Shopsmith

Angle cuts and bevel cuts require tilting the blade (or the table on some models) to the correct angle. Usually this is done by turning a knob or loosening and fastening a lever. Adjust the table so that the blade is always in the center of the slot. For safety's sake, never make these adjustments while the saw is running. Then, run the wood through in the same manner as described above. (Figure 2.14)

**Radial saws** differ in that the saw is suspended above the wood and you pull the saw towards you, through the wood, rather than pushing the wood past the blade.

Radial saws range in size from 10″ to 12″ and larger, and usually have a 2 hp rating (although they may range upwards to 10 hp). In addition to crosscutting, ripping, beveling and mitering, they also can be used with attachments to rout, drum sand, plane, dado, mold and shape. In this sense, they are multipurpose tools. This chapter, how-

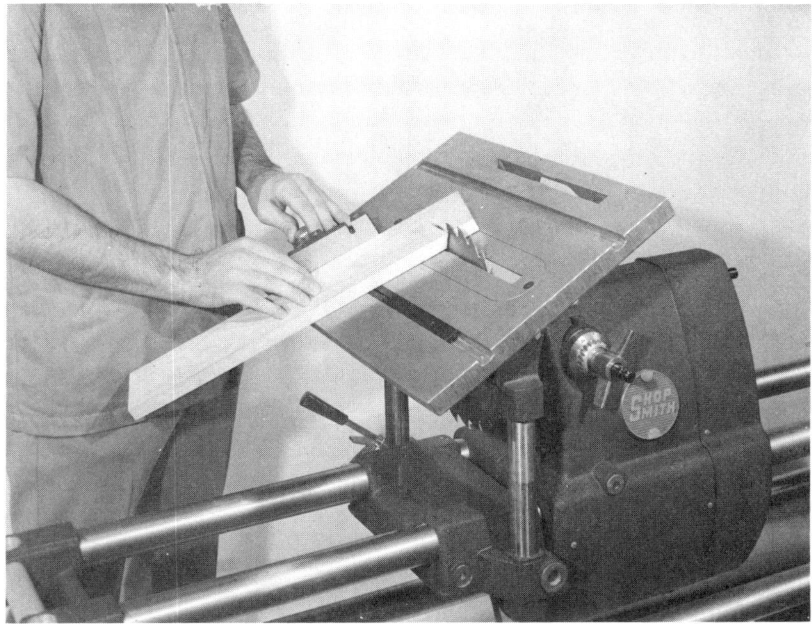


**2.14 Cutting a Compound Angle (Guards removed for photo)**
**Courtesy: Shopsmith**

ever, is only concerned with their most common use—as a saw.

To use the radial saw, adjust the depth of cut (maximum is usually 3″ at 90 degrees and 2¼″ at 45 degrees). Place the work in position on table. Turn the switch on and pull the saw towards you with one hand, keeping the wood steady with the other—out of reach of the blade. When you finish the cut, let the blade carrier return to its original position and shut the blade off. Wait until the saw blade stops moving before removing the wood. You will find that the radial saw is a safe and efficient way to crosscut up to 15″. Quality saws have an anti-kickback pawl to protect the operator.

There are limitations in ripping a long piece of plywood, but the blade can be revolved 360 degrees which will permit you to cut almost any kind of board you wish. With a radial saw you can make crosscuts, rip cuts, miter cuts and bevel cuts as well as combinations.

A **jigsaw** or scroll saw is a thin-bladed saw that can cut patterns in soft wood (up to 1½″ thick), hard wood (up to ¾″ thick) and acrylics, thin metal and other materials (leather, for instance). These saws operate at speeds of 3500 strokes a minute and more. The key measurement is throat depth; many machines will cut to the middle of a 28″ circle and some will cut to the center of a 36″ circle or more. (Figures 2.15 and 2.16)

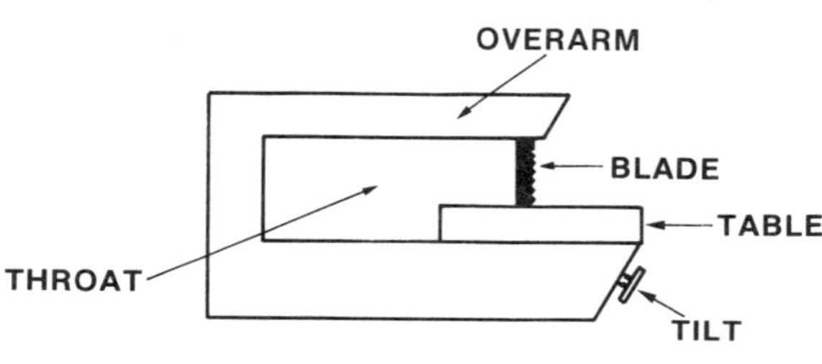


**2.15 A Jigsaw**

Although there is usually a variety of blades available, many inexpensive machines use one alloy steel blade for all materials. Most jigsaws take plain end blades 6″ long (shorter blades are made by snapping off the end), although some use pin-type blades ranging from 3″ to 6″. The more teeth per inch, the finer the cut; teeth range from 15 per inch (for fast cutting) to 25 per inch. Generally, better results are obtained by cutting metal with the blades having fewer teeth.

To use, turn the jigsaw on and let it run for 3 to 5 seconds to reach maximum speed. Start the work through slowly, letting the saw do the work. The guard holds the work down but you will need to guide it. You can make sharp turns left or right to make curves. The saw will cut very intricate scroll work and because the blade moves so fast, little sanding or other finishing is usually needed. When you complete sawing, remove the work before turning the saw off.

Although there are still some motor-driven hand-held coping saws or scroll saws on the market, they have been all but replaced by units which stand on a workbench top taking up only about 2 sq.′ of room. The reason for this is that much better control is obtained through the use of a stationary saw.

2.16 A Homemade Miter Gauge

## How to Select Your Jigsaw or Bandsaw

| General Features | Yes or No? (Two *No* answers mean the tool is is unacceptable) |
|---|---|
| Is there sufficient power? (At least ⅓ hp for the jigsaw and ½ hp for the bandsaw) | |

| | |
|---|---|
| Is the blade large enough? (Check for the work you want to do—6″ thick wood for bandsaw, 1¾″ thick wood for jigsaw) | |
| Are standard sized blades available? | |
| What is the maximum distance from the blade to the fence? (6″ for bandsaw, 4″ for jigsaw) | |
| What is the distance from the front of the table to the blade? (5″ is adequate) | |
| Is the table large enough? (8″ square is the minimum) | |
| Does the blade or table tilt? (0–45 degrees?) | |
| Is the fence square and self-locking? | |
| Is the miter gauge included? | |

## How to Service and Repair Your Jigsaw

1. If the speed is slow or erratic:
   a. clean the motor and replace the brushes

   b. check and replace drive belts (if needed)
   c. examine, clean, and lubricate the drive shaft and pulleys
2. If the blade guides are damaged or worn:
   a. straighten and clean
   b. replace (if parts are still available)
3. If the upper and lower blade shafts wobble:
   a. tighten blade tension lock
   b. replace worn bushings (if available)
   c. replace worn castings (if available)*
4. If the driveshaft is loose or wobbles:
   a. tighten
   b. replace worn bearings or bushings
   c. replace worn castings*
5. If the blade is out of alignment (vertically):
   a. adjust the overarm
   b. bend or replace damaged frame*
6. If table is damaged or out of square:
   a. locate and tighten loosened parts
   b. file the surface of the table trunnion (part on which it pivots)
   c. replace the table (if available)*

### Using Your Bandsaw

The **bandsaw** is very similar in its application to the jigsaw, except that it cuts much thicker wood. It operates on a different principle: a band of steel with teeth on one edge rotates on two wheels, almost like a large version of a belt sander. The blade is narrow—ranging from ⅛″ to ½″. (Figure 2.17)

A bandsaw can be used to cut compound shapes, intricate designs and bevel curves. In addition, it can be adapted to carve compound shapes, make spiral cuts and cut narrow kerfs or grooves so that the wood can be bent. With a speed reducing attachment, it will cut metal as well as wood. Use a ½″ sanding belt and you can sand any surface.

---

*means that this operation is very expensive

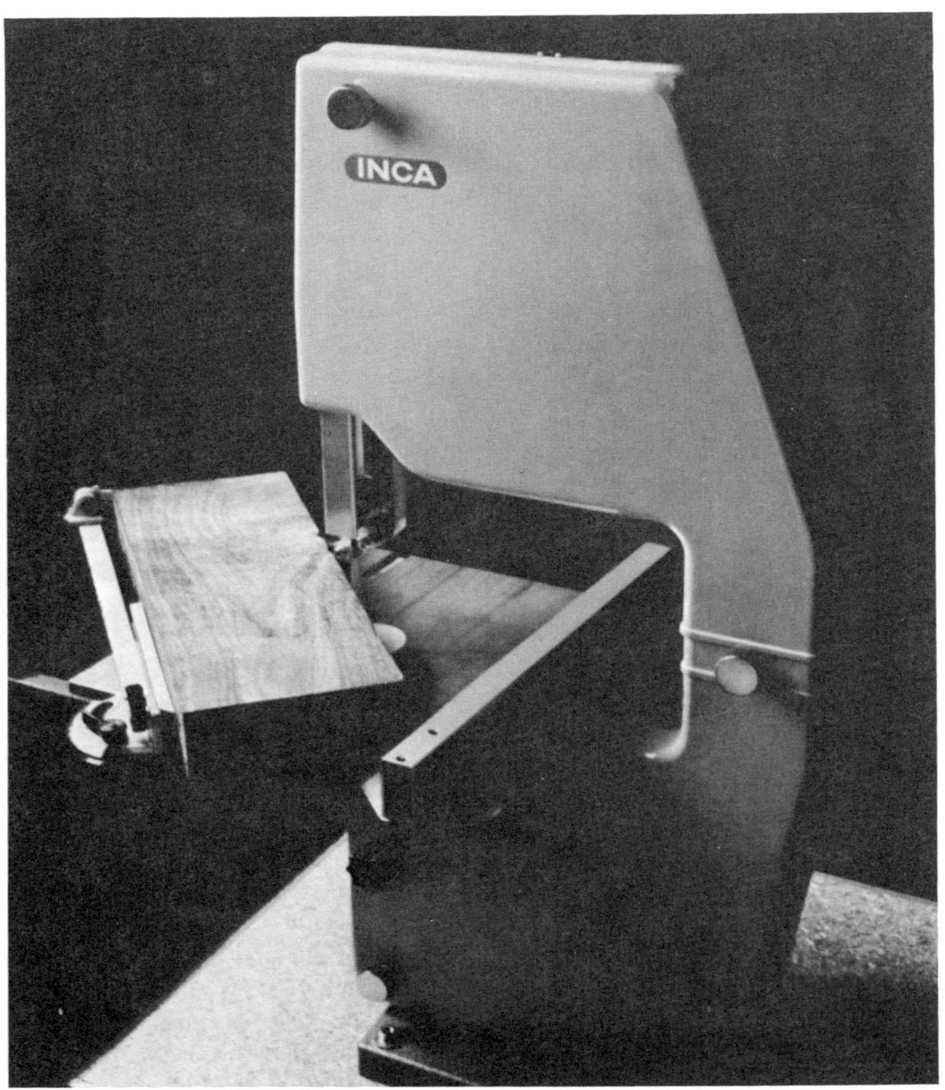


**2.17 A 10 inch Bandsaw**
**Courtesy: Garrett Wade**

A top quality bandsaw should be mounted on its own stand. Expect it to have 12″ drive wheels (on which the blade is mounted) and an adequate sized worktable at least 12″ square. It should be able to cut wood up to 6″ thick and 12″ wide. The table should tilt for bevel cuts.

To use, wear safety glasses. Adjust the fence and miter gauge if required. Start the motor and let it run for 5 seconds to attain maximum speed. Start the wood through, guiding it with the miter gauge and keeping your fingers well out of way of the blade. Stand so that the teeth of the saw face you. In rare cases when a blade breaks, it can come spinning out of the machine at a terrifying speed. However, it tends to spill out at right angles to the front of the machine (and you). Thus, keep in front of the teeth for safety's sake. Avoid twisting the work (and the blade) or forcing the work into the teeth. When your cut is completed, turn the switch off and wait until the blade stops moving before removing your project. (Figure 2.18)

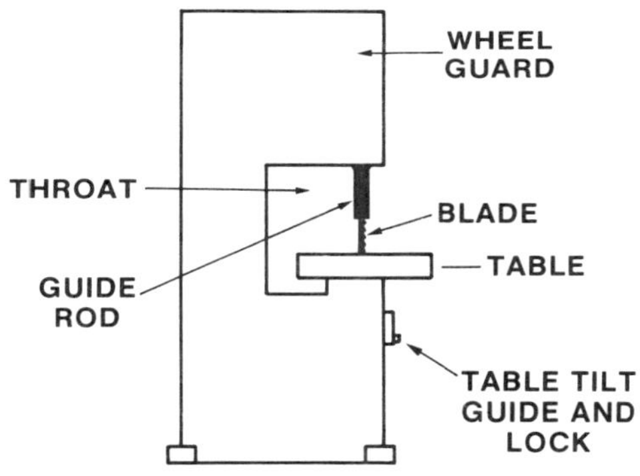


2.18 A Bandsaw

## How to Service and Repair Your Bandsaw

1. If the speed seems slow and erratic:
    a. clean the motor and replace the brushes (lubricate if possible)
    b. clean and lubricate the axle of both upper and lower wheels
    c. replace worn tires on both upper and lower wheels
2. If the machine vibrates:
    a. tighten all bolts
    b. check the wheels to see if they are in balance (repair or replace)*

*means that this operation is very expensive

c. check and replace the rubber tires on both upper and lower wheels
d. check and replace bearings (if available)*
3. If the blade does not stay on:
a. check to see that it is the correct size
b. fasten blade on wheels according to manufacturer's specifications
c. check and replace upper and lower wheel bearings (if available)*
4. If blade guides will not turn:
a. clean and lubricate them
b. replace (if parts are available)
5. If the machine runs noisily:
a. adjust blade to run near center of both wheels
b. tighten all bolts and lubricate (#10 motor oil)
c. check and replace wheel bearings (if available)*

## Part B: Metalworking

### Metal Cutting Saws: Their Use and Maintenance

For cutting light sheet metal (up to 1/16″ thick), use **tin snips** which range in size from 6″ to 14″. Grasp the snips in your hand and use them like a pair of scissors, cutting just outside the line (which will permit you to smooth or dress the work without altering the desired dimensions). For circles use **circle snips**, designed for this purpose. (Figure 2.19)

Avoid trying to cut heavy metals; this will spring the tin snips, making them useless. Keep them well-oiled and hang them up when not in use. Good care will make them last three times as long as snips left lying in a tool box.

**Bolt cutters** may be used for cutting bolts up to ½″; never attempt to use tin snips for this purpose. These giant shears (which range from

*means that this operation is very expensive

18″ to 36″ in length) drive the blades together with tremendous force. Wear safety glasses so the sheared-off end does not fly off and hurt you.

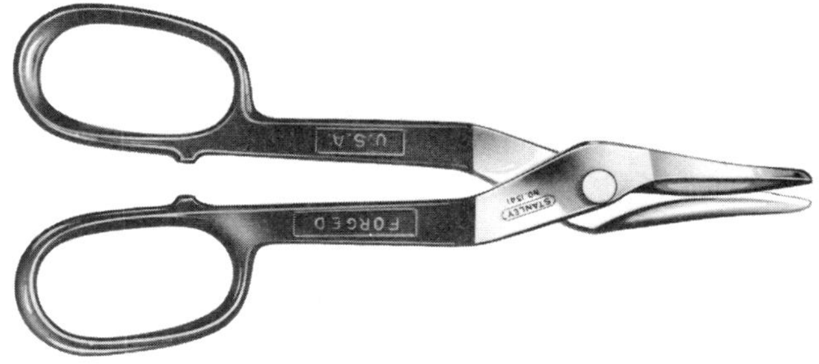


2.19 Tin Snips

**Hacksaws** cut metal which is too heavy to be cut by tin snips or bolt cutters (for example, metal bars). Many hacksaws are adjustable and take blades of different length; some have solid frames. Hacksaw blades are ½″ wide, 8″ to 16″ long and have 14 to 32 teeth per inch (the more teeth, the finer the cut). Blades are either all hard or flexible (only the teeth hardened) and are classified by set. Alternate set teeth are staggered, double alternate set teeth are staggered by two's, raker set teeth are staggered by two's, but every third tooth is straight—and with wave set teeth, the teeth seem to undulate from one side to the other. (Figure 2.20)

To cut with a hacksaw, place the material in a vise. Hold the hacksaw by gripping the handle and the front end. Apply pressure on the forward stroke but not on the return. Cut with long and steady strokes at a speed of almost one per second. Do not apply too much pressure or twist the blade—you may break the blade which can cause injury. Keep the blade drawn tight with the adjustment screw in the frame. To avoid vibration when cutting thin metals, enclose them in pieces of wood.

A new development is the **rod saw** blade which cuts through stainless steel and other hard metals by means of tungsten carbide particles bonded permanently to a rod that cuts on both forward and backward strokes. Use this in your hacksaw instead of a conventional blade and you will probably never use the old type blades again. This blade cuts sideways and is excellent for use in otherwise hard-to-reach spots. (Figure 2.21)

"Set" of hacksaw blade teeth.

14 TEETH PER INCH

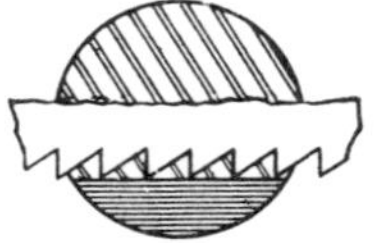

FOR LARGE SECTIONS OF MILD MATERIAL

18 TEETH PER INCH

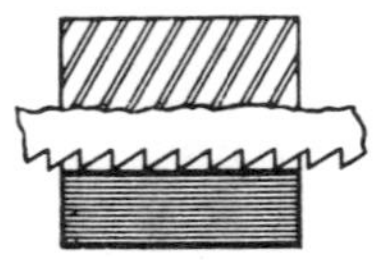

FOR LARGE SECTIONS OF TOUGH STEEL

24 TEETH PER INCH

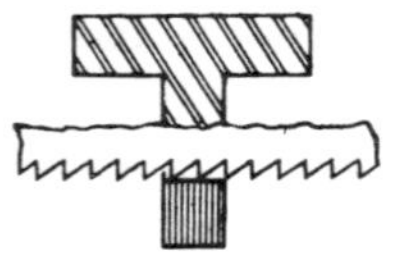

FOR ANGLE IRON, HEAVY PIPE, BRASS, COPPER

32 TEETH PER INCH

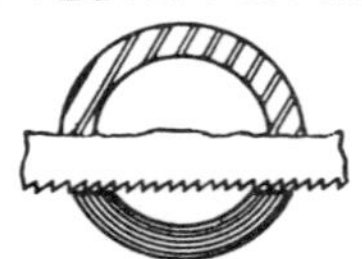

FOR THIN TUBING

KEEP AT LEAST TWO TEETH CUTTING TO AVOID THIS

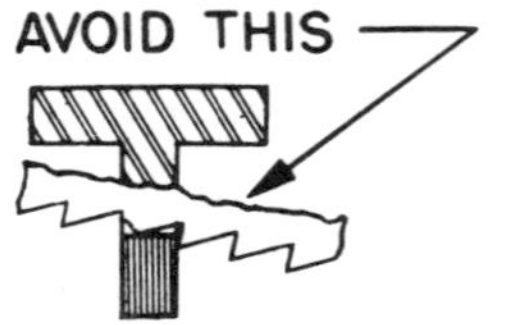

2.20 Selecting Hacksaw Blades

**Power hacksaws** and **metal cutting bandsaws** are rather specialized tools that will permit you to make miter cuts of metals as well as notching, contour cuts and slitting—some of which will cut up to 7″ round stock. In operation, these machines are like their wood-

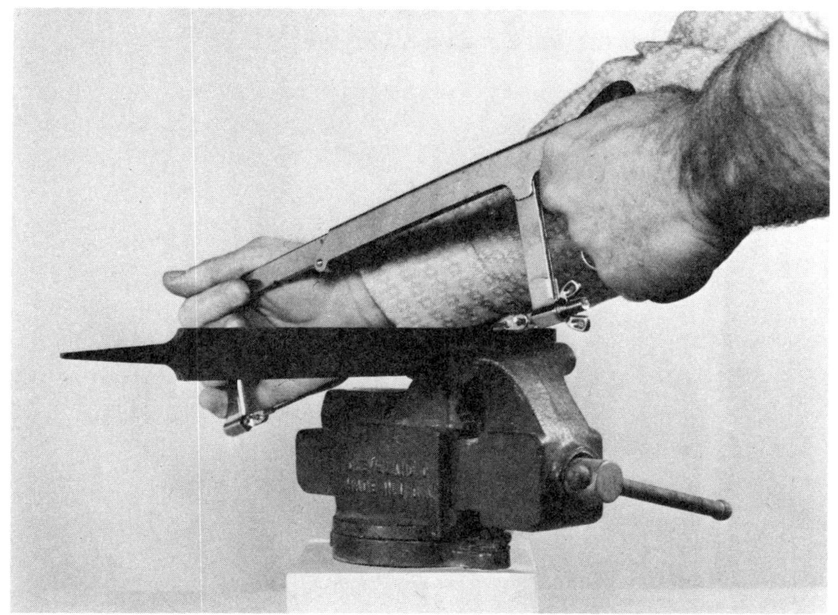

2.21 A Rod Saw
**Courtesy: Remington Arms Co., Inc.**

working counterparts—except that the metal is usually held in a vise and the equipment operates automatically without your feeding the material through. The cutting action takes much longer, of course, than cutting through the same amount of wood. (Figure 2.22)

*Aluminum* can be cut as easily as wood with any power saw. Thus, you may enjoy working with it more than any other metal. Be sure to let your saw cool between cuts, however, because high temperatures can cause particles of aluminum to weld themselves to the saw blade. Wear protective safety glasses and back up the aluminum with scrap wood for safety.

### Pipe Cutters: How to Use Them

Use **pipe cutters** to cut steel, brass, copper, iron and lead pipe. The #1 pipe cutter will cut pipe from ⅛″ up to 2″ and the #2 pipe cutter will cut pipe from 2″ to 4″. Open the jaws to the size of the outside diameter of the pipe and then tighten them as you place the pipe inside the cutter. Rotate the cutter around the pipe, tightening the screw as you go. The cutter works best if you add a small amount of oil directly into the cut. When you finish cutting through the pipe, you can thread it in much the same manner. (Figure 2.23)

**2.22 Cutting Through Fiberglass**
**Courtesy: Remington Arms Co., Inc.**

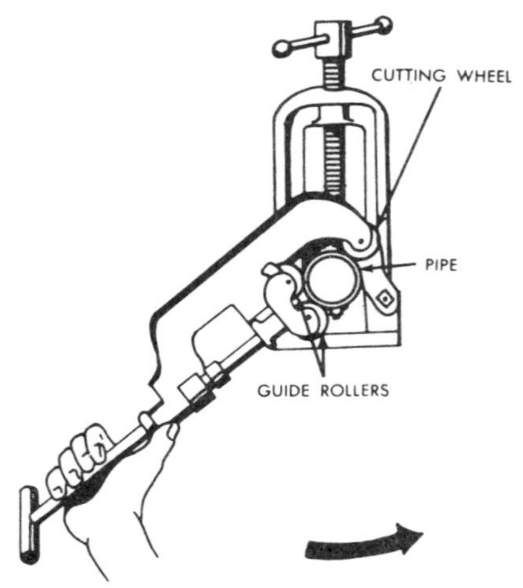


**2.23 Cutting Tubing**

Assuming that you have measured correctly (end to end measurements include the threaded portion; end to center means measuring from the free end to halfway through the threaded end; center to center means measuring from halfway through the center on each end), you need to file the outside ridge smooth and ream the inside ridge smooth with a reamer. Then, selecting the correct size pipe die, put the pipe through it and begin turning the die clockwise for right-hand threads. Apply lard oil for best cutting action and continue turning (and cutting) until the end of the pipe has gone through the die which cuts the outside threads, and is flush with the outside face. Unscrew the die and remove.

For cutting tubes (which are thin-walled pipes), use a **tube cutter** which looks like a pipe cutter and which comes in two sizes (⅛″ to ¼″ capacity and ¼″ to 1″ capacity). Use it in the same way you use the pipe cutter. Flaring tools (usually a block with holes matching the outside tubing dimensions and a screw device) are useful in expanding the outside edge of the metal smoothly and evenly. Remove burrs with a file or a reamer. Tubes are not threaded (the walls are too thin) but are connected by an outside bolt and nut. The flare is seated so that a seal is maintained.

### Cutting Metal with a Torch

If you intend to cut large areas of metal (say, for customizing a car by cutting or "chopping" the top), you would be wiser to have the work done by a professional. However, for occasional work around the average shop, you can use the small torches made by Solidox and Bernzomatic. These torches will cut through a ⅝″ bolt. (Figure 2.24)

Of course you should follow the manufacturer's instructions carefully. In general, however, the procedure is as follows. First, make sure that you are operating safely. Wear safety glasses or a welder's hood. Take adequate precautions to prevent fire and make sure that you have a fire extinguisher at hand.

After lighting the torch, direct the hottest possible flame at the metal you wish to cut. Heat the metal until it turns yellowish-white. At this point you are ready to begin cutting, so turn the propane off and let the torch continue to operate on pure oxygen which is used to cut the metal. Keep the area to be cut yellowish-white in temperature. Move the torch slowly and carefully, watching out for molten metal which is highly hazardous.

When you finish the cut, turn the torch off and let the metal cool.

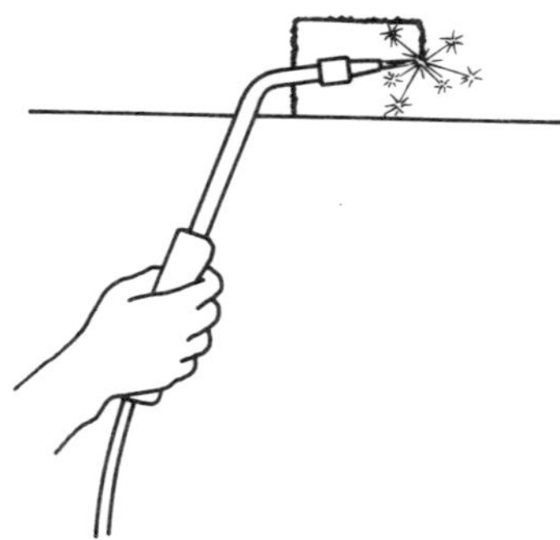

2.24 Torch

## SHOPBUILDER #2

Selections of sawing tools—
(Choose according to your needs/Build your shop step-by-step)

BASIC TOOLS

a. crosscut saw (26″ long, 10 points per inch)
b. ripsaw (26″ long, 8 points per inch)

AMATEUR TOOLS: (Include tool list above)

c. coping saw (5″ throat depth)
d. keyhole saw (10″ long, 10 teeth per inch)
e. backsaw (miter saw) (16″ by 3½″ with 11 points per inch)

ADVANCED AMATEUR TOOLS: (Include tool lists above)

f. 7″, 1¼ hp circular saw
g. ½ hp sabre saw
h. hacksaw (12″ blade)

PROFESSIONAL: (Include tool lists above)

i. 18″ bandsaw (1 hp)
j. 10″ table saw (2 hp)
k. table model jigsaw (12″ throat, ⅓ hp)

PROFESSIONAL CRAFTSMAN: (Include tool lists above)

l. 10″ radial saw
m. power hacksaw (1 hp)

## SKILLBUILDER #2

Use these tests to determine the level of your skill: CUTTING

| | |
|---|---|
| ADVANCED AMATEUR: | Saw through a two-by-four in one minute maintaining an accurate cut.<br>Cut a 3¼″ circle out of a piece of ¼″ plywood with a jigsaw. |
| PROFESSIONAL:<br>*Do the above plus* | Saw through a 1″ by 8″ pine board in 30 seconds accurately and squarely. Cut a piece of 2′ x 4′ plywood (½″ thick) into equal sections which match perfectly.<br>Using the bandsaw, cut an egg-shaped piece of wood 8-1/16″ long (at its longest point) and 5-5/32″ wide (at its widest point).<br>Using a hacksaw, cut a 45 degree angle from a piece of ⅛″ steel. |
| SKILLED CRAFTSMAN:<br>*Do the above plus* | Using a backsaw, cut 45 degree angles to make a picture frame from any suitable molding.<br>With the torch, cut through a ⅛″ bolt, making both ends equal. |

# 3

# Shaping Tools and How to Use Them

After you have cut the rough shape of the project out of wood or other material, you will need to shape it more carefully to its final dimensions. If this is done with carefully selected shaping tools, you will find that the job of finishing it will be much easier.

## Part A: Woodworking

### Judging the Type of Shaping Tools Required and How to Use Them

Planes and chisels are used in woodworking to shape the project. Planes shave wood. The most useful small shop planes are bench planes and block planes.

The **bench plane** has a handle and a knob. Grasp both and push the plane ahead of you, guiding it with your hand on the knob. The frame of this plane carries a sloping, sharpened iron blade which goes through a slot in the sole of the frame. A screw or knob on the front of the iron blade adjusts the depth of the cut. The lower edge of the iron fits in the plane, bevel side down.

Adjust the plane in two ways: up and down (by moving the adjustment nut) and from right to left (by moving the lateral adjustment lever).

Since the longer the plane, the more uniformly flat the surface: a **smooth plane** (usually 9″ long) will plane a smooth but not true surface; the **jack plane** (14″ long and the best all-around plane), will give a smooth and fairly true surface; and a **jointer** (or fore or gauge plane—usually 20″ to 24″ long) will give a smooth and true surface. (Figures 3.1 and 3.2)

Another type of plane is the **block plane** which is used to cut off ends of stock since it cuts across the grain. (Figure 3.3)

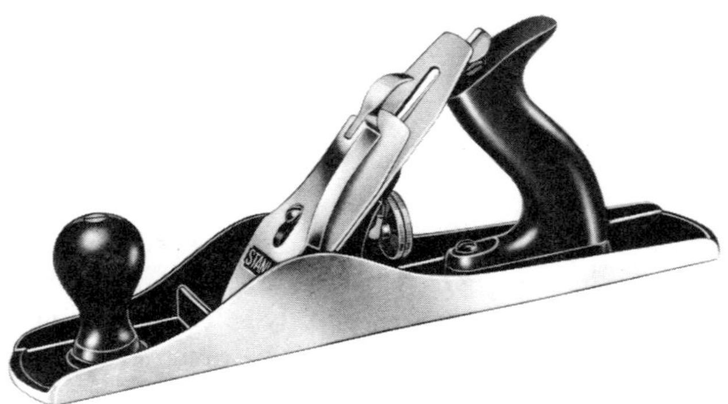

**3.1 A Jack Plane**
**Courtesy: Stanley Tools**

**3.2 A Bull Nose Rabbet Plane**
**Courtesy: Stanley Tools**

You will have to sharpen your planes frequently. Commercial devices which hold your plane at the correct angle will simplify your task, although you can do it by hand if you keep the bevel at 25 degrees. Dip the tool into water as you grind to keep the temper. Read the information in the chapter on the use of the grinding wheel for best results as to the procedures involved. (Figures 3.4, 3.5 and 3.6)

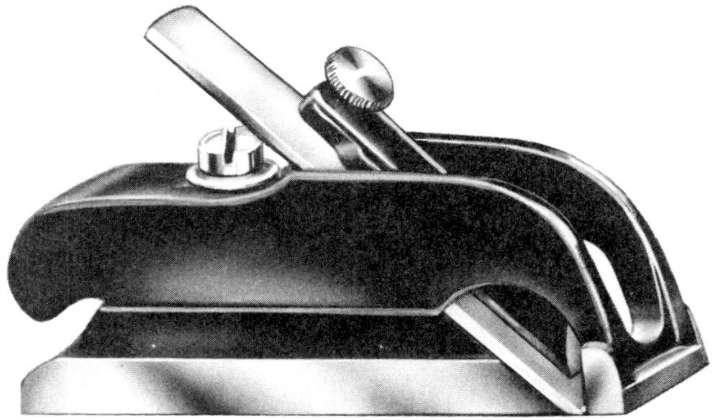

3.3 A Block Plane
**Courtesy: Stanley Tools**

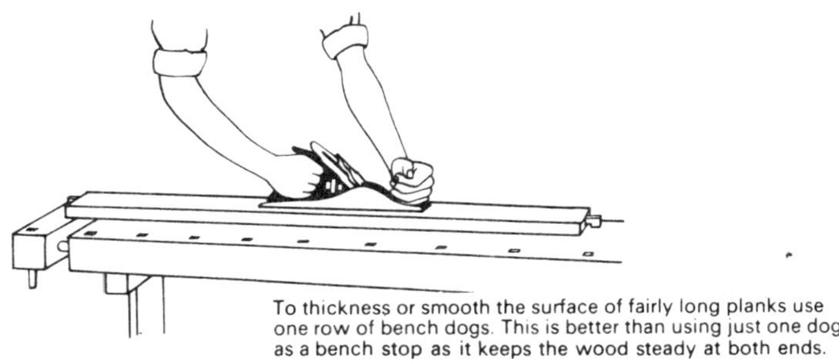


3.4 Using Your Workbench

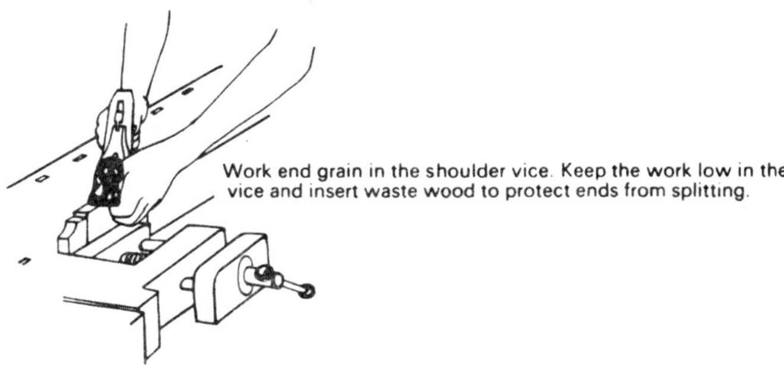


3.5 Using Your Workbench
**Courtesy: Leichtung, Inc.**

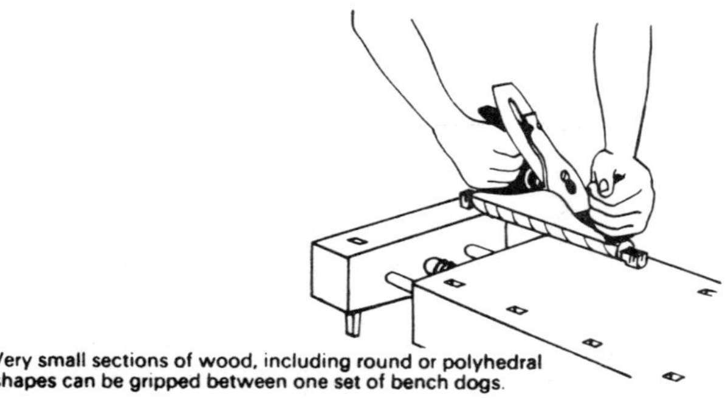
Very small sections of wood, including round or polyhedral shapes can be gripped between one set of bench dogs.

**3.6 Using Your Workbench**
**Courtesy: Leichtung, Inc.**

Next, use a whetstone, checking the edge with a square to make sure it is straight. Square it by rubbing it on the edge of the oilstone, then whet the bevel side and the flat side. (Figures 3.7 and 3.8)

Power planes level surfaces almost automatically. Top quality machines use razor sharp blades spinning at 15,000 rpm to smooth surfaces with fewer passes. To operate, you set the dial for the depth of cut you want, press the trigger switch (grasping the device much as you do a regular plane) and after letting the motor run for 5 seconds to reach maximum speed, touch it down to the surface. In a few passes, you will see that it operates like an ordinary plane. At the end, raise the plane up and release the motor trigger so that the motor stops after you raise it from the surface of the wood.

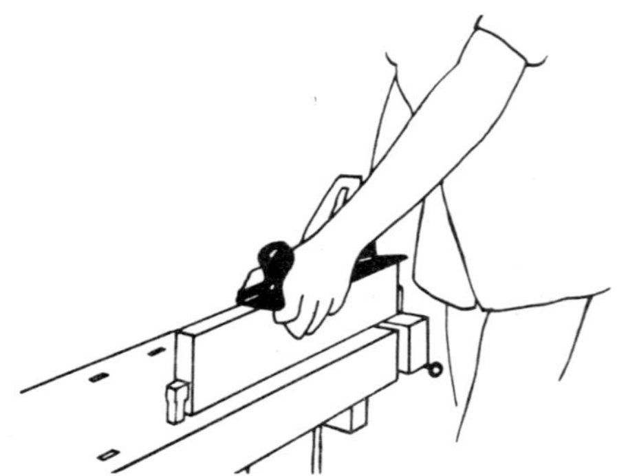
For edge planing all but the shortest timbers the bench dogs are again the best hold. The best position when squaring. Very small pieces in the shoulder vice.

**3.7 Using Your Workbench**
**Courtesy: Leichtung, Inc.**

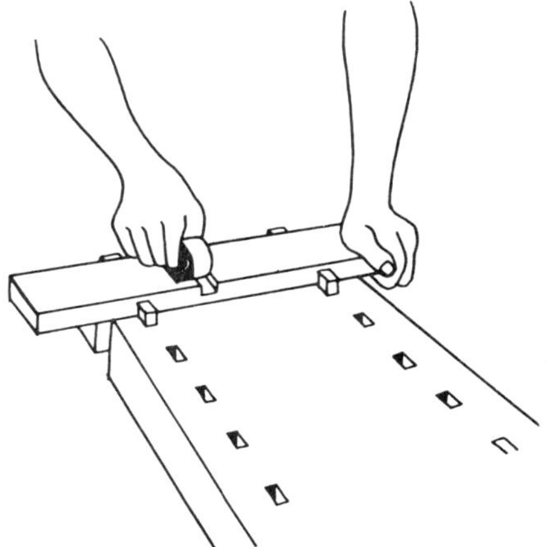
The same piece is equally well secured for trimming with a side rebate plane or router.

**3.8 Using Your Workbench**
**Courtesy: Leichtung, Inc.**

The blades are removable for sharpening in the same manner as conventional hand tools. Use a wrench to remove and insert them.

You will use this tool a lot when you see that you can plane the broad side of a two by four in just one pass! In addition, you can bevel edges usually for a uniform 45 degree cut and make rabbet cuts in one pass as much as 15/64″ deep and 11/32″ wide.

Other hand tools used in shaping are **scrapers** and **chisels**. Scrapers are used after planing and in cleaning off old paint on old surfaces. They are pushed or pulled to make smooth surfaces across the grain of hardwoods—they are of little use on soft woods.

A **wood chisel** is made of steel and has a plastic or wooden handle. There are two basic types: **tang chisels** (in which part of the chisel is inside the handle and is used by the hand only) and **socket chisels** (in which the handle enters into part of the chisel and is to be struck with a hammer).

A further means of classifying chisels is by the work they do. A **firmer chisel** is designed for all work and has a strong rectangular cross-section blade similar to a framing chisel (which is a bit stronger). A **paring chisel** is thinner and used for paring. A **butt chisel** has a short blade for use in tight quarters and is most often used for butt hinges on doors. A **mortising chisel** looks like a firmer chisel but is narrower for chiseling out mortises and tenon joints.

To use, hold the back of the chisel (the flat side) towards the work and start slightly away from the guideline so that you finish at it. Use the chisel for finishing work; let the saw do the roughing out.

For safety's sake, cut away from yourself, keeping both hands in back of the blade. Make sure that the wood is held securely and cut with the grain, making thin shavings. (Figures 3.9 and 3.10)

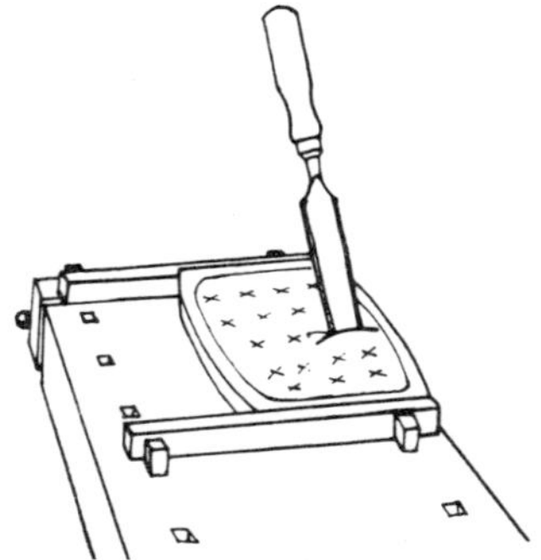

Pieces for gouging or hollowing out should be placed in the bench dogs, with a protective block between the dog and workpiece if necessary.

**3.9 Using Your Workbench**
**Courtesy: Leichtung, Inc.**

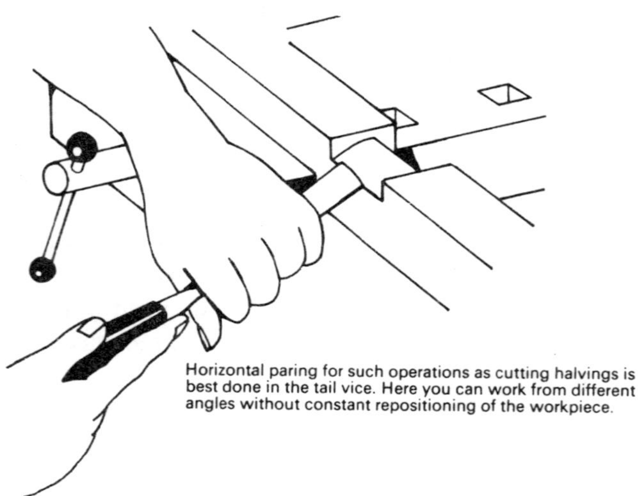

Horizontal paring for such operations as cutting halvings is best done in the tail vice. Here you can work from different angles without constant repositioning of the workpiece.

**3.10 Using Your Workbench**
**Courtesy: Leichtung, Inc.**

### How to Sharpen Your Hand Chisels

Sharpen wood chisels on a sharpening stone. Secure the stone and put a thin coat of light machine oil on the coarse side. Rub the chisel back and forth parallel to the surface of the stone, using the entire surface. After a dozen strokes, repeat the process on the fine side of the stone.

### Simplifying Shaping with Power Tools

**Routers** are useful tools which can cut circular and edge grooves, copy letters and designs by carving them into wood, mortise hinges, dovetail, trim and do countless other tasks. (Figure 3.11)

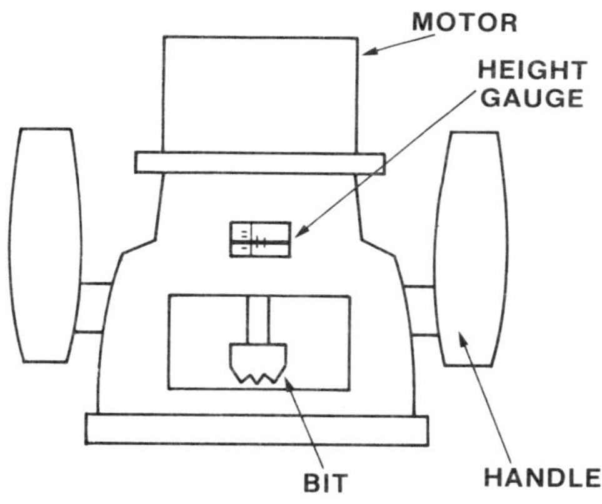


**3.11 A Router**

Router bits fit into a chuck connected to a ¼ to 3 hp motor running at 25,000 rpm and cut up to 1½″ deep. The types of bits are **straight bits** (used for slotting and grooving), **veining bits** (used for making ornamental cuts on the radius), **cove bits** (used to make concave cuts), **beading bits** (used to make convex cuts), **rabbetting bits** (used to cut steps or rabbets into wood), **dovetail bits** (to make dovetail joints) and **ogee bits** (to make both concave and convex cuts at the same time).

To operate your router, follow the manufacturer's instructions carefully. In general, the procedure is to select the correct bit, screw it into the threaded chuck and tighten it with a wrench. Next, adjust the depth of cut by loosening the motor (usually with a wingnut) or by turning the depth adjustment knob—depending on the type of router that you are using—until the visual depth gauge on the front of the router registers the correct setting. For example, most routers are adjustable by 1/32″ and a reading of ⅛″ would mean that the router will cut at a depth of ⅛″.

Secure the work firmly. Place the router on the work and turn the switch on. Work from left to right since the motor turns clockwise. When you are cutting, move slowly but steadily and think ahead so that you do not make any cuts in areas you wish to leave alone. At the completion of your cutting or when you want to change to another bit, turn the motor off and wait until the bit stops spinning before removing the router.

## How to Select Your Router

| General Features | Yes or No? (Two *No* answers mean the tool is unacceptable) |
|---|---|
| Is the motor adequate? (½ hp is O.K.; 1 hp is excellent) 100% ball bearings used? | |
| Is the chuck self-extracting? (Accepting standard sized ¼″ bits?) | |
| Are the handles easy to grip and sturdy? | |
| Is there provision for accurate height adjustment? (1/32″ steps are adequate; 1/64″ steps are excellent) | |

| | |
|---|---|
| Will it cut deep enough? (1″ is sufficient; 1½″ excellent) | |
| Adequate chip deflection for eye protection? (Preferably a shield) | |
| Is the base smooth to protect the surface you are working on? | |
| Is the housing steady when you turn it over to change bits? | |
| Double insulated or otherwise electrically safe? | |
| Is the trigger switch easy to reach? | |

### Using Your Shaper and Jointer/Planer

A **shaper** is a larger version of a router in that it will cut rabbets, scallops, moldings and other contours. In this regard, it is also similar to a molder—a much more expensive piece of equipment. (Figure 3.12A)

The operation requires you to wear safety glasses. Select the correct size shaper-cutter and attach it. Turn the motor on and let it run for 10 seconds to reach maximum speed. Press the edge of the project against the fence and begin to guide it by using your wooden hold-down blocks past the cutters, keeping your hands safely out of the way. Use the miter gauge, if possible, to guide the wood. Use small blocks of wood as pushers to move the project safely past the cutting head. You will find that a good shaper will cut so cleanly that little or no sanding will be needed. Turn the machine off at the end of the operation.

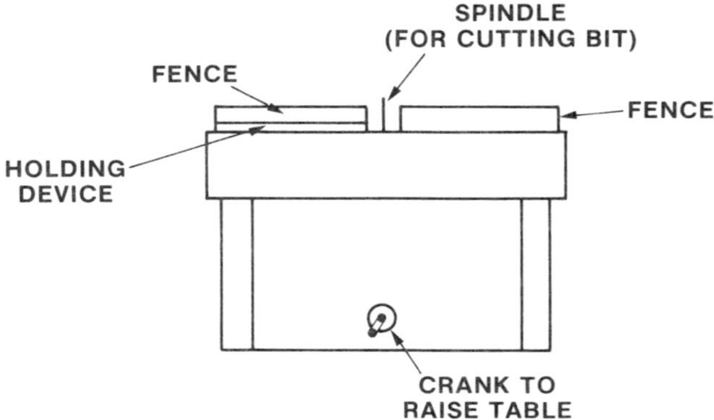


3.12A A shaper

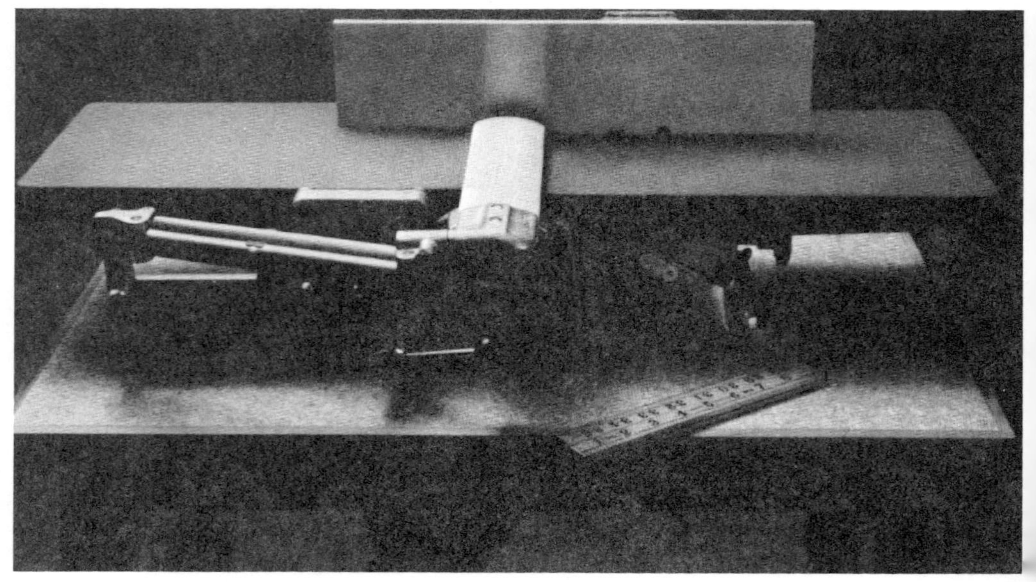

3.12B A Jointer/Planer
**Courtesy: Garrett Wade**

A jointer/planer is used most often to plane long lengths of wood. However, it will also give you smooth, true edges for flush fitting joints. (Figure 3.12B)

For protection, wear your safety glasses. Set the height by raising or lowering the infeed table (on most models). Check to see that the fence is in the correct position. Turn the switch on and push the board through with your wooden hold-down blocks. *Never attempt to push the project through with your hands for any reason whatsoever.*

When the pass has been made, shut the motor off and do not attempt to remove the wood until the motor has stopped completely.

## How to Select Your Shaper

| General Features | Yes or No? (Two *No* answers mean the tool is unacceptable) |
|---|---|
| Is the motor adequate? (½ hp is acceptable; 1 hp is excellent) | |
| Is the cutting height adequate? (2″ is excellent) | |
| Does it deliver sufficient rpm? (7,500 is the minimum; 9,000 rpm is better; 14,000 and up is better) | |
| Is the table large enough? (12″ by 14″ is sufficient) | |
| Does it come with a stand or do you have a stand? | |

| | |
|---|---|
| Is a miter gauge included? | |
| Are the half-fences adjustable?<br>(Left to right, front to rear?) | |
| Do the spindles accept standard sized cutters of ½″? | |
| Does the spindle adjust sufficiently?<br>(⅞″ is adequate) | |

## How to Select Your Jointer/Planer

| General Features | Yes or No?<br>(Two *No* answers mean the tool is unacceptable) |
|---|---|
| Is the motor adequate?<br>(½ hp is adequate) | |
| Can deep enough cuts be made?<br>(⅛″ is adequate; ⅜″ is excellent)<br>Can it plane 6″ boards in one pass? | |
| How many knives?<br>(3 are an adequate number) | |
| Is the cutter head driven by a timing belt for more accurate cutting action? | |

| | |
|---|---|
| Can lateral and bevel adjustments be simply made? (45 degree and 90 degree adjustments?) | |
| Are the cutters well-guarded to maintain safety? | |
| Is there a reset overload protector to avoid burning out the motor? | |
| Are the bearings permanently lubricated for long life? | |
| Are the knives easily accessible for removal for sharpening? | |

## How to Service and Repair Your Jointer/Planer

1. If the speed is slow and erratic:
   a. check to see if the house current is adequate
   b. clean and lubricate the motor (if possible) and replace brushes
   c. check to see that the knives are attached correctly
2. If the knives are dull:
   a. sharpen or replace them
3. If the fence is out of line
   a. adjust by use of knob
   b. bend into shape (if only minor alignment is needed)
   c. replace
4. If the machine is noisy:
   a. tighten all parts

   b. check for worn bearings (usually not replaceable)
   c. check to see if knives are worn
5. If the table is out of line:
   a. replace it*

## How to Service and Repair Your Shaper

1. If the motor speed is too slow or erratic:
   a. see if belt on pulley is slipping or damaged
   b. clean and lubricate motor (replace brushes)
   c. see if spindle is cracked or damaged (replace)*
2. If machine does not cut satisfactorily:
   a. sharpen or replace blades
   b. examine spindle threads for damage (replace if parts are available)*
   c. replace bearings and bearing housing if available*
3. If fence slide does not move:
   a. lubricate
   b. examine for damage (repair or replace)*
4. If table operates incorrectly:
   a. adjust table-raising knob or lock
   b. clean and lubricate raising mechanism and lock
   c. replace mechanism*
5. If the hold-down components do not work:
   a. bend into shape
   b. replace

---

*means that these operations are very expensive

## How to Select Your Lathe

| General Features | Yes or No? (Two *No* answers mean the tool is unacceptable) |
| --- | --- |
| Is the motor included in the price? Is it adequate? (¼ hp is O.K.) | |
| Are the motor speeds variable? (Belts and pulleys, O.K.; variable speed motor best) | |
| Is the turning capacity sufficient? (12″ diameter over bed is O.K.) | |
| Is spindle mounted on permanently lubricated ball bearings? | |
| Is there adequate distance between centers? (36″ is fine) | |
| Is the tool rest large enough to use in comfort? | |
| Does it come with a workbench or do you have one that is suitable? | |

| | |
|---|---|
| **Is it made by a well-known manufacturer in case you need to replace some parts?** | |
| **Are accessories available?** | |

**How to Use Your Lathe**

A lathe is used to make turnings of wood for posts, spindles, and chair and table legs. A variable speed motor turns the project (clamped at both ends) while various cutting tools are moved along its length. (Figure 3.13)

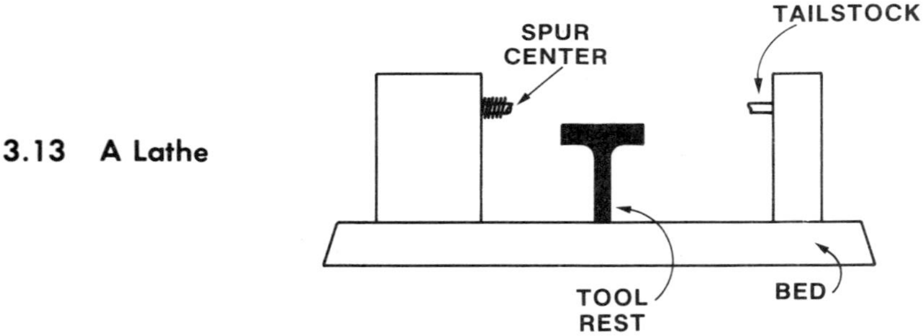


**3.13 A Lathe**

With a wood lathe, you can shape bowls with plain or fancy discs and rims, turn wheels, drawer knobs and other small projects, and even—with attachments—sand, drill and buff.

A good quality lathe will have pulleys and belts to use in changing speeds; a superior quality lathe will have a variable speed motor. A lathe which runs at one speed only is of very limited use; you won't be happy with it.

In addition, you will need a good selection of wood turning tools. A recommended selection would be:

1″ skew chisel
½″ skew chisel
⅛″ parting tool
½″ round nose
½″ spear point

} for spindle turning

| | |
|---|---|
| ¾″ gouge<br>½″ gouge | for general use |
| half-round<br>full-round<br>left skew<br>right skew | for internal turning |

With this selection of cutting tools, you will be able to turn almost any project imaginable.

Although turning projects on a lathe requires some practice, with care you should be able to turn out satisfactory simple work at the start—if you plan carefully and do not try to rush the job.

Use a sharp tool to round off the square edges of the wood block that you wish to turn. Center the stock by drawing lines from each of the four corners of the end so that they intersect in the middle at the exact center. Counter-punch the mark at dead-center so that you can see it easily.

Drive the centers into the work. One center is called a *live center* (this is where the motor is attached to turn it) and the other center is called a *dead center* (no power is attached to it). (Figure 3.14)

Adjust the tool rest so that it does not hit the work but is within ½″ of it. Make sure that the work is firmly fastened. Wear your safety glasses and make sure that any loose clothing is securely fastened so the machine won't catch it.

Turn the machine on at its *slowest* speed. Let the lathe run for 60 seconds or more while keeping out of the way so that if the project should be thrown off, you won't be hurt.

Rest the gouge on the tool rest, holding it firmly with the point raised slightly. Make several cuts 3″ apart so that waste stock is easily removed. Then, using whatever cutting tools are needed, move them along the tool rest so that the wood is cut no more than 1/16″ deep at any one time. Move the tool rest as required if the project is longer than can be reached in one spot. (Figure 3.15)

*Sanding* can be done by holding sandpaper by both ends over the wood as it revolves. Do not bear down too hard or you may burn the wood. You can trim the ends with a skew and even cut off the work (by running the skew in at the headstock—the live end—not the other end). However, this is an operation which is better done with a saw, off the lathe.

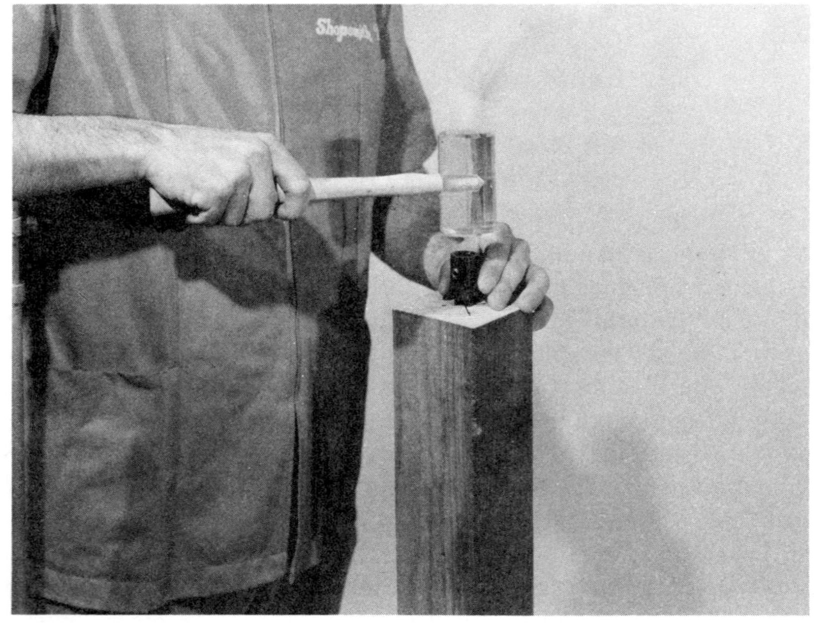

3.14 Seating the Drive Center
**Courtesy: Shopsmith**

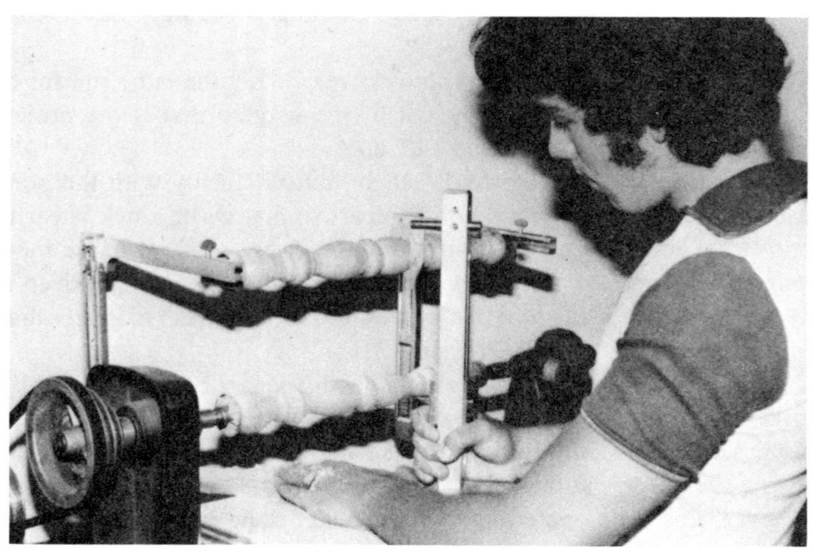

3.15 Replicating Spindles
**Courtesy: Turn-O-Carve Tool Co.**

### How to Service and Repair Your Lathe

1. If the speed seems slow or erratic:
   a. clean the motor and replace the brushes (lubricate if possible)
   b. check pulley belts and replace if necessary
   c. clean and lubricate the drive shaft and/or spindle
   d. lubricate the bearing cap
   e. check the speed control (if the lathe has one) and repair or replace if needed
2. If the internal headstock tapers and tailstock sleeve tapers are worn or damaged:
   a. file slightly to smooth
   b. replace them (if parts are available)
3. If lathe bed is gouged or damaged:
   a. smooth with file and emery cloth
4. If the threads on the spindle are damaged or worn:
   a. re-thread with same size thread
   b. replace*
5. If the spindle is loose or wobbles:
   a. tighten
   b. check and replace bearings or bearing housings (if available)*
6. If the spindle and tailstock center are out of alignment:
   a. adjust them
   b. bend or move them
   c. replace them*

## Part B: Metalworking

Shaping metal is done with chisels and by turning on a lathe. Your lathe can be used for metalworking as well as woodworking. If you

---

*means that this operation is very expensive

select the right carbide-tipped turning tools, you will be able to cut and shape non-ferrous metals. (Figure 3.16)

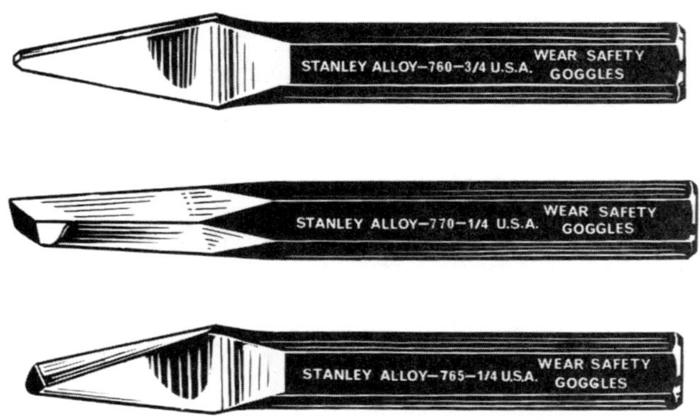


**3.16 Shaping with Metal Chisels**
**Courtesy: Stanley Tools**

## Using Your Lathe to Turn Metal

Set your lathe to the slowest speed possible (usually 700-900 RPM) and use carbide-tipped tools to cut metals. Generally, only small pieces of non-ferrous metal can be successfully turned; as for example, small drawer pulls or knobs.

Since most jobs are time-consuming and require the use of specialized tools, you will only want to turn objects that cannot be duplicated in any other way.

Mount the metal to be turned in the lathe. Since it won't splinter like wood, you can even mount it so that it is attached only to the live end of the lathe (which means that it is almost like turning the metal in a power drill chuck). Obviously, round off any edges. Wear your safety glasses.

Turn the tool rest so that it is ¼″ away from the revolving metal. Rest your carbide-tipped cutting tool on it just as if you were cutting wood. Do not try to cut too much or you will cause the work to chatter and maybe even do extensive damage to your cutting tool as well as the work.

Hold the tool on the rest so that it faces *downward* slightly into the metal as it revolves. You can make this cut freehand. However, for more precise work, you will need to build a jig which will turn the cutting blade to the right height by means of a screw.

## SHOPBUILDER #3

Selections of shaping tools (woodworking)—
(Choose according to your needs/Build your shop step-by-step)

BASIC TOOLS:

a. set of four chisels:
   ¼″ x 6¾″
   ½″ x 6¾″
   ¾″ by 7⅛″
   1″ x 7½″
b. smooth plane (9″ x 2″)

AMATEUR TOOLS: (Include tool list above)

c. jack plane (8″ x 1½″)
d. block plane (6″)
e. wood mallet

ADVANCED AMATEUR: (Include tool lists above)

f. 1¼″ chisel
g. 12″ lathe and tools (½ hp motor)
h. router (1 hp) and bits

PROFESSIONAL: (Include tool lists above)

i. 6⅛″ jointer/planer (½ hp motor)
j. high speed shaper (½ hp motor)
k. power planer (½ hp motor)

PROFESSIONAL CRAFTSMAN: (Include tool lists above)

l. floor model planer-molder (2 hp motor) and bits
m. Foundryette furnace

## SKILLBUILDER #3

Use these tests to determine the level of your skill: SHAPING MATERIAL

| | |
|---|---|
| **ADVANCED AMATEUR:** | **Plane the surface of a rough, 1′ long two-by-four to a finished surface in 10 minutes.** |
| **PROFESSIONAL:**<br>*Do the above plus* | **Continue planing the above two-by-four to a finished size that measures the same at any point along its width.**<br>**Using hand chisels, cut out a 1¼″ x ¾″ slot 1″ deep in a two-by-four. (No time limit.)**<br>**Using the router, cut five different types of cuts *or* with the lathe, turn a 6″ spindle in 20 minutes. (½″ in diameter.)** |
| **SKILLED CRAFTSMAN:**<br>*Do the above plus* | **Using the shaper or jointer/planer, turn out two different-shaped edges in 15 minutes that do not need to be sanded.**<br>**Using the metal Foundryette, make a casting by the lost wax process. (Optional)** |

### Making Metal Castings

You can make metal castings using cast iron, bronze, aluminum, brass, pewter, silver, gold, copper and other metals. Two-part sand mouldings are used for the simplest castings and the lost wax method is used for more complex designs.

Basically, **sand casting** means making an opening in sand into which metal is poured. The metal, when cooled, will take the shape of the sand cavity it has filled. Using two-part moulds the object will have two parts. Water is troweled through the specially selected sand and the pattern pressed into the sand. The same is done with the second half of the project. Molten metal is then poured into the sand cavity after the project has been removed.

In the **lost wax process**, a model is made of wax, it is surrounded with a plaster cast, the wax is melted out and the cavity is refilled with molten metal. When the metal cools, it takes the shape of the mould.

Both processes are surprisingly easy and relatively safe—if you use common sense. The only difficulty is in getting a furnace which will produce the necessary high temperatures ranging from 1000 to 2000 degrees and more.

The Foundryette (available from Kansas City Specialties Co., Inc., 2805 Dewey Court, Middleton, Wisconsin 53562), is an excellent small furnace which operates on natural gas or propane, butane and other fuels. The manufacturer claims it is as safe to operate as your kitchen stove. (Figure 3.17)

**3.17 The Foundryette and Its Components**
**Courtesy: Kansas City Specialties Co., Inc.**

# 4

# Sanders and Other Finishing Tools: Methods of Use

Professional sanding differs greatly from amateur work. Truly fine projects have almost a silky feel to them.

## Part A: Woodworking

### The Basic Tools for Sanding

Sandpaper is paper coated with glue to hold particles of flint, quartz or garnet (red in color and the longest lasting). It comes in grades ranging from 8/0, the finest grit, to #3, the coarsest grit. You will most commonly use numbers 2/0 or 00, 0, ½, 1 and 1½; starting with #1½ which will leave large scratches on the surface of the wood after planing or scraping. Then use #1, #½, #0 and possibly #2/0 (#00) or #3/0 (#000)—in that order—to give a satin sheen to your work's surface.

Sand with the grain. However, you can speed your work up somewhat if you sand at a slight angle to the grain. Fold or tear your sheets into quarters and wrap them around a small block of wood or insert them into ready-made holders available at any hardware store. Rap the holder sharply against the workbench every so often to knock the wood particles out of the paper. If you have to sand scrolled-edges, wrap a small piece of sandpaper around a pencil and use the same procedure as with a block of wood. (Figure 4.1)

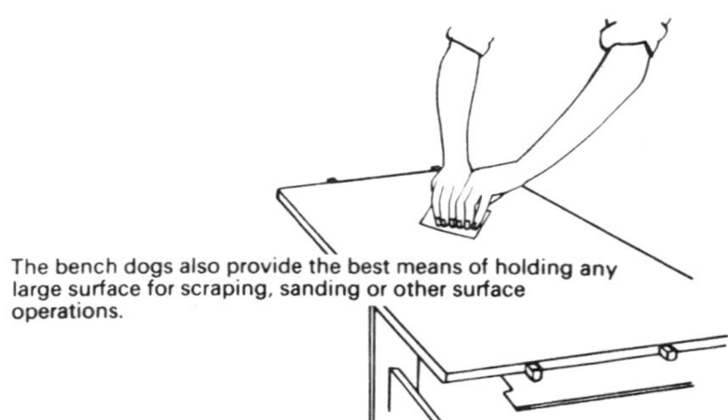


4.1 Using Your Workbench
**Courtesy: Leichtung, Inc.**

## Belt and Disc Sanders: Their Use and Maintenance

The **disc sander** is often used by the amateur for the one purpose for which it is *not* intended—to create a mirror smooth finish. The best use for a disc sander is to remove scaling for painting preparation.

### How to Select Your Sander

| General Features | Yes or No? (Two *No* answers mean the tool is unacceptable) |
|---|---|
| Is the motor adequate? (Belt sanders require 1 hp minimum; disc sanders ½ hp; small hand-held sanders 1/5 hp) | |
| Does it use standard size sandpaper? (Usually ⅓ sheet for hand-held sanders; 7″ discs for disc sanders; 3″ x 21″, 3″ x 24″, 4″ x 24″ or 4″ x 36″ for belt sanders)* | |

*although this list can be used to evaluate vertical belt sanders they use different size belts; usually 1″ by 42″.

| | |
|---|---|
| **Does it have a vacuum or similar device to reduce dust?** | |
| **Is it well-balanced and are the controls easy to find and use?** | |
| **Is it versatile? (Will it sand flush against various surfaces?)** | |
| **Is it double insulated or otherwise made electric-shock proof?** | |

To use, move the disc constantly so that it does not cut into or gouge the surface. For finishing wood, use the other types of sanders. (Figure 4.2)

**Belt sanders** are used to give a fine surface to lumber used in finished work such as interior trim, furniture and cabinets. In addition, floors are sanded with belt sanders. This tool uses endless belts which are available in many different grades or grits and are 2″ to 4″ wide. They can be changed easily.

To use, be sure that the object to be sanded is firmly secured—nail down loose floor boards first, before sanding. Start the motor and make sure that the belt is tracking correctly. Turn the machine off and then upend it. Start the motor briefly and check the direction in which the belt tends to move. Be sure that the belt is not hitting the housing striking bar because it will wear it through. The striking bar can be removed and turned around if it is accidentally damaged, but frequent examination should prevent this from happening. To bring the belt to the correct position, adjust the tracking knob on the side of the sander or on some models, adjust with aligning screws. Do all adjustments with the machine turned off.

Hold the sander with both hands, one on the front knob and one on the handle. Turn the motor switch on and let the belt spin for a few seconds. Then, touch down the rear of the sander and level it as you move it forward. Do not press down; the weight of the sander is adequate for the job. Instead, guide the machine back and forth, always with the grain. Overlap your strokes. Do not stop in any one spot or tilt the sander. When you finish, lift the machine off the work before turning off the motor.

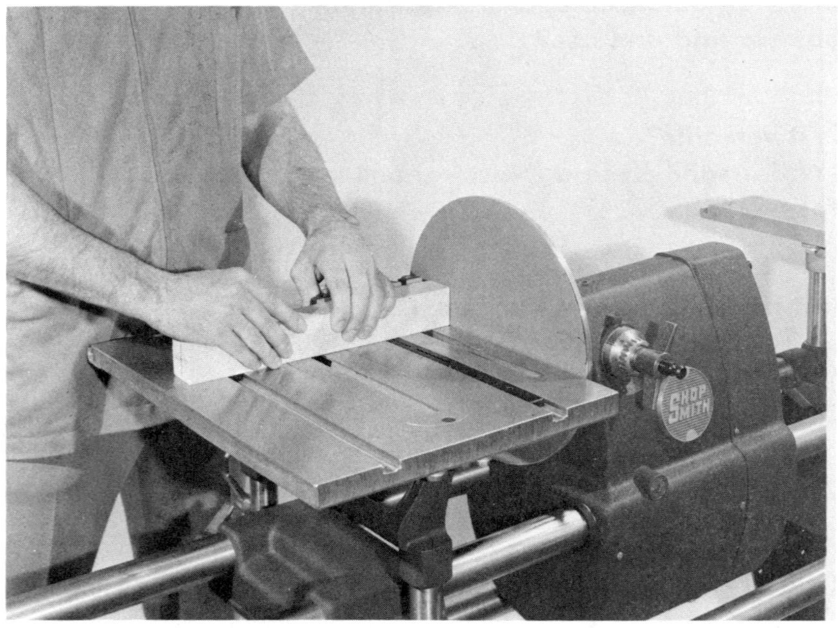


**4.2 A Disc Sander**
**Courtesy: Shopsmith**

If you need to install a new belt, unplug the machine. Then, press and tilt the front left side until the pulley retracts and locks (you may need to loosen the belt adjusting knob). Slide out the old belt and slide in the new one. Arrows on the belt will show you the correct direction of belt travel. Then, press the front right side to return the pulleys to their correct position. Turn the machine on and check the tracking adjustment.

**Orbital sanders** are easily used and are thus popular tools. The sandpaper is placed on a pad which vibrates so that it sands in all directions. This type of sanding motion is useful because it leaves almost no scratches and can be used in very tight quarters. (Figure 4.3)

4.3 An Orbital Sander

Sanders are designed to take one-third of a standard 9″ by 11″ paper. Use papers no coarser than ½ to 60 grit. Try coarser grit first and then change to finer grit, using open-coat aluminum oxide or garnet paper. The quality of the finish is determined by the quality of the paper that you use, so select it carefully.

To attach paper, first unplug the sander and pull the sheet, paper side down, over the edge of a table to curl the ends. Two types of clamps are used on orbital sanders: knurled rollers or clamps. For sanders with knurled rollers, insert the paper between the roller and the top of the platen base plate, turning the roller with a screwdriver until the paper is rolled in and firmly seated. Then, repeat the same procedure with the rear knurled roller. Tighten the paper as much as possible. (Figure 4.4)

If your orbital sander has clamps, lift the front clamp and insert the paper as far as it will go. Press the clamp down firmly. Repeat the same thing with the rear clamp, tightening the paper as much as possible. Obviously, the sander must be unplugged.

Turn the machine on before touching it to the surface. Then, move slowly in a straight line, lifting the sander off the surface at the end of a stroke. Some craftsmen move the sander in a concentric circle—the pattern used in mowing a lawn by starting along the edges and working towards the center. Pressing down on the sander will overload it and reduce sanding quality.

For polishing, use a lamb's wool pad. After every use, clean the sawdust out with a vacuum cleaner.

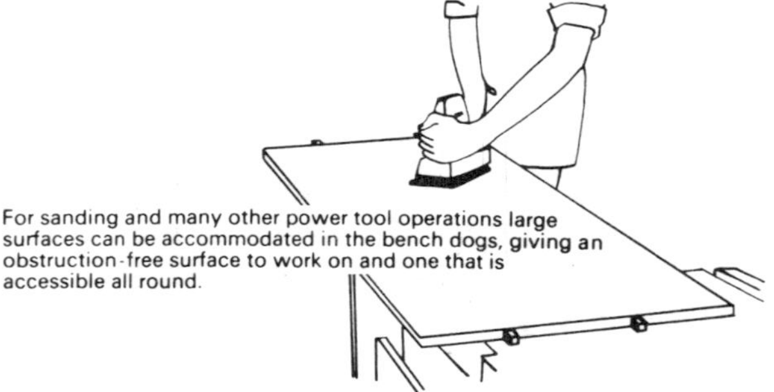


4.4 A Workbench
**Courtesy: Leichtung, Inc.**

## How to Service and Repair Your Sander

### BELT MACHINES

1. If the belt will not stay on track:
   a. adjust tracking controls
   b. clean, adjust or replace guides
   c. clean drums and lubricate axles
   d. check for bent shaft (replace if available)*

### DISC MACHINES

1. If the disc vibrates:
   a. clean and tighten
   b. inspect for bent shaft (replace)*

### GENERAL

1. If the motor speed is too slow or erratic:
   a. clean and lubricate motor (replace brushes if possible)

*means this operation is very expensive

b. check to make sure the paper is not slipping because it is improperly attached.
c. check house voltage to see if it is adequate

2. If the sander is too noisy (and vibrates too much):
a. tighten all components
b. lubricate where possible
c. check and replace bearings (if possible)*

## Three Key Ways to Sand Safely with Your Power Sander

Use these three ways to protect yourself from danger in using any power sander.

*First*, use safety glasses or goggles. Do not even start sanding a small area without them. Never break this rule when using any power tool, especially a sander.

*Second*, get a power sander that uses a vacuum bag to pick up the

4.5 A Homemade Sanding Table

*means that these operations are very expensive

fine sawdust, thus keeping it out of your lungs. If the sander that you are using does not have one, arrange your shop vacuum cleaner so that the nozzle will pick up the dust as fast as possible.

*Third*, make sure that the sander is grounded properly. Do not use any tool—even for just a few seconds—if it is not plugged into a properly grounded three-prong socket.

Keeping these three key safety pointers in mind, use common sense to avoid injury in handling the tool and the items you wish to sand. (Figure 4.5)

## Part B: Metalworking

Although metal can be sanded, the process usually is too rough for sandpaper. Tough emery cloth is sometimes used, but its usefulness is limited. Generally, metalwork that needs to be smoothed down is ground with a series of files and a grinding wheel.

### Finishing Metal: The Tools You Need and How to Keep Them in Good Shape

It's easy to use files to shape and smooth metal. Files range in length from 3″ to 18″. **Single cut files** have rows of teeth which are parallel to each other 65 degrees from center and are used for sharpening tools, finishing work and sheet metal. **Double cut files** have rows of teeth which criss-cross each other and are used for rough work.

The fineness and coarseness of the cut is rated as follows: dead smooth (very fine teeth), smooth (fine teeth), second cut (coarser) and bastard cut (very coarse). Obviously, the length of a file makes a difference because the smaller file has more teeth per inch than a larger file.

**Flat files** and **mill files**, used for general work, are tapered in width and thickness. **Square files**, tapered on all sides, are used to file rectangular holes; **triangular files** are used to square the corners of such holes. **Round files** are used to file round holes. **Half round files** are used for filing flat surfaces with the flat side and round surfaces with the rounded side. (Figure 4.6)

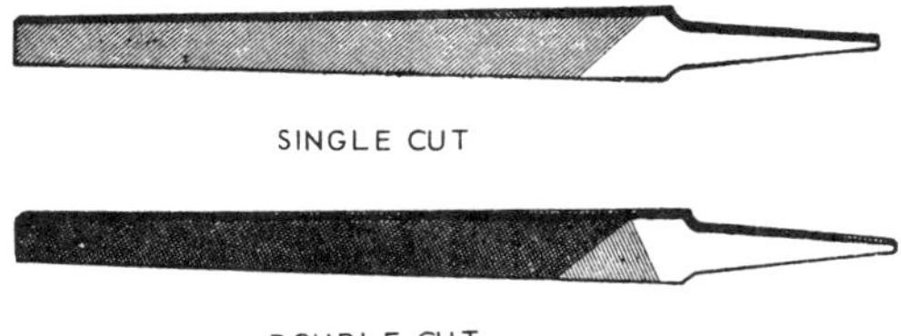


A. SINGLE AND DOUBLE-CUT FILES

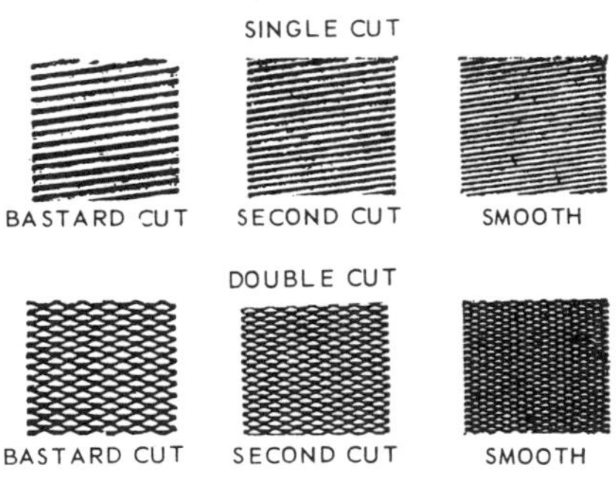


B. DESIGN AND SPACING OF FILE TEETH

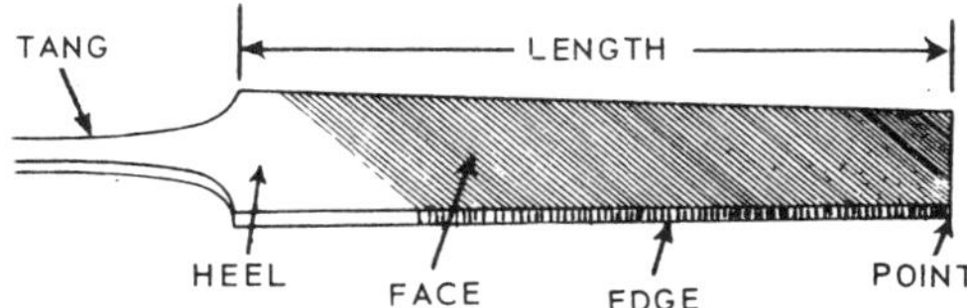


C. FILE NOMENCLATURE.

D. CROSS-SECTIONAL SHAPES OF FILES

**4.6 Files**

The file cuts as you push it, so lift it off the surface on the return stroke. Move across the project at a 45 degree angle and then repeat in the opposite direction. Use emery cloth for a fine finish. Wrap a piece around a block of wood and sand the metal as if you were sanding wood.

Clean your file with a brush. Chalk serves as a lubricant if you rub a bit on the file. Never use oil; it clogs the teeth of the file.

Files are difficult to keep in good shape. Store them in a rack if you can or wrap them in cloth. Files are brittle, so avoid dropping them or using them as levers because they will break. Never rap them on the workbench to clean the teeth for the same reason. Use a handle with every file to avoid cutting or puncturing your hand.

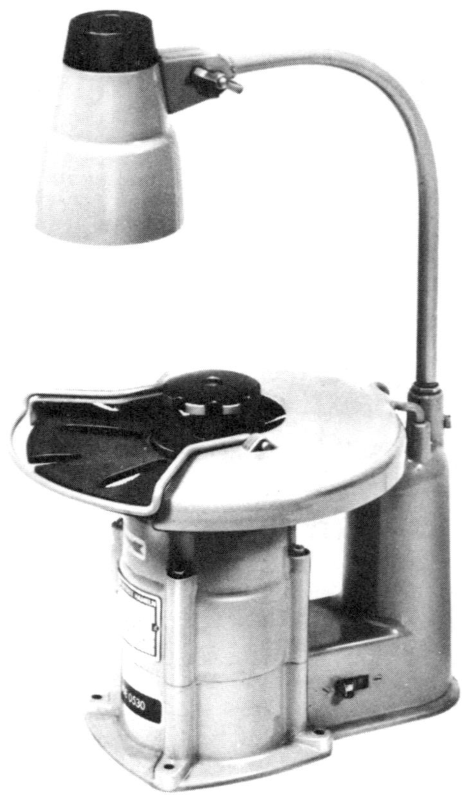

**4.7 Examine Work Through Wheel Slots on New Grinder**
**Courtesy: Leichtung, Inc.**

**Grinders** are power driven tools that can be used to shape metal quickly. Although the grinder is usually used to sharpen tools, it is also used to shape parts and to smooth them as well. (Figure 4.7)

## How to Select Your Grinder

| General Features | Yes or No? (Two *No* answers mean the tool is unacceptable) |
|---|---|
| Is the motor adequate? (¼ hp is adequate; 1 hp is excellent) | |
| Will it take standard sized wheels? (6″, 7″ or 8″?) Are they changed easily? | |
| Does a light come with the grinder? | |
| Are there adjustable tool rests of adequate size? | |
| Is it equipped with a quench tray (for water)? | |
| Are there clear plastic shields to prevent eye injury? | |
| Is it double insulated or otherwise made safe from electrical shock hazards? | |

| | |
|---|---|
| **Is it permanently lubricated?** | |
| **Is it shock mounted or otherwise vibration-proofed?** | |

Like sandpaper, a grinding wheel is composed of abrasive grit held with a bonding agent. However, unlike sandpaper, when these grits become worn, they fall away exposing a new surface.

There are numerous shapes and sizes of grinding wheels available for your use. Furthermore, there are many different types of abrasives, variations in hardness, structure and types of bonding material. Manufacturers often give you no choice in the types of grinding wheels which come with your grinder, but you should know a bit about them in order to get the best possible use out of them.

On each wheel there is a standard mark of 6 units of numbers or letters which shows the following:

**FIRST UNIT: Abrasive Type**

A—Aluminum Oxide (for grinding steel)
B—Silicon Carbide (for grinding non-ferrous metals and carbide tools)

**SECOND UNIT: Grain Size**

10–24 Coarse (for softer metals)
30–60 Medium
70–180 Fine (for harder metals)
220–600 Very fine

**THIRD UNIT: Bond grade (hardness)**

A—Soft to Z—Hard

**FOURTH UNIT: Structure**

1 (dense) for rough or coarse work to 15 (open) for fine work

**FIFTH UNIT: Bond Type**

V—Vitrified
S—Silicate
R—Rubber (for fine finish)

B—Resinoid (for rough grinding)
E—Shellac
O—Oxychloride

**SIXTH UNIT: Manufacturer's Record Number or Letter**

If you select a grinding wheel to suit the type of grinding that you do most often—a typical selection might be **A 24 H 8 V** for the type of surface grinding described in this chapter—you will find that mounting it is a relatively standard procedure. Test the wheel before mounting to see that it is all right. Old-timers tap the wheel with a piece of hard wood to see that it rings instead of thuds. (Figure 4.8)

Mount the wheel by using this procedure. Insert the inner flange (at least ⅓ wheel size); the paper blotter (.025″ or less), rubber or leather blotter (.125″ or less); the wheel (maintain .002 to .005 clearance on the wheel, reaming the center wheel bushing, if necessary); the outer blotter (same as the inner blotter); the outer flange; washer and nut. Then tighten. (Figure 4.9)

4.8 Sharpening a Chisel

4.9 Sharpening a Drill Bit with a Guide

Dressing or cleaning the wheel is done with a **grinding wheel dresser**, available at any good hardware store. Use it by pressing it against the wheel and moving it back and forth.

Truing the grinding wheel means making the wheel run straight with respect to the driving shaft. This can be done by dressing it. Afterwards, check to see that the 1/16″ clearance between the wheel and the tool rest is maintained.

To grind a piece of metal, turn the machine on only after you have donned your safety glasses. Let the motor run for at least 5 seconds to reach its maximum speed. Keeping the object parallel with the center shaft of the grinder and resting it on the tool rest, move it across the face of the wheel with a firm but steady pressure.

To grind a beveled edge, hold the object at the required angle, resting it against the tool rest. For more precise work, a device is available which will hold the object at the precise angle. (Figure 4.10)

To grind a rounded edge, hold the object by resting it against the tool rest and then move the object in the required arc steadily and carefully.

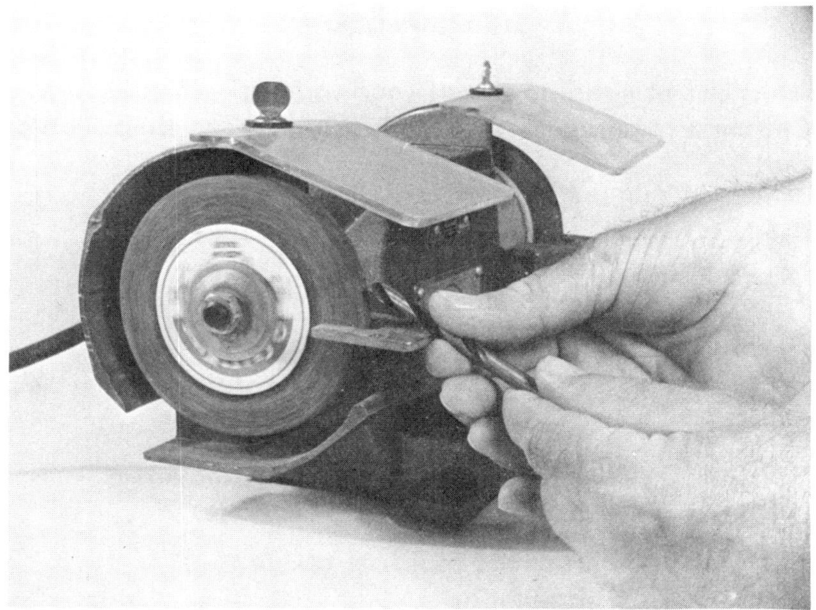

4.10 Sharpening a Drill Bit Freehand

Further smoothing is done by wrapping emery cloth around a block of wood and sanding the surface.

### Safety in Using the Grinder and How to Observe It

The grinder is a potentially dangerous tool, so follow these seven basic rules for safe operation:

1. Wear safety glasses and respiratory filters.
2. Inspect the machine before operation to see that it is in good condition and set correctly.
3. Remove rings and jewelry, fasten or remove loose clothing, and wear headgear to secure long hair.
4. Stand back until the wheel reaches full speed.
5. Maintain light but steady pressure on the object being ground.
6. Grind only on the face—not on the side of the wheel.
7. Use coolant if required for the operation you are performing.

As soon as you are finished, turn the grinder off. Do not leave it running while you walk away for a few moments. You will never regret being overly cautious in working with this important tool.

## SHOPBUILDER #4

Selections of sanding tools (woodworking)—
(Choose according to your needs/Build your shop step-by-step)

BASIC TOOLS:

a. sandpaper
b. sandpaper block or holder

AMATEUR TOOLS: (Include tool lists above)

c. sanding disc attachment for ¼″ drill
d. small power sander (⅓ sheet size—1/5 hp)

ADVANCED AMATEUR: (Include tool lists above)

e. belt sander (1½ hp; 24 sq.″ surface)

PROFESSIONAL: (Include tool lists above)

f. 2½ hp edger-sander
g. heavy-duty 8″ hp drum sander

PROFESSIONAL CRAFTSMAN: (Include tool lists above)

h. belt-disc sander

## SKILLBUILDER #4

Use these tests to determine the level of your skill: SANDING AND FINISHING MATERIAL

ADVANCED AMATEUR: *Part 1*: Sand (by hand) a 1′ long piece of two-by-four—keeping the edge sharp on one side and rounded on the other—to piano top smoothness in 10 minutes. *Part 2*: Repeat the identical task with any type of power sander in 5 minutes.

| | |
|---|---|
| **PROFESSIONAL:**<br>*Do the above plus* | Using any type of power sander, sand a rough 2′ x 2′ plywood surface smooth (including edges) in 10 minutes.<br>Using an appropriate file, smooth the edges of a recently cut piece of steel to a mirror finish (squared off, of course) in 10 minutes. |
| **SKILLED CRAFTSMAN:**<br>*Do the above plus* | Using any suitable wheel, sharpen a set of chisels to "like new" condition in 10 minutes. |

# 5

# Ways to Use Hammers and Other Fastening Tools

## Part A: Woodworking

Putting professional-looking projects together requires skill and good tools. Although simple work can be nailed together, most fine craftsmen prefer using screws and glue. Other materials and techniques are used in working with metal. No matter what the project, select your tools with care—they can make the job easy or almost impossible.

### Hammers for Woodworking

Several types of hammers are used in working with wood: a nail hammer or claw hammer (which has either a curved or a flat claw), a tack hammer, a soft-faced hammer (with screw-on replaceable plastic faces) and a mallet. Sledge hammers and wood chopper's mauls are also used in woodworking to drive wedges when splitting wood. Hammers are striking tools; they are used chiefly to drive nails into projects made in the average workshop. (Figures 5.1, 5.2 and 5.3)

**Claw hammers** have tempered steel heads (16 ounces is the most popular weight) with a hickory handle. Hammers with metal handles are stronger but more tiring in use because wood tends to absorb shocks better. However, metal hammers are excellent for use in pulling nails. New fiberglass-handled hammers are as strong as steel hammers and absorb shock so that little is transmitted to your arm. Choose one that feels good in your hand and then determine whether you want a hickory handle or one made of metal or fiberglass. Most professionals still prefer wooden-handled hammers!

**5.1 A Hammer**
**Courtesy: Stanley Tools**

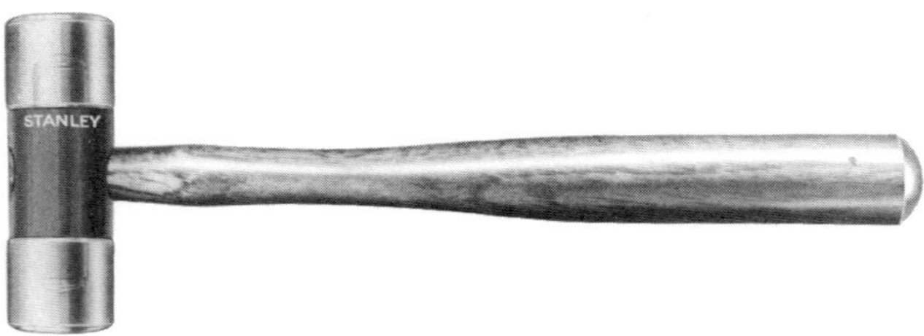


**5.2 A Mallet**
**Courtesy: Stanley Tools**

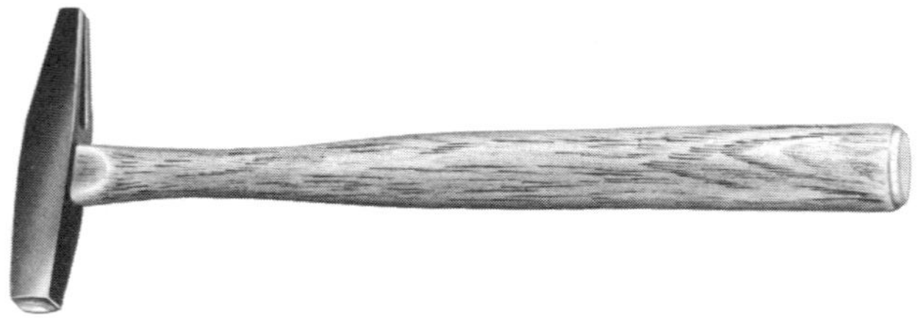

**5.3 A Tack Hammer**
**Courtesy: Stanley Tools**

**Tack hammers** are similar to claw hammers in the materials used in their construction, but they are much lighter. In addition, the face of the tack hammer usually is not beveled or crowned (the face of the claw hammer is formed in this manner to prevent chipping). Tack hammers are seldom made with a claw; a separate tack puller is used to remove tacks. Much of the function of these small hammers has been taken over by stapling guns and small nail guns. Even though you can purchase magnetized tack hammers (which make it easier to drive small nails or tacks in tight quarters), you will find that most jobs go smoother with the use of a fine quality stapler. In doing upholstery work, you will still find it useful to have a small tack hammer in your tool kit—especially if you want to drive decorative brads or nails.

**Wooden mallets** are used for driving chisels in shaping wood. Many craftsmen also use metal hammers with modern chisels which have a metal core and a metal top. (For further information about mallets and chisels, see Chapter 3.) Mallets are generally not used as fastening tools and neither are sledge hammers or mauls—although in rare situations, they can be used for driving nails (as in fastening railroad ties). *Ball peen* and other metalworking hammers are discussed in Part B of this chapter.

Obviously, hammers are used to drive nails; most hammer faces are bell-shaped to make this job easier. But, how do you avoid bending the nail when you hit it? First, hold the hammer near the end of its handle. Grasping the hammer near the head changes the arc at which the hammer strikes the nail and increases the likelihood of bending it. You also waste energy instead of letting the hammer do the work. Second, drive nails straight by using the old-timer's trick of keeping the hammer face smooth and free from nicks (by sanding or filing it lightly). Third, tap the nail gently until you've gotten it started, and then increase the power of your strokes. If you hammer too hard on the first two strokes, you will bend the nail. Most nails can be driven flush with four to five strokes. In finished work, use a nail set (a pencil-shaped metal object) to countersink or drive the nail below the surface of the wood without marring it.

Select a nail of the proper size so that you won't split the wood or come out through the other side. Depending on the strength you require, drive nails every 3″ to 6″ (obviously, the closer the nails, the stronger the joint). Nails are available for a variety of purposes such as: finishing, roofing and flooring. Select the proper nail for the job at hand—there is a difference. (Figure 5.4)

To pull a nail out, use the claw of the hammer. Fit the nail into the "V" (which should be sharply formed in a good hammer). Don't try to pull the nail out in just one pull—you'll bend it and leave an enlarged hole. Instead, insert a small wooden block under the head of the hammer to give you leverage on your second pull, and the nail will come out straight. In removing tacks, use a tack puller (which looks like a bent screwdriver). For rough work use a crowbar or a nail-puller (which is usually 18″ long or more). Bent nails can be straightened out by pounding them, but you will find that they are more likely to bend when you try to drive them the second time.

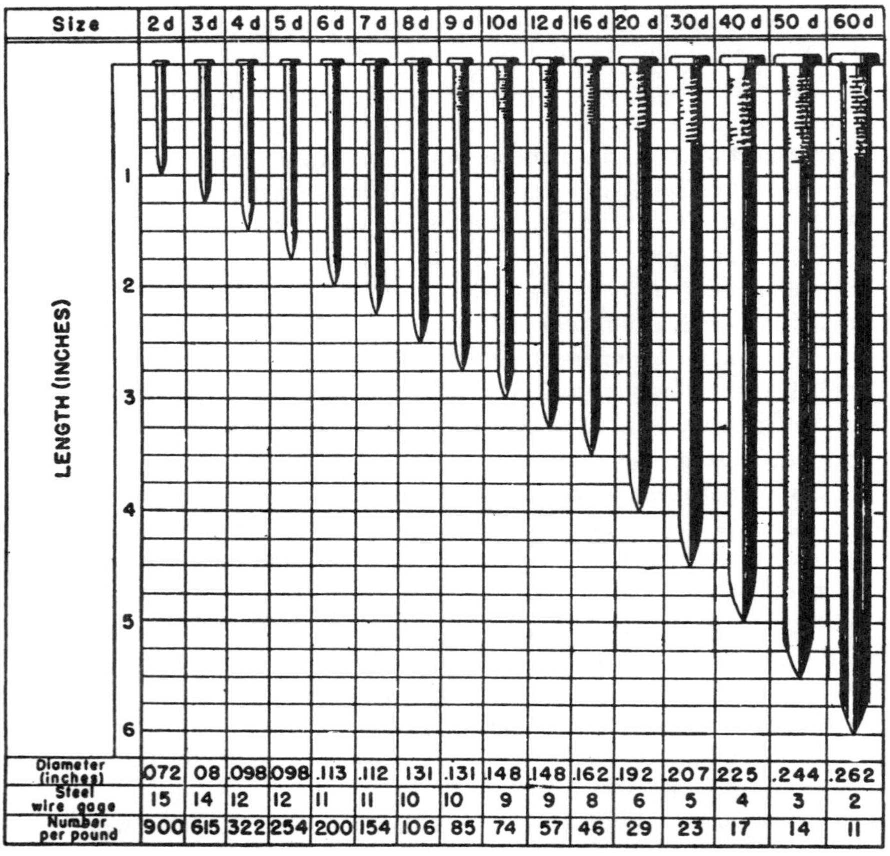


| Size | 2d | 3d | 4d | 5d | 6d | 7d | 8d | 9d | 10d | 12d | 16d | 20d | 30d | 40d | 50d | 60d |
|---|---|---|---|---|---|---|---|---|---|---|---|---|---|---|---|---|
| Diameter (inches) | 072 | 08 | .098 | 098 | .113 | .112 | 131 | .131 | .148 | .148 | .162 | .192 | .207 | 225 | .244 | .262 |
| Steel wire gage | 15 | 14 | 12 | 12 | 11 | 11 | 10 | 10 | 9 | 9 | 8 | 6 | 5 | 4 | 3 | 2 |
| Number per pound | 900 | 615 | 322 | 254 | 200 | 154 | 106 | 85 | 74 | 57 | 46 | 29 | 23 | 17 | 14 | 11 |

5.4 Nail Sizes

### Staplers and Safe Ways to Use Them

Staplers or staple guns drive staples of various lengths ($^1/_4''$, $^5/_{16}''$, $^3/_8''$, $^1/_2''$, $^9/_{16}''$) into wood and other materials. Most jobs which used to be done with a small tack hammer are now done better with a staple gun. In fact, staplers are used in fastening an amazing variety of items from upholstery to crates. The device is simple—it pushes a wire staple into an object with great pressure.

It also can be dangerous if it is not used with care. Do not shoot staples into the air. Do not *squeeze* the lever because you will find it tiring and because you will find that the staple gun may slip away from the spot you are stapling. Instead, place the staple gun flat against the surface you are going to staple. Grip the gun with one hand and place that hand comfortably on the lever so that the pressure will come from the heel of your hand. Then, press the lever down with the heel of your hand in a snapping motion with your weight leaning behind it. Be sure that you keep the gun solidly against the work.

No maintenance is necessary except to remove a jammed staple on occasion. You can usually avoid this jamming if you always keep a minimum of twelve staples in the gun. However, if jamming does occur, use a pair of needle-nosed pliers to pull the staple out of the gun. Don't forget to wear your safety goggles! Do not use a screwdriver or a similar tool in an attempt to pry the bent staple out. You may injure yourself or damage the staple gun.

### How to Select and Use Nail Guns

Nail driving tools are useful if you are doing extensive nailing, as, for example, in installing wall paneling. Although there are some very high powered nail guns on the market (one actually fires a ten penny nail by means of a gun powder charge), the most popular one in use drives brad type nails ($1^{1}/_{32}''$ in length) by means of a sturdy spring. (Figures 5.5 and 5.6)

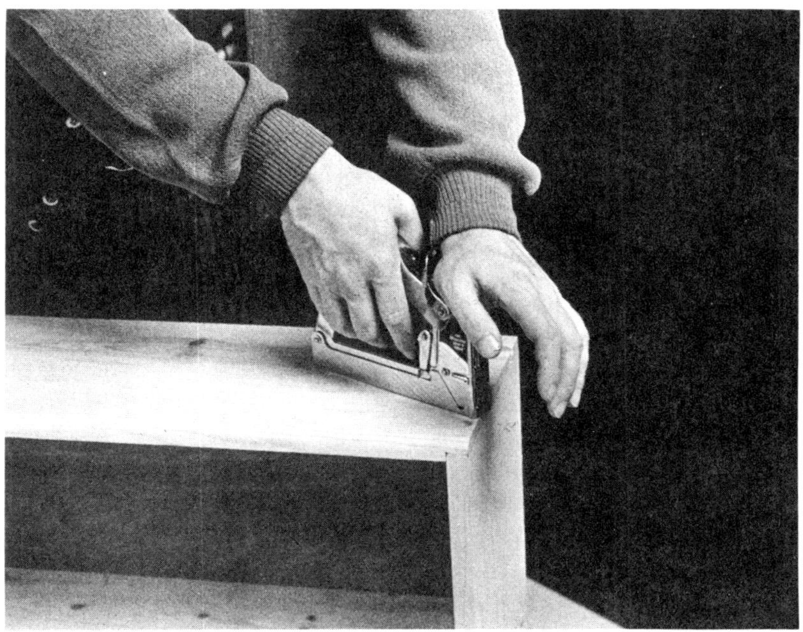

**5.5 A Nail Driving Tool**
**Courtesy: The Swingline Co.**

5.6 A Nail Driving Tool

The nail gun will drive nails flush or countersink them with ease. The device works like a stapler. Place it flush against the surface to be nailed. Hold it with one hand and place the other hand on the power lever. Press downward firmly (don't squeeze), making sure that the gun does not slip or slide. Let the handle return to its original position. Lift the gun—do not slide it to the next spot or you may mar the finish.

Treat the nail gun with respect in order to avoid injuries. Do not fire it into the air. Fire nails only into solid surfaces—for safety and to keep the firing mechanism in proper order.

There are several tricks you should know about to improve your skill with a nail gun. If fewer than three nails are left in the gun when it is opened for reloading, the nails may fall sideways in the bottom of the feed channel. This can jam the gun. To avoid this happening, always hold the gun upside down and shake it before reloading.

Guns have a safety guard which must be released before firing. When storing the gun, however, remove the nails, depress the handle until the gun fires and then set the safety lock. If the gun is not fired before locking it, the safety lock may be damaged or broken from the pressure of the handle.

If the nail gun drives the nail in only halfway (as sometimes happens when nailing into dense materials), unload the gun, close the base and carefully place the gun over the nail. Snap the power in the conventional manner and the nail will be driven all the way in.

Select a nail gun only if you are going to do an extensive amount of nailing. It will not pay for itself if you are going to use a variety of nails in a number of different situations.

There is little care required in keeping it in working order. The nail gun works on the lever principle—lifting an internal ram that is driven forward with tremendous force by a ram spring. A safety lock keeps the ram from moving by accident.

If a nail should jam the gun (this may happen from hitting a knot in a piece of wood), swing open the bottom plate and allow the nail to fall out. If you cannot open the bottom plate, pull back the loading hatch, insert the safety guard and open the bottom plate by turning the safety guard downward.

With care, your nail gun should give you many years of service with little or no trouble. Use it to install floor covering, insulation, molding and paneling. You can also use it to construct boxes and furniture from plywood. Although the manufacturer suggests that you can use it to hang pictures, you will probably shy away from using the gun just to drive a single nail. It is only worthwhile when you have at least a dozen nails or brads to drive.

Remember that nails are generally used for quickly assembled projects or in situations where permanence is the major consideration. For many other tasks, you will prefer screws.

### Screwdrivers

Screwdrivers are often used for many purposes for which they were never intended such as stirring paint, prying open lids and windows, and scraping. Small wonder these screwdrivers never work effectively when used to drive or remove screws! (Figure 5.7)

In addition, cheaply made screwdrivers are difficult and tiring to work with. They are not well-finished and the rough handles cut your hands and make them sore; their tips do not fit the slots of the screws; they are too long or too short, giving you improper leverage.

**5.7 A Screwdriver**
**Courtesy: Stanley Tools**

Insist on using fine quality screwdrivers. Select brand name tools with well-finished handles. You will find sets of assorted lengths—commonly 1/8″ by 4″, 3/16″ by 4″, 3/16″ by 9″, 1/4″ by 6″ and 3/8″ by 12″. In addition to these standard blade-type screwdrivers, get some **Phillips screwdrivers** (which have tips shaped like an "X") which come in numbered sizes. The most useful sizes are 0 (2 1/2″ long), 1 (3″ long), 2 (4″ long) and 3 (6″ long). A set of screwdrivers like this will fit almost any job you'll ever encounter. If you intend to do any fine work, get a set of **Jeweler's screwdrivers** which are usually numbered (a good selection will range from #1 to #6) and range in size from .040 to .100. You will seldom, if ever, need these in woodworking.

Additional screwdriver types you may find occasional need for include: the **reed prince screwdriver** (for cross-recessed screws), **Robertson style screwdriver** (for the recessed square slotted screws used in mobile homes), **clutch head screwdriver** (for screws similar to Robertson style screws, except for their indented centers) and **Pozidriv® screwdrivers** (to drive screws with heads similar in shape to Phillips head screws).

You will also find offset screwdrivers with a variety of tips (to use in hard-to-reach spots), ratchet screwdrivers, screwdriver bits (for use with a hand brace), insulated screwdrivers (for electrical work), magnetized screwdrivers and screwdrivers with small clips attached (designed to hold a screw while starting it).

Keep these tools in a central place and take the time to find the right size and type whenever you need to use it. That way, you will never damage a screwhead or a screwdriver.

Craftsmen prefer screws for most projects because they hold better than nails and are easy to remove in cases where repairs are needed.

Wood screws are turned by a screwdriver and may be flat-headed (to facilitate countersinking them below the surface of the wood), round-headed (when the screw head can be above the surface) and oval-headed (when the screw is countersunk but is slightly raised above the surface). Sizes range from ¼″ to 4″. To install, bore a hole slightly smaller than the diameter of the screw; do not drive it into the wood without drilling or you will split the wood. In addition, you will find it hard to move the screw into the wood. (Figure 5.8)

| Diameter | | | Threads Per Inch | | |
|---|---|---|---|---|---|
| No. | Inch | Decimal Equivalent | NC | NF | EF |
| 0 | ---- | .0600 | --- | 80 | --- |
| 1 | ---- | .0730 | 64 | 72 | --- |
| 2 | ---- | .0860 | 56 | 64 | --- |
| 3 | ---- | .0990 | 48 | 56 | --- |
| 4 | ---- | .1120 | 40 | 48 | --- |
| 5 | ---- | .1250 | 40 | 44 | --- |
| 6 | ---- | .1380 | 32 | 40 | --- |
| 8 | ---- | .1640 | 32 | 36 | --- |
| 10 | ---- | .1900 | 24 | 32 | 40 |
| 12 | ---- | .2160 | 24 | 28 | --- |
| --- | 1/4 | .2500 | 20 | 28 | 36 |
| --- | 5/16 | .3125 | 18 | 24 | 32 |
| --- | 3/8 | .3750 | 16 | 24 | 32 |
| --- | 7/16 | .4375 | 14 | 20 | 28 |
| --- | 1/2 | .5000 | 13 | 20 | 28 |
| --- | 9/16 | .5625 | 12 | 18 | 24 |
| --- | 5/8 | .6250 | 11 | 18 | 24 |
| --- | 3/4 | .7500 | 10 | 16 | 20 |
| --- | 7/8 | .8750 | 9 | 14 | 20 |
| --- | 1 | 1.0000 | 8 | 14 | 20 |

**5.8 Screw Threads Per Inch**

To speed the job up, use either a ratchet screwdriver or a power drill with a screwdriver attachment. Ratchet type screwdrivers use the push-pull principle to turn the screw. Simply grasp the tool in one hand and push and pull the handle with the other hand. In soft woods, plaster and similar material, you can use small bits which come with the drill to avoid drilling with a brace and bit or a power drill. Ratchet type screwdrivers use both standard tips and Phillips tips.

Maintenance of these simple hand tools is not difficult. Use common sense and do not store your hammers and screwdrivers in a wet or very hot place or you will find the handles coming loose and rust forming. You can replace the handle of a hammer by driving it into the head and then hammering a steel wedge into the end, inside the hammerhead. It is impossible to repair or replace a loose screwdriver handle.

### Power Tool Screwdrivers and Ways to Use Them Safely

Do not attempt to put a screwdriver bit directly in your power drill without using a device of some sort to slow down the speed; it is far too dangerous. To be safe, use a **speed reducer** which will reduce the speed of the drill from 11 to 1 (the reverse speed will be cut from 4 to 1). Most speed reducers come complete with both a standard bit and a Phillips bit. Attach them as if you were inserting a bit into your drill. Put the screw into the holder on either side of the screwdriver bit and put the tip of the screw into the pre-drilled hole. Press the drill trigger and the screw will be driven in effortlessly. Quality speed reducers employ a clutch to disengage the screwdriver bit once the screw is driven all the way in.

An alternative device is a **motor speed control unit** which works like a rheostat to drop the speed of your power drill without decreasing its torque (to maintain its power). Most units have a constant speed feature which allows you to adjust the speed from zero to full speed in any variation you wish. Usually operating from 5 to 7.5 amps load, you will find that the best speed is the slowest speed—for driving screws.

Some newer drills have a built-in speed control and all you need to do is press the trigger and lock it in place. In such units, simply insert a screwdriver bit and set the drill at its slowest speed.

Obviously, the first step is to drill a hole slightly smaller than the screw. You should also drill a second hole slightly smaller than the shank or top portion of the screw. Skilled craftsmen know that by drilling two holes, the screw will sit better and hold more firmly.

To be safe, wear goggles when using your screwdriver bit in your power drill. Even at a slower speed, the equipment is still potentially dangerous; the head of the screw could snap off, for instance. Be safe—not sorry—and protect your eyes. Keep your fingers away from the top of the screw as you start to drive it in; otherwise, you may receive a nasty cut. Unplug the drill or keep your fingers away from the trigger when inserting a screw into the screwdriver bit holder. Remember that it is as easy to be safe as it is to be careless.

Maintain your power equipment in good shape by keeping it clean and storing it in a dry place. Since this equipment is lubricated for life, you have no need to service it.

## Rivets and Assorted Fastening Devices—How to Use Them

**Rivets** (soft metal slugs that are hammered flat) are not used in woodworking; however, you may find occasion to use them in attaching plastic or leather strips. Simply flatten them with a hammer after insertion. Metal grommets are also used to fasten plastic and leather together—usually in cases where you can insert a rope or cord after installation. Hammer the grommets carefully or use a plier-like tool that comes with them. (Figures 5.9 and 5.10)

You will also find that pieces of plastic can be fastened by specialized tools that heat the plastic sufficiently to melt it and thus fuse it together. This equipment is seldom seen in the average shop; its purpose is too specific. On the few occasions on which you will need to fasten plastics together, you will be better off gluing them together as described in Chapter 8.

## Keeping Your Fastening Tools in "Like New" Condition

Unlike saws, shapers and sanders, most fastening tools are simple and require little or no maintenance. However, use common sense. Do not store your tools in a wet or hot place—either one will cause handles to loosen, making the tool less efficient and actually dangerous. Sounds obvious, doesn't it? Yet most workshops are cluttered with tools damaged by thoughtless storage.

To be absolutely sure that your tools will not be subject to dampness or extreme heat, get a dehumidifier. Automatic units are relatively inexpensive and require no maintenance, removing 2 to 3 quarts of water from the air in an average workshop in an 8-hour period. Although some units require emptying by hand, it is a simple matter to rig up a drain hose.

Clean your tools after use. It takes only a few seconds to brush debris from your hand tools or even your power tools after you unplug them. Wipe metal parts lightly with an oily rag when you finish a job

**RIVET-IT IS A PROFESSIONAL TOOL ANYONE CAN USE TO FASTEN ALMOST ANYTHING TO ANYTHING.**

**HERE'S HOW TO PUT THE EASY-TO-USE RIVET-IT PROFESSIONAL TO WORK:**

**1**

**Determine proper diameter and length of rivet to be used as follows:**

**a.** Determine size of predrilled hole. Use the rivet that matches the size of the hole. Example: 1/8″ rivet for 1/8″ hole.

**b.** On jobs requiring drilling of new holes, rivet diameter is best determined by strength required. Swingline rivets are available in steel and aluminum, and in three diameters. Steel rivets are much stronger than aluminum rivets. Use steel rivets for very heavy duty jobs and when riveting steel to steel. Use aluminum rivets for lighter weight jobs such as aluminum to aluminum, fabrics, plastics, etc. Aluminum rivets do not rust. We suggest:

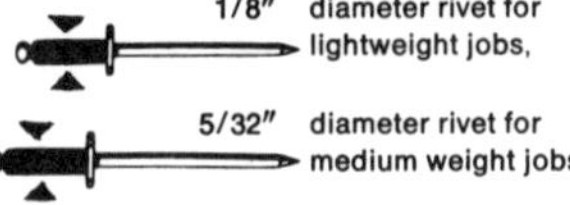

1/8″ diameter rivet for lightweight jobs,

5/32″ diameter rivet for medium weight jobs

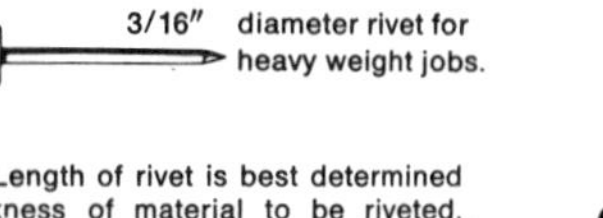

3/16″ diameter rivet for heavy weight jobs.

**c.** Length of rivet is best determined by thickness of material to be riveted. Rivet lengths available are:

SHORT – for work up to 1/8″ thick

MEDIUM – for work up to 1/4″ thick

LONG – for work up to 3/8″ thick

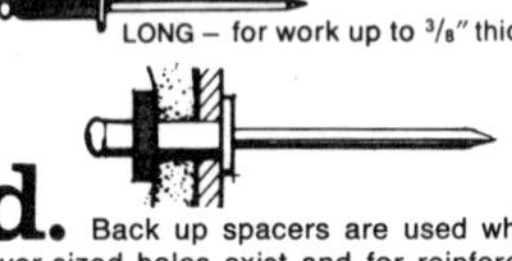

**d.** Back up spacers are used where over-sized holes exist and for reinforcing soft material such as: canvas, leather, plastic, and fabric.

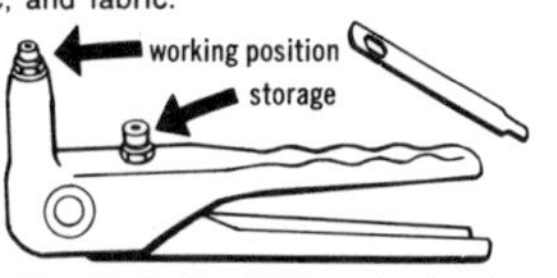


**2** Your Swingline RP-3 professional riveting plier comes equipped with two nosepieces, the smaller size for 1/8″ diameter rivets is in the working position. The larger one for 5/32″ and 3/16″ diameter rivets is stored in the body of the tool. Use the wrench supplied to change nosepieces. Make sure nosepiece is tight.

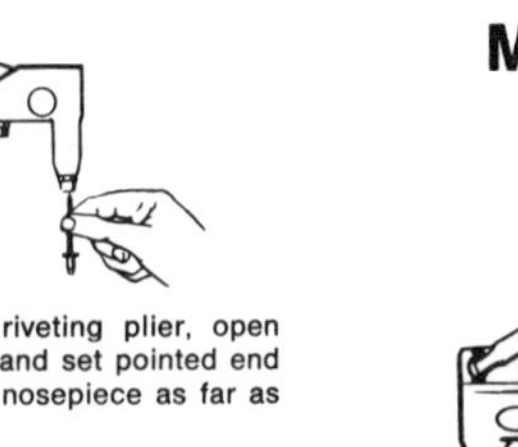

**3**

To insert rivet into riveting plier, open handles completely—and set pointed end of rivet into hole of nosepiece as far as it will go.

**4**

Squeeze handles of tool firmly until rivet stem is broken off. Repeat action if stem does not separate on first squeeze.

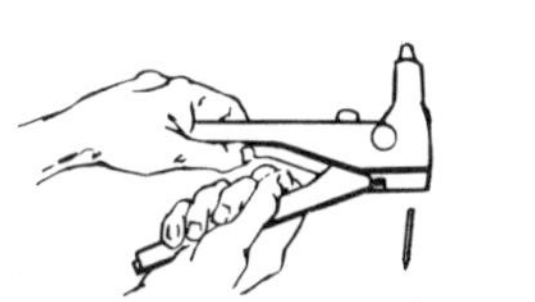

**5**

To remove separated stem from tool open handles completely and turn tool over. Separated stem will fall out of the riveting plier. *Warning:* Be sure to remove separated stem to accept the next rivet and to prevent separated stem from being expelled into the air.

## Maintenance

Occasionally a drop of oil on the moving parts is desirable. Also, it is advisable to clean the jaws. The jaws are easily removed by unscrewing the retainer screw.

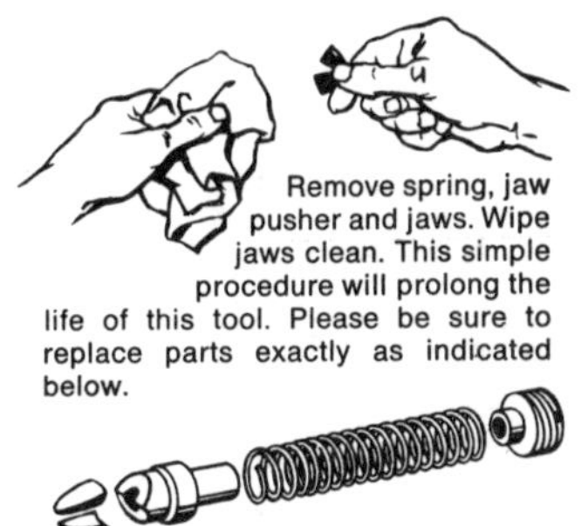

Remove spring, jaw pusher and jaws. Wipe jaws clean. This simple procedure will prolong the life of this tool. Please be sure to replace parts exactly as indicated below.

**5.9 Rivets**

**Courtesy: The Swingline Co.**

and remove rust when you spot it. Use modern chemically treated cloths or rotten-stone (which looks like a small bar of soap) to erase rust quickly and easily before the tool is ruined.

Finally, another bit of common sense advice—store your tools in their proper place after use. That way, you will not run the risk of losing, dropping or otherwise damaging them. Thus, after you have selected your fastening tools, you can keep them for a lifetime with good care.

5.10 Rivets
Courtesy: The Swingline Co.

## Part B: Metalworking

Metal is held together with metal screws or nuts and bolts. In addition, rivets, glues, welding and brazing are also used.

### Holding Metal Together

Metal screws are screws which cut their own thread after being inserted into a hole slightly smaller than their diameter. They are effective for light work, but are easily torn out and cannot be removed and replaced very often without losing their holding power. Nuts and bolts are used for work which undergoes more stress. Welding and/or brazing is used for work which must be rigid and strong.

When using metal screws, you can slightly improve their strength under stress by staggering them so that they are not in a precisely straight line.

Nuts and bolts do not need to be inserted into threaded holes, although sometimes bolts are so inserted alone. Washers of various sizes are used to keep the bolt from loosening. In addition, new chemical compounds are available which keep the bolt from loosening by applying it to the threads before tightening.

Hammers have some use in fastening metals. Riveting hammers, weighing 4 to 12 ounces are the most useful. However, other hammers are used in metalworking such as the ball peen hammer (used to straighten dents and to strike cold chisels and star drills) and setting hammers (with a perfectly square face—used to form metal corners).

Wrenches are tools used to turn nuts, bolt heads, studs and pipes. The finest are made of chrome vanadium steel and are both light and unbreakable. More common wrenches are made of forged carbon steel or molybdenum steel; they are heavier and bulkier. There are many kinds of wrenches, each designed for a specific application.

**Open-end wrenches** are solid and non-adjustable. They come in sizes ranging from $^5/_{16}''$ to 1″ and have their jaws parallel to the handle or at angles to it. These angles, which range all the way to 90 degrees but average about 15 degrees, permit you to work in tight quarters. There are other variations on the straight shaped wrench—some are curved like an "S" and some have off-set handles which permit you to work on bolts and nuts that are below the surface.

**Box wrenches** completely surround the nut or bolt head. You will find this is safer than an open-end wrench because it won't slip off the nut or bolt. However, there is a disadvantage in that the box-end wrench must be lifted off the nut or bolt every time there is not enough clearance to turn the wrench in a full circle. Box wrenches usually have a 12 point head (notched inside in 12 places to permit swinging in a minimum area). In addition, 16 point wrenches are available for light work and 6 and 8 point wrenches for heavy duty work.

**Combination wrenches** have one end as an open-end wrench and the other end as a box wrench. The reason is that once a nut is freed, it can be turned more quickly with an open-end wrench than with a box wrench. However, it is easier to break a nut free with a box wrench because there is little chance it will slip.

## Common Size Combinations of Open-End Wrenches

$^{3}/_{16}$ x $^{1}/_{4}$
$^{1}/_{4}$ x $^{5}/_{16}$
$^{3}/_{8}$ x $^{5}/_{16}$
$^{3}/_{8}$ x $^{7}/_{16}$
$^{7}/_{16}$ x $^{1}/_{2}$
$^{1}/_{2}$ x $^{9}/_{16}$
$^{1}/_{2}$ x $^{19}/_{32}$
$^{9}/_{16}$ x $^{5}/_{8}$
$^{5}/_{8}$ x $^{3}/_{4}$
$^{19}/_{32}$ x $^{11}/_{16}$
$^{5}/_{8}$ x $^{11}/_{16}$
$^{11}/_{16}$ x $^{3}/_{4}$
$^{11}/_{16}$ x $^{25}/_{32}$
$^{3}/_{4}$ x $^{7}/_{8}$
$^{13}/_{16}$ x $^{7}/_{8}$
$^{7}/_{8}$ x $1^{1}/_{16}$
$^{15}/_{16}$ x 1
$1^{1}/_{16}$ x $1^{1}/_{8}$
$1^{1}/_{16}$ x $1^{1}/_{4}$
$1^{1}/_{4}$ x $1^{5}/_{16}$
$1^{3}/_{8}$ x $1^{7}/_{16}$

6mm. x 7mm.
8mm. x 9mm.

10mm. x 11mm.
12mm. x 13mm.
14mm. x 15mm.
16mm. x 17mm.
18mm. x 19mm.
20mm. x 22mm.
21mm. x 23mm.
24mm. x 26mm.

With all types of wrenches, *pull*, but don't push. On rare occasions when you must push, keep the hand open and push with your palm. That way, if the wrench slips, you won't bruise your knuckles.

**Socket wrenches** have a handle with a ratchet device and sockets which are hollow and fit over the nut or bolt. In addition, there are usually bar extension adapters available which will permit you to turn a nut or bolt in a seemingly inaccessible spot.

Sockets are usually available in either 6 or 12 point sizes. The advantage to the 12 point size is that it has to be swung only after as far as the 6 point socket before it must be lifted for another grip. Thus, it can be used in close quarters where there is less room to move the handle (of course, a ratchet handle does not have to be taken off the socket). (Figure 5.11)

Sockets are sized according to the drive side, which is the square hole in which the drive lug of the handle fits (¼", ⅜", ½"). The side which fits the nut or bolt (usually graduated in $^{1}/_{16}$" or 1 mm. sizes) is called the socket end.

There are four types of handles which snap into these sockets. The **ratchet handle** has a reversible lever which operates a pawl inside the tool head that engages the ratchet teeth to turn the socket. When the handle is moved in the other direction, this pawl slides over the teeth, backing up without moving the socket. Each small movement of the handle thus can tighten (or loosen) a bolt. The **hinged handle** can be moved to a position at right angles to the socket which gives greater leverage for frozen bolts. After loosening the bolt, it can then be moved to its original position. The **speed handle** is used like a woodworker's brace to remove the nuts quickly. The **sliding T-bar handle** allows you to attach the socket at any point along the bar.

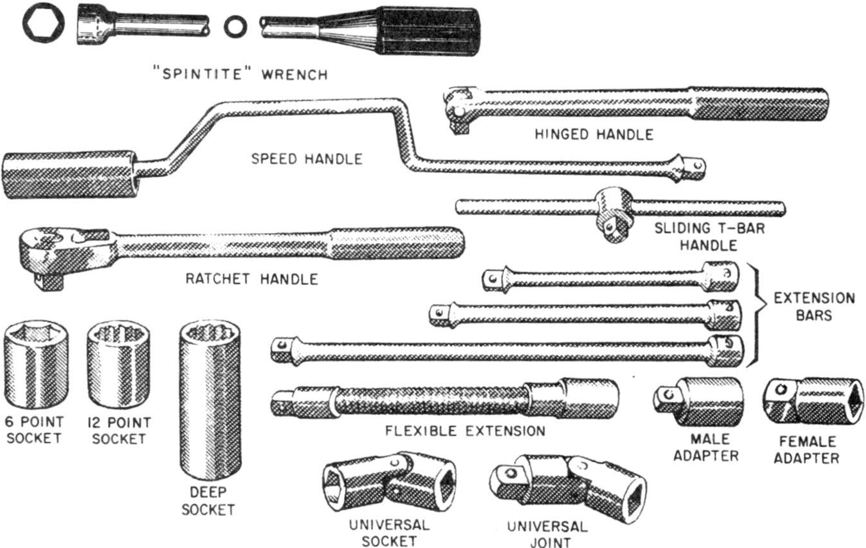


**5.11 A Socket Wrench Set**

Extension bars are made in different lengths (usually 3″ and 6″) to extend the distance from the socket to the handle. Universal joints (allowing the nut to be turned with the handle at any angle), universal sockets, flexible handles, drive size adapters (which let you use a ⅜″ handle with a ¼″ drive socket) and screwdriver handle drive sockets are some of the many accessories that are available to make the job of using socket wrenches easier.

**Nut drivers** look like miniature sockets with screwdriver handles attached. They are used for lighter work than the socket wrench. Available in both fractional and metric sizes (usually $^3/_{16}$″ through ½″ and 4 mm. through 11 mm.), they are used most often by electronic servicemen for the types of nuts and bolts used on radio and television chassis. (Figure 5.12)

Metal can also be glued together with epoxy or it may be riveted. Aluminum is easy to work with and can best be fastened to itself or to other objects with pop rivets. Using a pop riveting tool requires that you have access to only one side of the work. These tools use hollow rivets. A pin or mandrel on one end is pulled through the rivet until it imbeds the head and secures the rivet. For best results, use aluminum rivets when working with aluminum. You will find it perfect for attaching sheets of aluminum to tubing quickly, efficiently and securely.

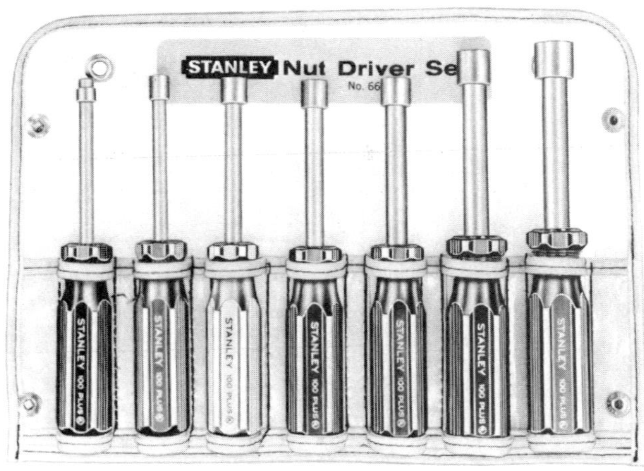


**5.12 A Nut Driving Set**
**Courtesy: Stanley Tools**

## Cutting Threads with Taps and Dies

**Taps** are used to cut internal threads. **Dies** are used to cut external threads. The most common types of taps are the **taper** (used for tapping through holes and starting a tap), **plug hand taps** (used after the taper tap has started a thread) and **bottoming hand taps** (used for threading the bottom of a hole that cannot be reached from the other side). **Pipe taps** are used for tapping pipes. **Rethreading tap sets** are used to recut damaged threads. **Dies** cut threads on the outside of cylindrical objects such as bolts or metal pipes. (Figures 5.13 and 5.14)

Select taps and dies made of tempered carbon steel or heat-treated high speed steel, so that they will stay longer and be able to cut accurately. You need both a fractional set and a metric set. Unless you intend to do a lot of work with heavy pipe (plumbing, for example), you need only purchase sets containing 12 to 50 pieces going from 3 by .60 mm. to 18 by 2.50 mm. (the first number is the amount of threads per millimeter) and from $^{5}/_{16}$″ by 18 to ¾″ by 16 (the second number being the number of threads per inch).

Taps and dies cannot be sharpened except by highly qualified specialists. Keep them oiled, clean and stored in a safe spot.

**Screw and tap extractors** are useful in removing broken screws and taps. They look like screws and are used by boring a hole into the

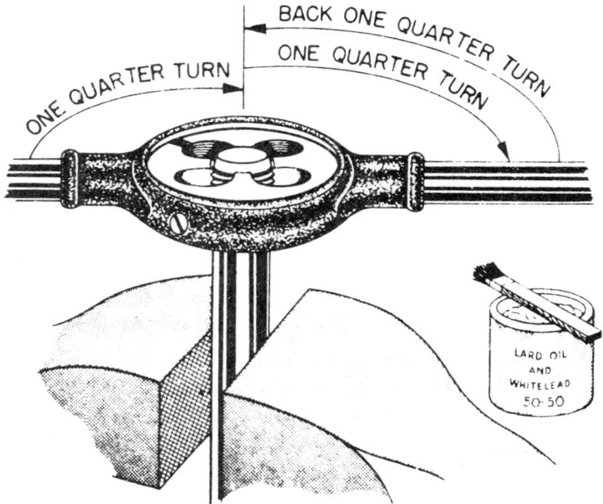


5.13 Cutting Outside Threads

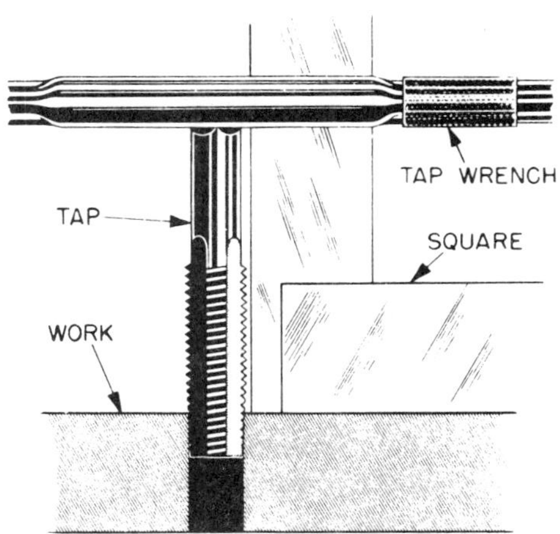


5.14 Cutting Inside Threads

broken screw or tap (the size of the hole required is stamped into the extractor itself). Insert the extractor into the hole and turn counterclockwise to remove the damaged part. A **straight tap extractor** is used if the part has broken off at or below the surface. Place the tap extractor over the broken tap and move the bottom sliding prong into it. Slide the bottom collar down to lock the tool into place. Work or jar the tap loose.

## Soldering, Brazing and Welding

**Soldering** is the process of joining two metal parts (usually wires) by heating them just hot enough to melt the binding metal (1000 degrees Fahrenheit), but not hot enough to melt the parts. **Brazing** is a process in which the two parts of metal are heated just below their melting point and another metal is melted, causing it to flow and join them as one. **Welding** is the process of joining metal by heating both metal parts to the melting point and making them flow together to become one. In the latter two processes, temperatures as high as 5000 degrees Fahrenheit are reached.

To solder, you need only solder and a soldering iron, the tip of which is made of copper. You tin it by letting solder melt on it. If you are soldering electronics parts, use rosin core solder—not acid core solder (useful in soldering some other metals). Heat the metal—not the solder—until the solder flows onto the metal. Remove the soldering iron but do not move the parts until they have cooled (about 30 seconds). (Figure 5.15)

To braze, you need a brazing torch. Although professionals have rather expensive equipment, you can do excellent work on a small scale with equipment now being sold by Solidox and Bernzomatic. However, if you have extensive work to do, you will be better off having it done by a professional. For brazing iron, nickel and copper base metals, you must heat the work (after following the manufacturer's recommendations for lighting the torch)—usually by igniting the oxygen and then igniting the propane. When the metal reaches an orange glow, touch the filler rod (any type except aluminum) to the joint, causing it to flow into the joint. If it does not, heat the metal further. Flux is necessary to clean the joint, ensure correct coating by the alloy and provide protection during cooling. Many welders dip the rod into the can of flux to apply it directly to the joint. Let cool and dip in water.

To braze aluminum, use aluminum rods. This, however, is a very difficult process and you need to practice before you attempt it on anything important. Do not melt the aluminum rod with the flame from the torch. Instead, brush the rod across the heated surface of the joint. Let cool but do not dip into water.

To weld, you must apply the torch to the joint until the metal melts and flows together. In some cases, you can use rods of the same metal to flow into the joint. Welding is more difficult than brazing, but with practice, you can make a good solid joint. Flux is not needed.

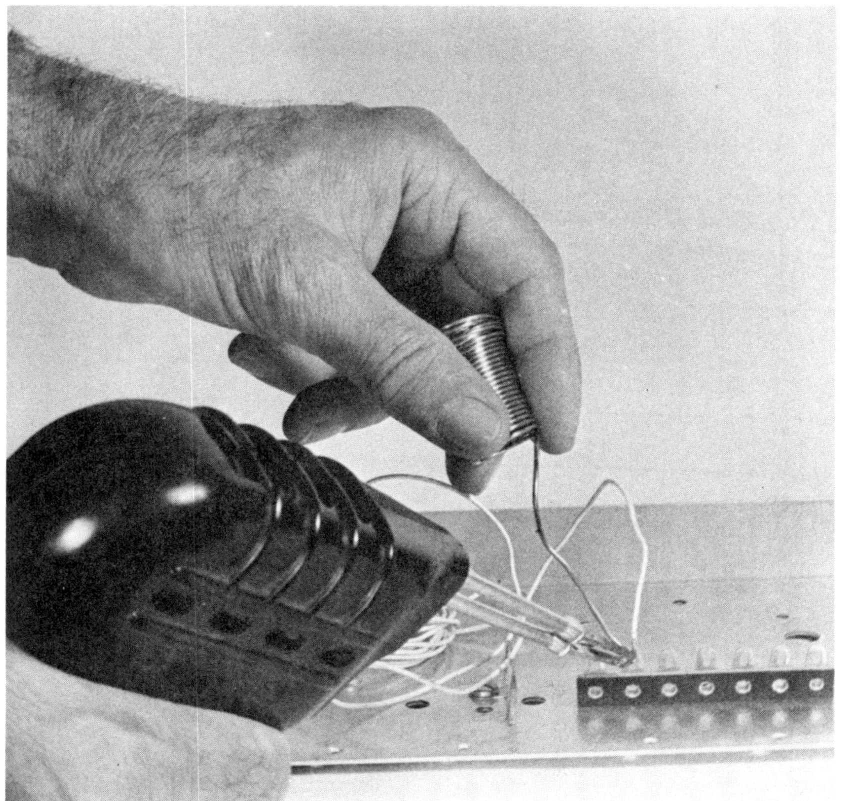

5.15 In Soldering, Heat the Terminal, Not the Wire

Aluminum can be welded as can many other metals. However, some metals, like cast iron, are tricky to handle because they must be packed in sand in order to cool evenly and prevent cracking. Furthermore, you must be careful to avoid welding galvanized steel and cadmium-plated steel (unless the coatings are removed), because dangerous and lethal fumes are emitted from them. (Figures 5.16 and 5.17)

Needless to say, you should always wear welding gloves and other protective clothing, a welding helmet with dark glasses to protect your eyes, and work in a well-ventilated area. Be sure that you have an area that is safe from fire and that you have fire extinguishers nearby.

Brazing and welding, unlike soldering, are techniques that require careful study of the instructions supplied by the manufacturers of the current popular small welding/brazing/cutting torches. Although rela-

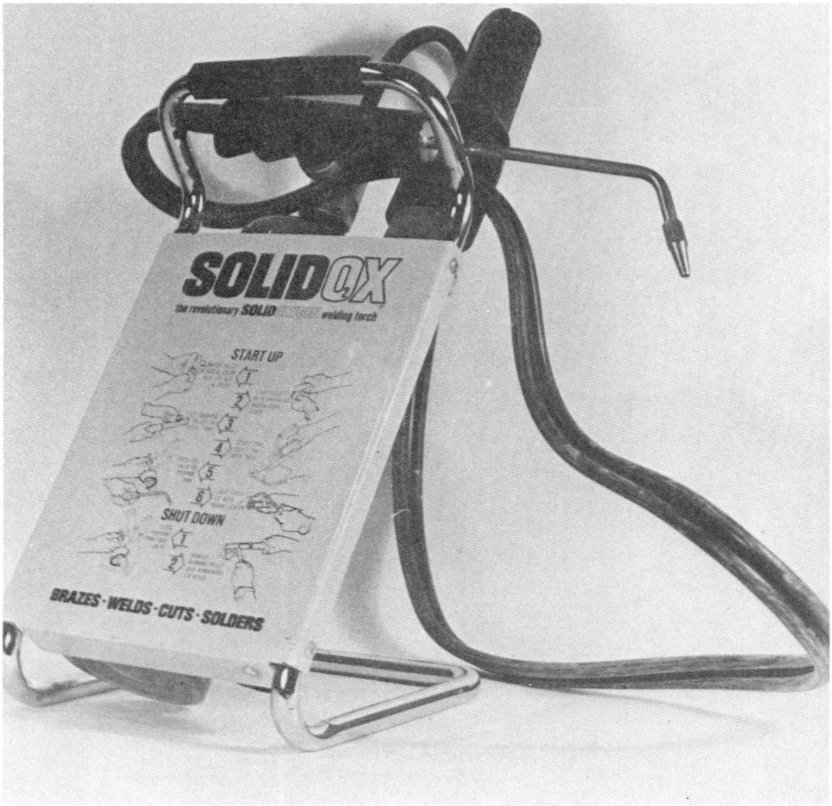

5.16 A Small, Effective Welding Unit

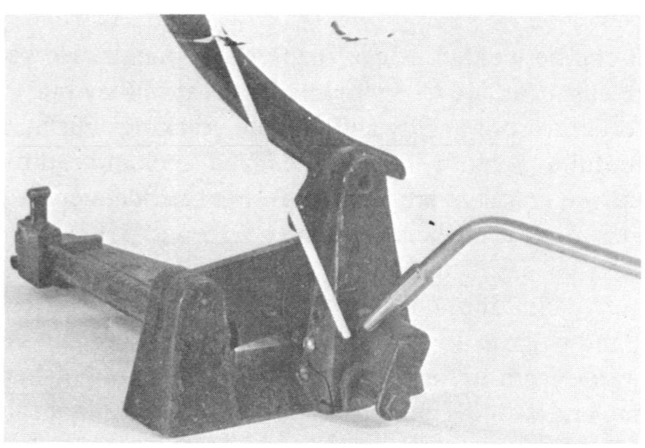

5.17 Welding

tively safe when these instructions are followed, there is potential danger from flashback (the flame disappearing back into the torch where it will burn its way through), injury from melting metal, and fire from careless handling of the torch or metal. However, these problems can be solved through care in watching what you are doing.

## SHOPBUILDER #5

Selections of wood fastening tools—
(Choose according to your needs/Build your shop step-by-step)

BASIC TOOLS:

a. 16 oz. curved claw hammer (hickory handle recommended)
b. 6″ x 1/4″ standard slotted blade screwdriver

AMATEUR TOOLS: (Include tool list above)

c. 4″ x 1/8″ standard slotted blade screwdriver
d. 4″ x 3/16″ standard slotted blade screwdriver
e. #3 Phillips screwdriver
f. 8 oz. tack hammer

ADVANCED AMATEUR TOOLS: (Include tool lists above)

g. 3/16″ x 9″ standard slotted blade screwdriver
h. 3/8″ x 12″ standard slotted blade screwdriver
i. wooden mallet
j. speed reducer for power drill (with screwdriver bits)
k. #0 Phillips screwdriver
l. #1 Phillips screwdriver

PROFESSIONAL TOOLS: (Include tool lists above)

m. #2 Phillips screwdriver
n. ratchet screwdriver (with assorted bits)
o. motor speed control unit (to fit your power drill)
p. dual compression stapler kit
q. nail gun (using 18 gauge 1 1/32″ brads)
r. tack puller
s. crowbar or nail puller (18″ minimum)

PROFESSIONAL CRAFTSMAN TOOLS: (Include tool lists above)

t. soft-faced hammer (with replaceable faces)
u. nail set
v. countersink bit for power drill

## SKILLBUILDER #5

Use these tests to determine the level of your skill: NAILING

| | |
|---|---|
| ADVANCED AMATEUR: | Drive 3 tenpenny nails without bending them, into a two-by-four in 5 minutes. Pull them out without leaving an enlarged hole. No more than one nail may be bent when pulling them out. |
| PROFESSIONAL: | Drive 5 tenpenny nails without bending them, into a two-by-four in 5 minutes. Drive 5 eightpenny finishing nails into a piece of hardwood flooring without bending them. Remove all nails without bending and without leaving an enlarged hole. |
| SKILLED CRAFTSMAN: | Drive 5 tenpenny nails in 3 minutes without bending them, into a two-by-four. Drive 5 eightpenny finishing nails into hardwood without bending them, in 5 minutes. Drive 5 sixpenny finishing nails into hardwood in 3 minutes. Countersink all finishing nails so that no damage is done to the surface. Remove the 5 tenpenny nails leaving no visible marks. |

# 6

# Drills and How to Use Them for Boring

## Part A: Woodworking and Plastic Work

Boring holes of various sizes is almost as common a task as cutting pieces of material to size. There are a variety of tools that will make your work easier. However, you need to know how to use them and how to keep them in tiptop shape. Otherwise, you will make even the simplest task much more difficult.

### The Brace and Bit and Ways to Use Them

**Bits**—often called drills—are used after inserting them into a holder called a **brace** to bore holes for screws and other fasteners. Common bits vary according to the job at hand, but they have six essential parts: **the screw** (which starts the bit into the wood), **the spurs** (which score the circle), **the cutter** (which cuts the wood within that circle), **the twist** (which carries the wood chips out of the hole, depositing them around the hole), **the shank** (which connects the cutting part of the bit into the brace) and **the tang** (a squared-off top section which keeps the bit from slipping or twisting in the brace). (Figures 6.1 and 6.2)

Bits with a steep pitch in the screw (more threads to the inch) that draws the bit through the wood—move faster than those with a fine pitch. Steep-pitched bits throw out larger chunks of wood and move more quickly through the material, making them best for rough work. Fine-pitched bits move more slowly, making it less likely for the wood to splinter and are thus best for more finished work. For all-around use, medium-pitch bits serve most functions. (Figures 6.3, 6.4 and 6.5)

To bore a hole after selecting the correct size needed, insert the auger bit into the chuck (opening the jaws by grasping the chuck and turning the handle). Insert the bit into the chuck as far as it will go and then tighten by turning the handle the other way. Usually the chuck has a square hole into which the bit fits; if it does not, the inside of the chuck is grooved to hold the bit.

For best results, use a center punch or a nail to mark the exact center so that the bit can be placed without error. Then, start turning the brace. To avoid splintering the wood, use a fine bit and turn it backwards two or three times as you bore. Use another piece of wood behind the one that you are boring. When the screw of the bit breaks

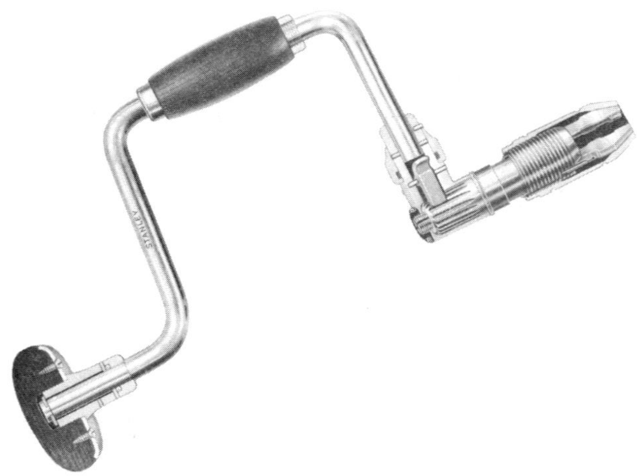


**6.1 A Brace**
**Courtesy: Stanley Tools**

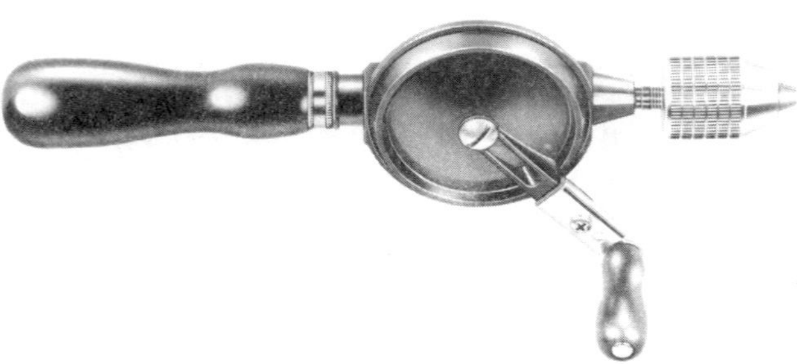

**6.2 A Drill**
**Courtesy: Stanley Tools**

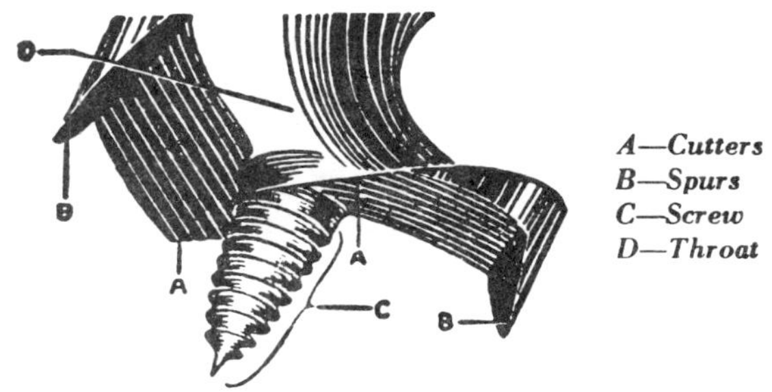


6.3 Parts of a Bit
**Courtesy: Irwin Auger Bit Co.**

6.4 Parts of a Bit
**Courtesy: Irwin Auger Bit Co.**

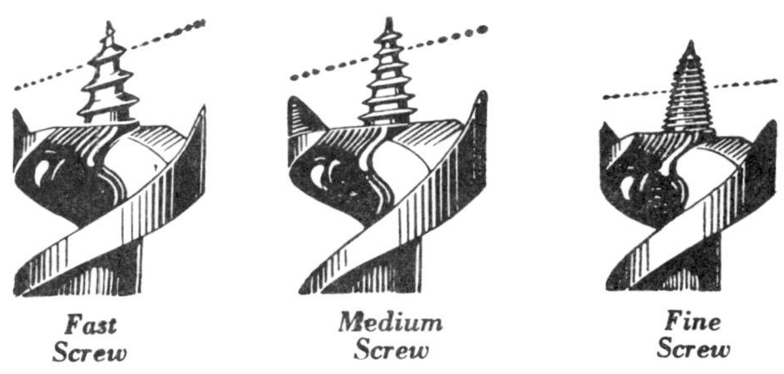


6.5 Types of Threads
**Courtesy: Irwin Auger Bit Co.**

through the other side, stop, turn the board around and begin boring from the opposite side. In this manner, you will not splinter the wood.

If you bore with a twist drill, follow the same procedure. With a breast drill, use the same method, but press your chest against the drill to maintain pressure as you turn the crank by hand.

Although usually you will want to bore at a right angle, you can also bore at other angles as well. Thus, you will line up your drill by using a try square, but you will need to bore through a small block of wood and then cut it off to the required angle before attempting to bore into your project. Subtract the angle desired (say 20 degrees) from 90 degrees and then cut the block to fit the remainder (in this case, 70 degrees).

Auger bits range in size from $^{1}/_{16}$″ to 1″. Larger size holes are usually bored by an expansion bit—a bit with an adjustable blade spur and cutting edge which can bore a hole up to 4″ in diameter. Larger holes than this are cut out with a saw. The size of each individual bit is stamped on the tang in sixteenths-of-an-inch: 6 means $^{6}/_{16}$-of-an-inch.

Braces are holders for the bits which do the actual cutting. The most common braces are those that are held with one hand and turned with the other. There are also breast drills against which the user presses his chest. These, however, are seldom used today. The third and final type of hand drill is the twist drill or push drill which uses a ratchet mechanism to drive the bit into the material. (Figure 6.6)

To bore a hole after selecting the proper size bit, insert it into the chuck of the brace as far as it will go, opening the jaws of the chuck by grasping the chuck and turning the handle. Then, turn your hand the other way to tighten the bit in the chuck. Usually, the chuck has a square hole into which the tang fits; if it does not, the inside of the chuck will be grooved to hold the bit. (Figure 6.7)

For best results in boring, use a center punch to indent the exact center so that the tip of the bit screw can be inserted without error. Start turning the brace, moving slowly and carefully as the spurs begin to score the wood so as not to split it. For further assurance that the wood won't split, turn backwards two or three times as you bore through the piece. (Figure 6.8)

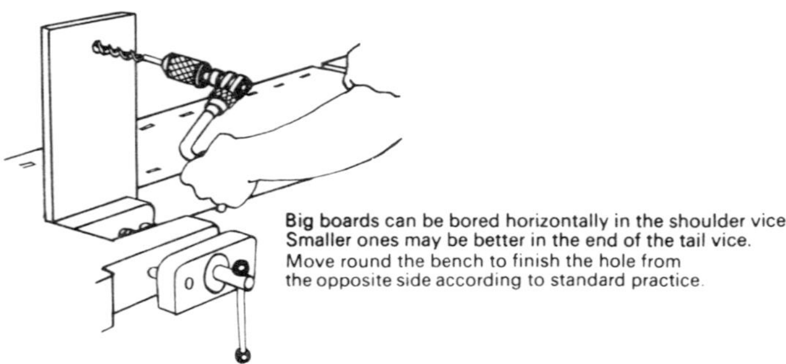


**6.6 Using Your Workbench**
**Courtesy: Leichtung, Inc.**

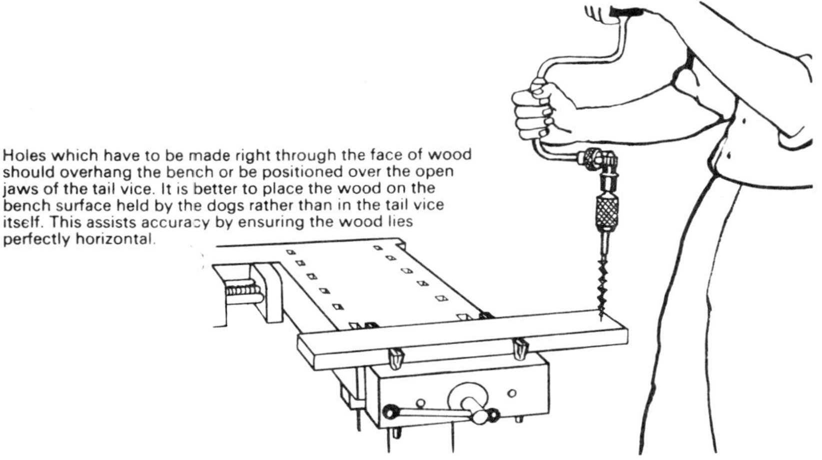


**6.7 Using Your Workbench**
**Courtesy: Leichtung, Inc.**

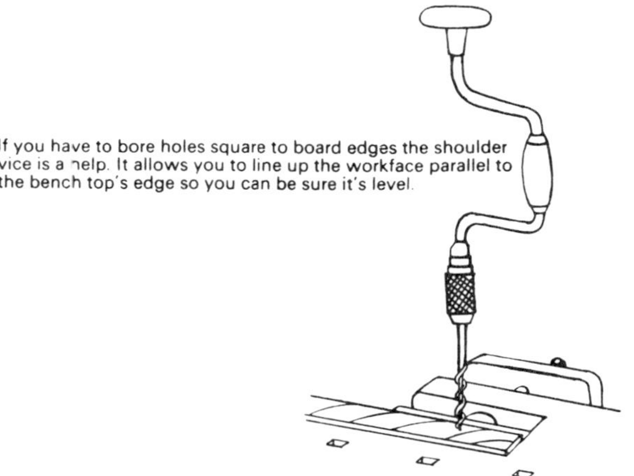


**6.8 Using Your Workbench**
**Courtesy: Leichtung, Inc.**

Always back up the wood you are boring through with another piece of wood. When the screw tip of the bit breaks through the other side of the board, stop and turn the board around and bore from the other side. In this manner, you will always avoid splitting the wood. Needless to say, you should always use well-sharpened bits to make your cut as clean as possible.

Bits are not as easy to sharpen as twist drills, but the process is mastered after a little practice. Be careful, because filing too much will reduce the boring quality. Rest the bit with the screw facing up and lightly file the inside of the spur (never the outside). Then, with the screw facing down, file the upper edge of the cutters, making both equal. There is no need to achieve razor sharpness.

You can best determine whether a bit needs sharpening if you examine the chips. If they are uneven (both thick and thin) the cutters are not equally sharp. If the chips have rough edges, the spurs need to be touched up.

If you find that you can choose between different types of bits, you will find that the twist and straight bore drills will do a fine job cutting hard woods and the double twist drills serve better in cutting soft woods. For the general run of the mill work, however, single twist drills are more than adequate. If you intend to bore into the end of wood pieces a great deal, you should use a Forstner bit (which looks like a sharp-edged jar lid attached to the shank) which can even cut through knots cleanly.

Other bits for specialized purposes are the **bell hanger's drill** (a drill designed for use in wood but which can also be used on metal), a **gimlet bit** for boring screw holes, a **ship's auger bit** (which range from 16″ to 24″ in length), **dowel bits** (short bits used to bore dowel holes) and **expansion bits** (which can change the size hole they bore by adjusting a screw).

## Push Drills and How to Make Use of Them

**Push drills** look similar to a screwdriver and, in fact, can usually be used as a screwdriver. Use them to bore small holes for starting screws without bothering to drag out your drill and plug it in.

The drill bits are usually stored in the handle. Select one, and you will notice that it works on a principle different from ordinary bits which are shaped like enormous screws. Push drill bits are grooved on both sides. They can be sharpened on a grinder.

To use a push drill, hold the handle of the drill in one hand, release the magazine and select your bit. Loosen the chuck as far as possible, insert the bit and tighten. Center the drill and press down firmly. A small button on the side will change the direction (to reverse or stop altogether).

Use this drill only with wood and similar soft materials like plaster. The drill is excellent for use in installing drapery rods, for example. Push the drill down and the ratchet action will return it. Guide the tool with one hand while pushing with the other. Do not attempt a one hand action because the drill may slip away from the material and gouge your hand.

### Your Power Drill: Its Use and Repair

Power drills are the most frequently used tool in the home. In addition to drilling and boring, they can be used for driving screws, sawing, buffing and polishing, mixing paint, and numerous other jobs with the use of adapters.

Usually, the holes bored with power drills range from 1/16″ to about 1″. The most common power drill is a ¼″ drill which uses a bit with a ¼″ shank. Popular ⅜″ and ½″ drills have ⅜″ and ½″ shanks, respectively.

The size of the hole that is bored, however, can be larger or smaller than the shank. In fact, sets of drills are available to drill almost any size hole. Also, there are adjustable cutters that can be used with power drills to cut holes up to 2½″ in diameter.

You need a ¼″ drill for the most simple jobs about the house; larger drills are required for heavier work. If you intend to drill masonry or steel, you also need a larger drill.

The use is simple, but for safety's sake, unplug the drill before inserting a bit into it. Select the correct size bit, and, in some cases, the correct type for the material you wish to drill. Center punch the material and turn the drill on before you touch the bit to the project. If you turn the drill on after the bit touches the wood, you will cause the bit to wander, scratching the surface.

If the drill stalls while you are drilling, you are applying too much pressure. This will also be seen if the drill smokes or the wood is scorched. This can cause damage to your drill or bit. In addition, the bit may snap off or bend. For these reasons, it is wise to wear goggles or protective eye shields even when boring a single hole. Although the drill usually works too fast to bore from the other side, you should still back it up with another board.

With standard drills, speed varies only with the amount of load. However, there are some drills which vary their speed as you increase the amount of pressure you put on their trigger. Their speed may be slowed by the amount of load, but you need only press the trigger harder. Still other drills, called full-torque variable-speed drills, automatically increase their speed when they sense an increased load. (Figure 6.9)

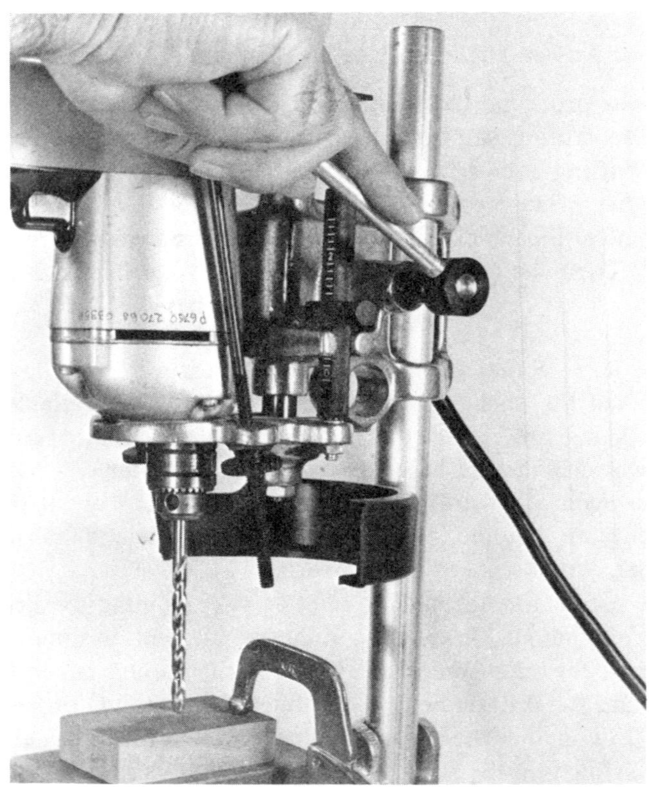

**6.9 A Hand Drill Press**

Generally, a power drill has one major control—a trigger which can be locked in the on position by pressing in a small red button located above it. Pressing the trigger again unlocks the button and turns off the power. Some more sophisticated models have a reverse control. Reversing the rotation of the drill is particularly useful in performing such jobs and removing screws with the proper attachment.

Drill speed is important in performing the best possible job. For example, driving screws is dangerous to attempt at the normal speed of 3600 rpm. Instead, you need to slow the rpm down to about 700. On the other hand, a high speed of 3000 rpm is useful in drilling a ¼″ hole through a ¼″ board.

Insert bits and accessories into the chuck with care. Unplug the drill, open the chuck all the way, insert the bit as far as it will go and tighten by hand. Then, tighten with the chuck key *using it in all three holes*.

To unfasten the chuck, unplug the drill. Insert the chuck key and turn. Then untighten the rest of the way by hand. Remove the drill.

To remove the chuck itself is seldom necessary, but if you have a need to do so, close the chuck jaws and insert the chuck key into any of the three holes. If you have a reversible drill, you will find a screw inside the chuck which must be removed. Tap the chuck key with a mallet in a counterclockwise direction and unscrew by hand. When replacing the chuck, you need only to tighten by hand.

## How to Service and Repair Your Hand Power Drill

1. **If the speed seems slow and erratic:**
   a. **check tightening of the drill bit in the chuck**
   b. **clean the motor, replace the brushes and lubricate, if possible**
   c. **check the house current**
2. **If the chuck is damaged or wobbles:**
   a. **tighten and clean chuck**
   b. **replace chuck**

Please note that many inexpensive hand power drills are glued together, which makes it almost impossible for you to take them apart and then put them back together. In effect, these small power tools are throwaway tools. When something goes wrong, it is actually cheaper to throw them away than to repair or rebuild them. Fortunately, with care, even these cheap power drills should last you a long period of time. However, when the drill stops operating, you will have to replace it.

## How to Select Your Drill Press

| General Features | Yes or No? (Two *No* answers mean the tool is unacceptable) |
| --- | --- |
| Is the motor included? (Minimum ⅓ hp) | |
| Is a stand or bench included? | |
| Are the bearings steel? Lifetime lubrication? | |
| Rustproofing? | |
| Is variable speed available? Simple or complex in operation? (Dial controls are better than pulleys and belts) | |
| Safely constructed? (Enclosed belts? Guarded on and off switch?) | |
| Are the controls clearly marked or labeled? | |
| How much floor space is required? | |

| Specific Features | Yes or No? |
| --- | --- |
| Is the table large enough? (6″ square is adequate) | |
| Can the table or motor be tilted to permit precision boring to at least a 60 degree angle? | |
| Is the capacity sufficient? (You should be able to drill to the middle of a 12″ circle) | |
| Is the distance of the chuck to the table adequate? (12″ is the minimum acceptable distance) | |
| Is the distance of the chuck to the floor (in large floor-mounted presses) at least 40″? | |
| Is the quill feed at least 4″? | |

## Drill Presses and How to Select, Use and Service Them

For more accuracy in boring holes, your shop should be equipped with a drill press. This tool is basically a motor-driven drill, mounted on a pole which gives it rigidity as it forces the drill bit into the project. (Figure 6.10)

For operation, select the correct bit, put on your safety glasses, and adjust the height of the head (if necessary). Insert the drill bit into the chuck and tighten. Fasten the work to be bored by C-clamps or similar devices and test the position of the drill bit (with the power off) to see if the hole will be bored correctly.

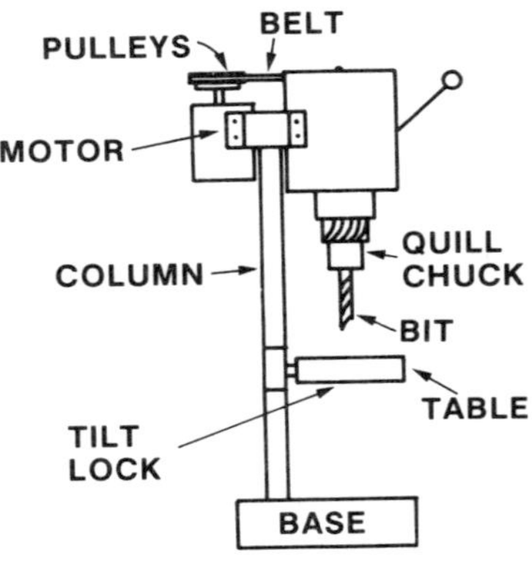


**6.10 A Drill Press**

Turn the switch to ON and grasp the feed lever. Press downward with a steady and slow pressure. Erratic and jerky motions may damage the press or the drill bit. Bore the hole and let the feed lever return to its original position by keeping your hand on it so that it doesn't fly back. Turn the motor switch to OFF and wait until the spindle stops revolving before attempting to remove the project.

Usually the drill press is used to bore holes up to 1″ in diameter at right angles to the project. However, it is possible to bore holes at other angles by tilting the table (usually by loosening a lockpin or wingnut) to the required angle and locking it in place.

In addition, it is possible to drill a hole to a specified depth. Almost all drill presses have a 4″ stroke which means that is the deepest they can ordinarily drill. However, most quality machines have a drill depth device which can be locked at depths less than 4″. (Figure 6.11)

### Ways to Avoid Breaking Drill Bits

Check these points and you will avoid breaking your drill bits in using your power hand drill:

1. Select drill bits larger than 1/16″ (smaller holes must be bored with a drill press).
2. Check to see that the drill bit is not bent or misshapen.
3. Be certain that the drill is held correctly at the right angle.

| Drill | Decimal | Drill | Decimal | Drill | Decimal | Drill | Decimal |
|---|---|---|---|---|---|---|---|
| 80 | 0.0135 | 49 | 0.073 | 20 | 0.161 | H | 0.266 |
| 79 | 0.0145 | 48 | 0.076 | 19 | 0.166 | I | 0.272 |
| 78 | 0.016 | 5/64 | 0.078125 | 18 | 0.1695 | J | 0.277 |
| 1/64 | 0.0156 | 47 | 0.0785 | 11/64 | 0.171875 | K | 0.281 |
| 77 | 0.018 | 46 | 0.081 | 17 | 0.173 | 9/32 | 0.28125 |
| 76 | 0.02 | 45 | 0.082 | 16 | 0.177 | L | 0.29 |
| 75 | 0.021 | 44 | 0.086 | 15 | 0.18 | M | 0.295 |
| 74 | 0.0225 | 43 | 0.089 | 14 | 0.182 | 19/64 | 0.296875 |
| 73 | 0.024 | 42 | 0.0935 | 13 | 0.185 | N | 0.302 |
| 72 | 0.025 | 3/32 | 0.09375 | 3/16 | 0.1875 | 5/16 | 0.3125 |
| 71 | 0.026 | 41 | 0.096 | 12 | 0.189 | 0 | 0.316 |
| 70 | 0.028 | 40 | 0.098 | 11 | 0.191 | P | 0.323 |
| 69 | 0.0292 | 39 | 0.0995 | 10 | 0.1935 | 21/64 | 0.328125 |
| 68 | 0.031 | 38 | 0.1015 | 9 | 0.196 | Q | 0.332 |
| 1/32 | 0.03125 | 37 | 0.104 | 8 | 0.199 | R | 0.339 |
| 67 | 0.032 | 36 | 0.1055 | 7 | 0.201 | 11/32 | 0.34375 |
| 66 | 0.033 | 7/64 | 0.109375 | 13/64 | 0.203125 | S | 0.348 |
| 65 | 0.035 | 35 | 0.11 | 6 | 0.204 | T | 0.358 |
| 64 | 0.036 | 34 | 0.111 | 5 | 0.2055 | 23/64 | 0.359375 |
| 63 | 0.037 | 33 | 0.113 | 4 | 0.209 | U | 0.368 |
| 62 | 0.038 | 32 | 0.116 | 3 | 0.213 | 3/8 | 0.375 |
| 61 | 0.039 | 31 | 0.12 | 7/32 | 0.21875 | V | 0.377 |
| 60 | 0.04 | 1/8 | 0.125 | 2 | 0.221 | W | 0.386 |
| 59 | 0.041 | 30 | 0.1285 | 1 | 0.228 | 25/64 | 0.390625 |
| 58 | 0.042 | 29 | 0.136 | A | 0.234 | X | 0.397 |
| 57 | 0.043 | 28 | 0.1405 | 15/64 | 0.234375 | Y | 0.404 |
| 56 | 0.0465 | 9/64 | 0.140625 | B | 0.238 | 13/32 | 0.40625 |
| 3/64 | 0.046875 | 27 | 0.144 | C | 0.242 | Z | 0.413 |
| 55 | 0.052 | 26 | 0.147 | D | 0.246 | 27/64 | 0.421875 |
| 54 | 0.055 | 25 | 0.1495 | E | 0.25 | 7/16 | 0.4375 |
| 53 | 0.0595 | 24 | 0.152 | 1/4 | 0.25 | 29/64 | 0.453125 |
| 1/16 | 0.0625 | 23 | 0.154 | F | 0.257 | 15/32 | 0.46875 |
| 52 | 0.0635 | 5/32 | 0.15625 | G | 0.261 | 31/64 | 0.484375 |
| 51 | 0.067 | 22 | 0.157 | 17/64 | 0.265625 | 1/2 | 0.5 |
| 50 | 0.07 | 21 | 0.159 | | | | |

**6.11 Decimal Equivalents of Drill Sizes**

4. Clamp the work down securely.
5. Hold the drill steady and firmly without putting too much pressure on the drill bit.

In addition, watch for the warning sounds of a drill squeaking, the smell of burning or the sight of smoke wisping from the work. These are all signs that the drill is being driven too fast or at too high a rate of speed and is overheating. In such a case, the drill bit will break, lose its temper and become dull, or bend. In any event, these signs indicate that trouble is ahead if you continue using the drill at that speed.

## How to Use Your Drill Press on Metals

Since the hand power drill is difficult to use on precision projects, you will use your drill press instead. First, mark the hole carefully (using a template if you have more than one hole to drill) and mark the center with a punch. Select an appropriate drill and insert it into the drill press. Wear your safety glasses and run the press at the slowest speed possible for the size drill bit and the type of metal that you are boring. Clamp the project firmly and test the movement of the drill before you turn it on.

## How to Service and Repair Your Drill Press

1. If the speed seems slow or erratic:
   a. clean the motor and replace the brushes (lubricate if possible)
   b. check pulley belts and replace if needed
   c. check pulleys for alighment, wear or damage (replace if needed)
   d. check speed control (if equipment has one separate from pulley system)
2. If the chuck is damaged or wobbles:
   a. tighten and clean the chuck
   b. replace the chuck
3. If the table is damaged or out of alignment:
   a. straighten and clean
   b. file the surface of the table swivel
   c. regrind the table*
   d. replace the table (if part is available)*
4. If the drill runs noisily (pulley noise is normal):
   a. locate and tighten loosened parts
   b. lubricate sparingly (#10 machine oil)
   c. check for and replace bearing housings (if available)*

---

*means that this particular operation is very expensive

# Part B: Metalworking

Use your power hand drill to bore holes in metal safely. Although you can use a ¼″ drill, you will be better off with a ⅜″ or ½″ drill. These sizes refer to the diameter of the shank of the drill bit that can be inserted into them.

## How to Bore Holes in Metal

Generally, you will get the best results from high speed steel drills, although some craftsmen get by with carbon tool steel drills. High speed steel twist drills are often given fractional sizes by the manufacturer which may be stamped on the shank. However, some shanks bear metric sizes or numerical sizes (1 is the largest and 60 is the smallest, usually). If you purchase a fine quality set with a drill stand, you will have little trouble keeping them straight. A further caution on your purchase is that bargain drill bits are often off-center which makes it difficult to bore an accurate hole, wears the drill bit abnormally and is very hard on your equipment.

To work with metal, your drill should have variable speeds, because as a rule of thumb, the larger the drill, the slower the speed necessary to bore well. (Figure 6.12)

Unless you have some way of securing your hand drill and also securing the metal stock that you are boring, you will find it difficult to make a precision cut. Leave such work to your drill press. Use your hand power drill to make holes in non-critical places and on odd-shaped objects that would require a complicated jig on your drill press.

Wear your safety glasses and secure the work in a vise or with a C-clamp. Check to see that the selected drill bit (at least $^{1}/_{16}$″ in size) is not bent; otherwise, you are sure to break it. Press the trigger and then touch the drill to the metal. Do not force the drill or you will break the drill bit. Keep the drill steady and straight to avoid breaking the bit.

## How to Sharpen Your Drill Bits

Although you can purchase a bit sharpener which looks and works something like a pencil sharpener, you can also sharpen your drill bits on your grinder. There, it can be done freehand or with a holder.

| Diameter of Drill | Soft Metals 300 F.P.M. | Annealed Cast Iron 140 F.P.M. | Mild Steel 100 F.P.M. | Malleable Iron 90 F.P.M. | Hard Cast Iron 80 F.P.M. | Tool or Hard Steel 60 F.P.M. | Alloy Steel Cast Steel 40 F.P.M. |
|---|---|---|---|---|---|---|---|
| 1/16 (No. 53 to 80) | 18320 | 8554 | 6111 | 5500 | 4889 | 3667 | 2445 |
| 3/32 (No. 42 to 52) | 12212 | 5702 | 4071 | 3666 | 3258 | 2442 | 1649 |
| 1/8 (No. 31 to 41) | 9160 | 4278 | 3056 | 2750 | 2445 | 1833 | 1222 |
| 5/32 (No. 23 to 30) | 7328 | 3420 | 2444 | 2198 | 1954 | 1465 | 977 |
| 3/16 (No. 13 to 22) | 6106 | 2852 | 2037 | 1833 | 1630 | 1222 | 815 |
| 7/32 (No. 1 to 12) | 5234 | 2444 | 1745 | 1575 | 1396 | 1047 | 698 |
| 1/4 (A to E) | 4575 | 2139 | 1527 | 1375 | 1222 | 917 | 611 |
| 9/32 (G to K) | 4071 | 1900 | 1356 | 1222 | 1084 | 814 | 542 |
| 5/16 (L, M, N) | 3660 | 1711 | 1222 | 1100 | 978 | 733 | 489 |
| 11/32 (O to R) | 3330 | 1554 | 1110 | 1000 | 888 | 666 | 444 |
| 3/8 (S, T, U) | 3050 | 1426 | 1018 | 917 | 815 | 611 | 407 |
| 13/32 (V to Z) | 2818 | 1316 | 939 | 846 | 752 | 563 | 376 |
| 7/16 | 2614 | 1222 | 873 | 786 | 698 | 524 | 349 |
| 15/32 | 2442 | 1140 | 814 | 732 | 652 | 488 | 326 |
| 1/2 | 2287 | 1070 | 764 | 688 | 611 | 458 | 306 |
| 9/16 | 2035 | 950 | 678 | 611 | 543 | 407 | 271 |
| 5/8 | 1830 | 856 | 611 | 550 | 489 | 367 | 244 |
| 11/16 | 1665 | 777 | 555 | 500 | 444 | 333 | 222 |
| 3/4 | 1525 | 713 | 509 | 458 | 407 | 306 | 204 |

Figures are for High-Speed Drills. The speed of Carbon Drills should be reduced one-half. Use drill speed nearest to figure given.

6.12 Drill Speeds

Start the grinder and let it run for 10 seconds to come up to full speed, having adjusted the tool rest $^{1}/_{16}''$ from the face of the wheel. Hold the drill bit at an angle of about 60 degrees and turn the drill bit clockwise, increasing the angle to about 50 degrees. As you are grinding the drill bit and moving it in this manner, also move it downward, as well. Thus, you are moving it against the face of the grinder to the left, clockwise and downward. (Figure 6.13)

6.13 Sharpening Bits by Hand

A sharp drill bit has equal drill point angles and has cutting lips. These are difficult to achieve by hand and the task requires experience and skill. You must keep the temperature of the drill down so that you do not draw its temper (keep it cool enough to hold in your hand). Use a drill point gauge to check the angle of the chisel edge and the drill point as well.

Like most craftsmen, you will find that it is better to use a drill bit sharpener which will accurately sharpen drill bits from ⅛″ through ½″. Virtually no practice is needed to attain very close tolerances. (Figure 6.14)

6.14 Sharpening Bits with a Holder

### Attachments to Make Your Drill More Versatile

In addition to common twist drills, you can obtain a wide variety of other bits which will let you use your drill for many different jobs. A wire brush wheel attachment will give soft metals an interesting satin finish (be sure to wear your safety glasses). In addition, you will find a cloth buffing wheel can also be used to give a high gloss to other metal projects. Thus, you can turn your metal shop drill into a very valuable tool by adding to its ordinary use.

## SHOPBUILDER #6

Selections of boring tools (woodworking)—
(Choose according to your needs/Build your shop step-by-step)

BASIC TOOLS:

a. ratchet brace
b. steel bits (1/4″, 5/16″, 3/8″, 7/16″, 1/2″, 9/16″, 5/8″, 11/16″, 3/4″)

AMATEUR TOOLS: (Include tool list above)

c. steel bits (13/16″, 7/8″, 15/16″, 1″, 1 1/8″, 1 1/4″, 1 3/8″, 1 1/2″)
d. forstner bits (3/8″, 3/4″)

ADVANCED AMATEUR TOOLS: (Include tool lists above)

e. ¼″ power drill
f. set of drill bits (1/16″ to ¼″ by 64ths)
g. push drill and bits

PROFESSIONAL TOOLS: (Include tool lists above)

h. drill press (12″, 1 hp) and accessories
i. drill bits (¼″ to 1″ by 64ths)
j. circle cutters (⅞″ to 4″ diameter)
k. grinder and bit sharpener

PROFESSIONAL CRAFTSMAN TOOLS: (Include tool lists above)

l. hollow chisels (for use in drill press)
m. mortising bits (for use in drill press)
n. dovetail attachment (for use in drill press)

## SKILLBUILDER #6

Use these tests to determine the level of your skill:

ADVANCED AMATEUR: *Part 1*: Using a brace and bit, bore a ⅛″ hole through a two-by-four without splintering the edges in 2 minutes. *Part 2*: Using a power drill, bore three ⅛″ holes through a two-by-four—each center 1″ apart with no splintering in 2 minutes.

PROFESSIONAL: *Do the above plus* Using a drill press, bore two holes through a piece of ⅛″ steel in 3 minutes.

Using a brace and bit, bore a hole through a two-by-four into which any dowel (selected by you) will fit perfectly.

Cut a 2½″ circle through a piece of ¼″ plywood (any grade) with smooth edges.

**SKILLED CRAFTSMAN:**
*Do the above plus*

Bore a hole through a 8″ pine shaft with a horizontal drill press.

Cut a 1⅞″ circle through a piece of ⅛″ steel.

# 7

# How to Hold Projects with Clamps and Vises

Every job will be easier to work on if you can hold it firmly and securely in one place. In addition, you will make your workshop a much safer place to work in.

## Part A: Woodworking and Plastic Work

### Selecting Clamps to Fit Your Needs

Clamps are useful folding devices that are inexpensive but long-lasting. **C-clamps** (a piece of steel shaped like the letter "C" with a screw) are available in sizes from 1″ to 8″ and sometimes larger. Use them to clamp two pieces of wood together when you are gluing them, to hold work for boring at your drill press and for numerous other purposes. To avoid marking your project, insert small blocks of wood under the two ends of the clamp. You can also use strong rubber bands, shock cord, or even masking tape for small or light work. (Figure 7.1)

For gluing larger projects, use **hardwood screw clamps** (which have wooden screws or metal screws) for projects up to 10″ wide. Use gluing clamps that utilize ½″ or ¾″ threaded pipe for wider projects. For special purposes (such as gluing corners on picture frames), use **corner** and **miter box clamp sets**. All work on the same principle—tighten the screws until enough pressure is exerted to keep the object straight and steady. Be careful that too much tension is not exerted or you may force all the glue out of the joints in addition to damaging your project. Use common sense.

If you do not do a lot of gluing, it doesn't pay to purchase a wide selection of these larger clamps. Instead, you may rent them or use alternative methods of tying and clamping.

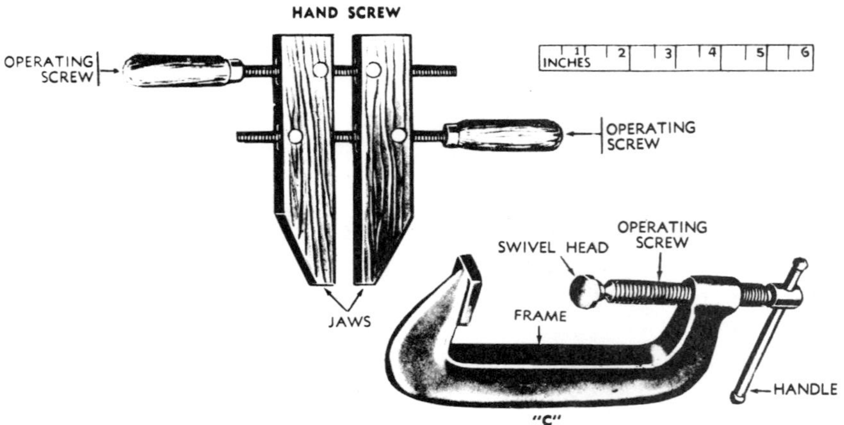


7.1 A Hand Screw and a C-Clamp

### Wood Vises: How to Use and Maintain Them

Wood vises are used to hold projects while you work on them with other tools. It is important that they grip your project firmly without denting, marring or otherwise damaging the surface. (Figure 7.2)

The jaws of a wood vise are broad. A useful size is a 7″ capacity vise with jaw faces of 4″ by 7″. A larger, popular size is a 12″ capacity vise with a 4″ by 10″ jaw face. These vises are generally installed so that their upper edge is flush with the top of the workbench. Some workbenches have holes in their surface into which you fit wooden or metal stops so that larger pieces of wood can be placed between them and the front lip of the wood vise.

A good wood vise is operated by sliding the front jaw closed on the project and then tightening it with a turn of the handle. Reverse the action and your project is free from the vise.

Although there are some models that clamp to the workbench, you will probably only be happy with one that is bolted to the bench and becomes a part of it. To keep it in good shape, clean after every use and keep the screw lubricated. (Figure 7.3)

7.2 A Tourniquet Clamp

## How to Improvise Clamps

For gluing, many projects can be held together temporarily with a strip of masking tape. If there is spring in the material to be glued, or if it is too heavy, it is best to use clamps. However, if none are available, improvise by using blocks of wood and rope or twine. Tie the rope around the article to be glued and insert the block of wood as if you were making a tourniquet. This exerts sufficient pressure to keep the parts in place. Afterwards, untie the rope to release the article. If the rope could possibly mar the object under pressure, place scraps of cloth under it at the various spots where damage may occur. (Figure 7.4)

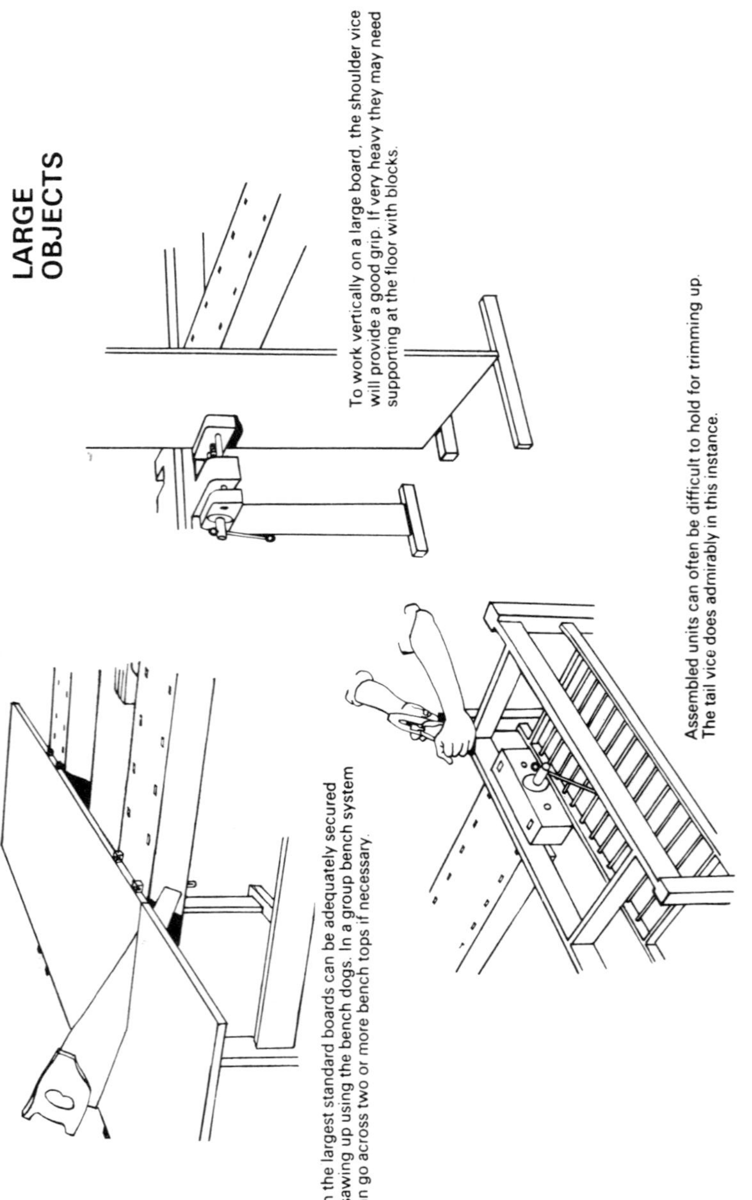


**7.3 A Bench Vise**
**Courtesy: Leichtung, Inc.**

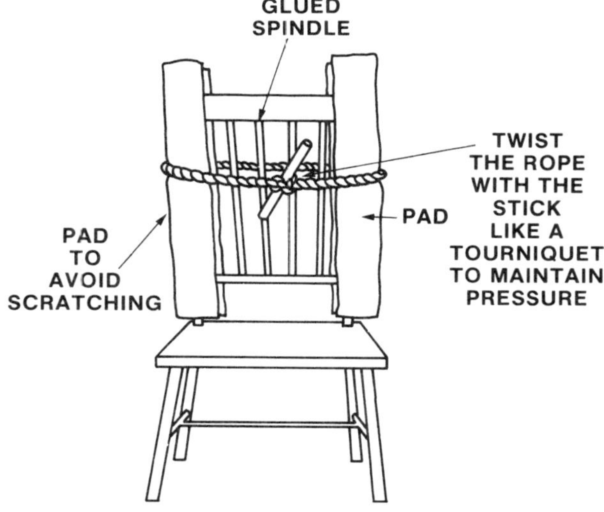


7.4 Holding Large Objects
**Courtesy: Leichtung, Inc.**

# Part B: Metalworking

## Machinists' Vises for Use in Metal Shops

There are more varieties of vises for use in metal shop work than there are vises for use in woodshop work. (Figure 7.5)

A **machinist's vise** is a large, heavy-duty bench vise usually made of cast iron reinforced at stress points. It has rough jaws designed to grip pipes. Some better models have screw-on replaceable faces for the jaws. In addition, there is a large anvil and anvil horn at the rear of the vise for hammering. The vises range in size from 3″ to 6″ in jaw width and more. Generally, these vises will open from 4″ to 10″ and scme weigh as much as 200 pounds. They are bolted to the workbench for safety.

Machinist's vises have swivel bases which allow you to turn them to the precise position you wish. The position of the work can usually be shifted and changed without removal from the vise. To use, turn the handle slightly, move the work and retighten.

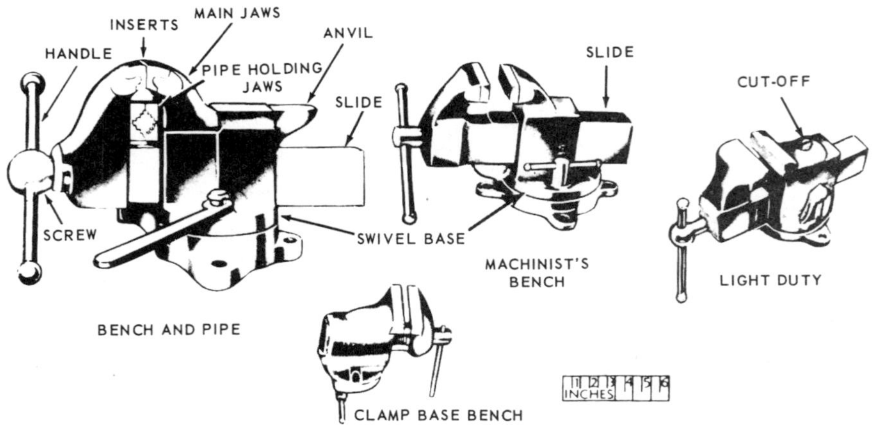


## 7.5 Vises

Smaller and lighter versions of this versatile metal shop vise are available that may be clamped to your workbench. In addition, a vacuum-based portable vise can be set up wherever you need it by applying slight pressure to the top of the vise while pulling the lever down. To detach it, lift the lever. Lightweight vises are useful for cutting and filing light work, but are not of much use in holding heavy objects like a cast iron water pipe. (Figure 7.6)

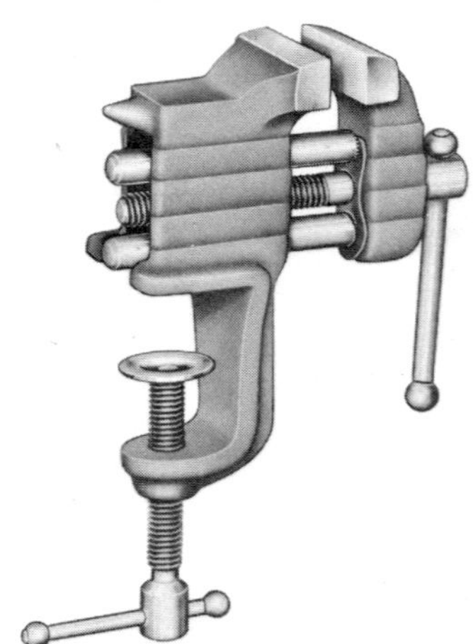

**7.6 A Portable Vise**
**Courtesy: Stanley Tools**

The best vise for holding pipe is a **bench-and-pipe vise** which is specifically designed for the job. This vise has a screw coming down from the top to clamp two curved surfaces together with the pipe in between. Any size pipe from ⅛″ to 8″ may be held securely depending upon the capacity of the bench-and-pipe vise you select. (Figure 7.7)

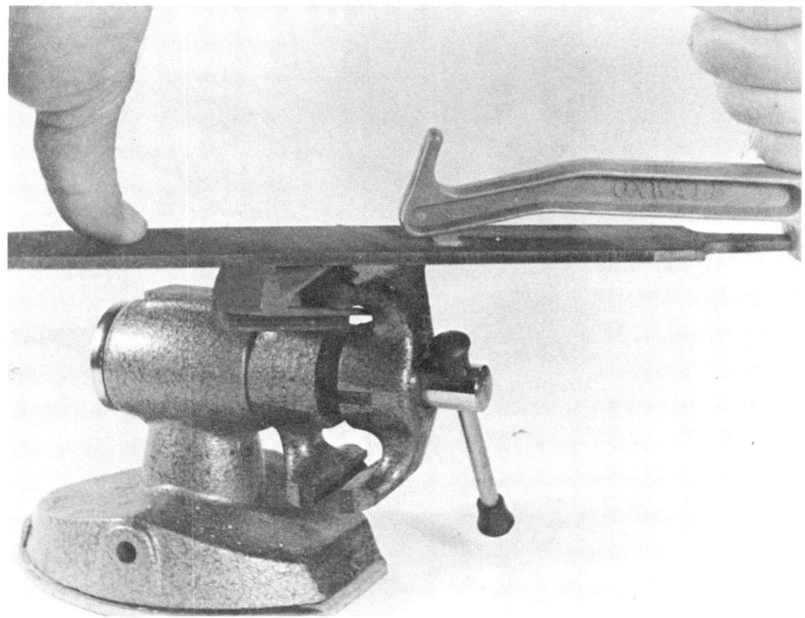

7.7 A Vise

A **blacksmith's vise** has a long metal leg attached to it which reaches to the floor. Since this type of vise is used for heavy hammering, the leg helps absorb the blows.

A good vise will last more than one lifetime if it is taken care of. To avoid springing the jaws, do not try to hold huge objects in a small vise and do not hammer on objects in vises which are lightweight and not designed for this.

Lubricate the screws and the slide but do not oil the swivel base; instead, merely clean it carefully. Do not clamp the jaws of your vise shut when it is not in use; leave them slightly open to allow for expansion of the metal if it gets warm.

## Clamps for Use in Your Metal Shop

The C-clamp, available in sizes from 1″ to 8″ (in increments of 1″), is an invaluable tool for use in holding objects in place as you work on them in addition to using your vise.

Even more versatile are the **Vise-Grip® clamps.** These well-designed devices adjust to grip any size work and then lock with a one-ton grip and stay locked without slipping. (Figures 7.8A–7.8I)

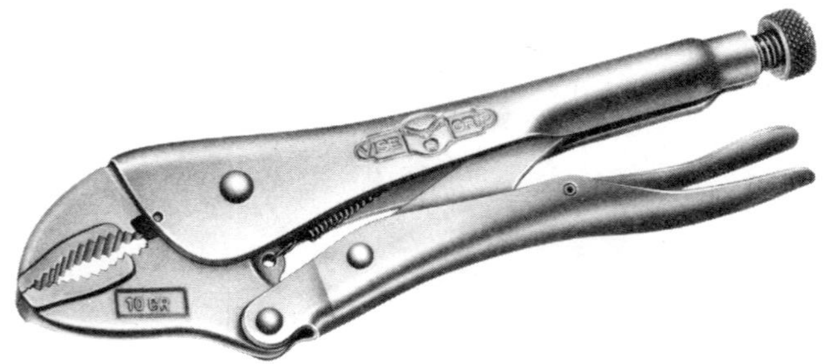


**7.8A Vise-Grip® Clamps**
**Courtesy: Petersen Manufacturing Co.**

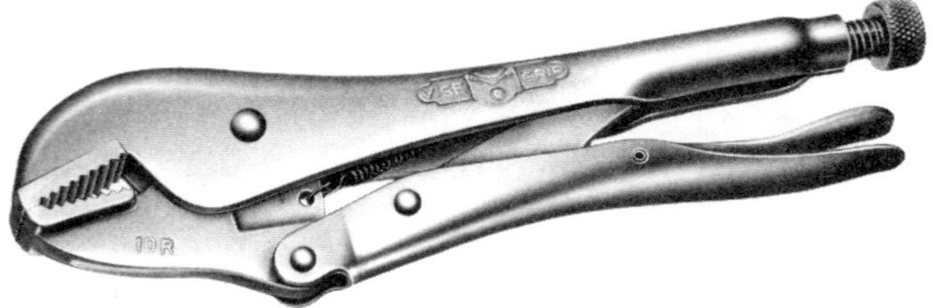


**7.8B Vise-Grip® Clamps**
**Courtesy: Petersen Manufacturing Co.**

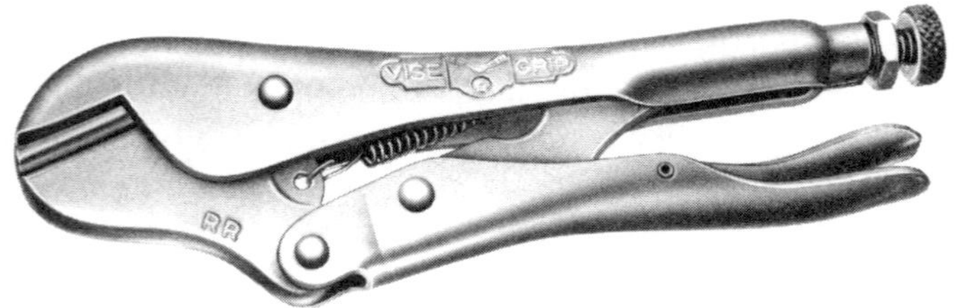


**7.8C Vise-Grip® Clamps**
**Courtesy: Petersen Manufacturing Co.**

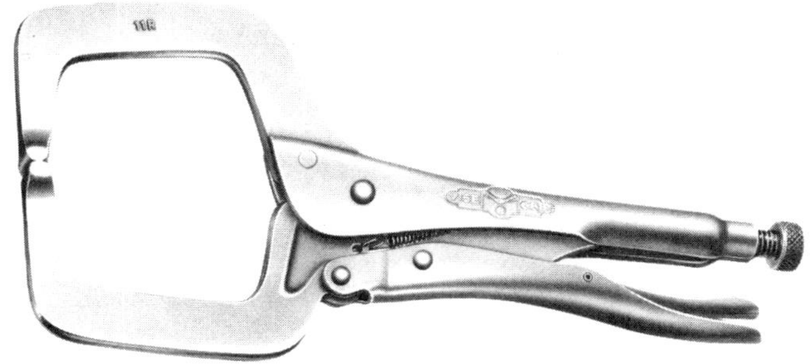

7.8D Vise-Grip® Clamps
**Courtesy: Petersen Manufacturing Co.**

7.8E Vise-Grip® Clamps
**Courtesy: Petersen Manufacturing Co.**

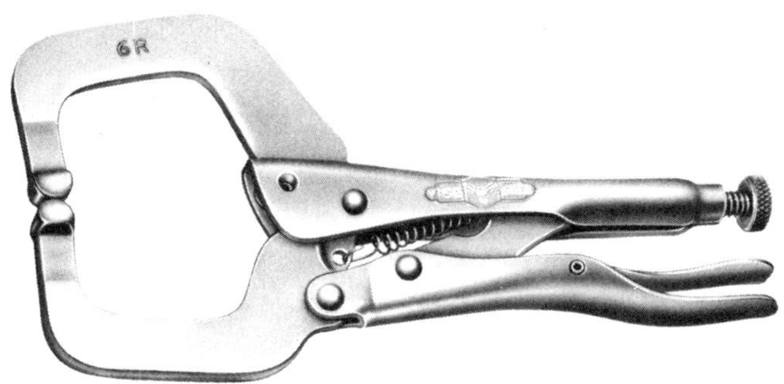


7.8F Vise-Grip® Clamps
**Courtesy: Petersen Manufacturing Co.**

7.8G Vise-Grip® Clamps
Courtesy: Petersen Manufacturing Co.

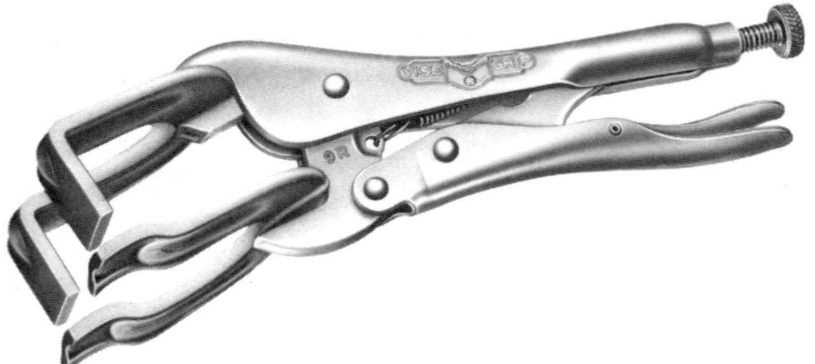


7.8H Vise-Grip® Clamps
Courtesy: Petersen Manufacturing Co.

7.8I Vise-Grip® Clamps
Courtesy: Petersen Manufacturing Co.

Adjust for the size you need by turning the bolt head in the handle. Select one from a wide choice of styles for sheet metal work (accurate bending, forming, crimping), for welding (holding parts in perfect alignment—even when the material is not identical in thickness), for pipework (chain clamps around any size or shape), cutting wire (progressive bites will cut a ¼″ bolt) and countless other tasks. (Figures 7.9, 7.10 and 7.11)

7.9 Clamping Work
**Courtesy: Petersen Manufacturing Co.**

When you are finished, the Vise-Grip® clamps are easily removed by a built-in quick release.

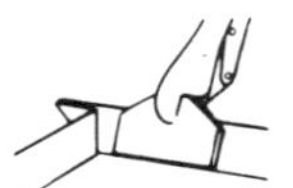
Use VISE-GRIP® Locking Sheet Metal Tool to form bread-pan corners.

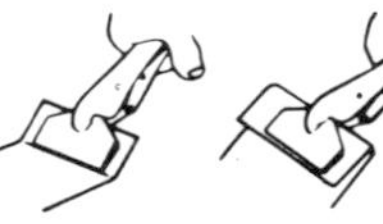
Use VISE-GRIP® Locking Sheet Metal Tool to crimp and double crimp.

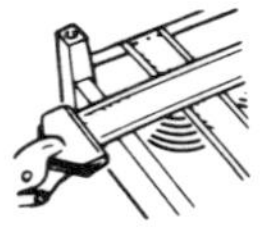
Use VISE-GRIP® Locking Sheet Metal Tool for upholstering.

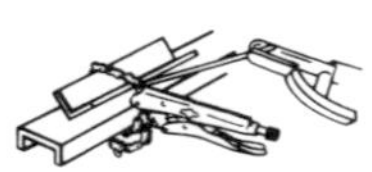
VISE-GRIP® Locking Chain Clamp holds odd shapes securely for welding, fabricating.

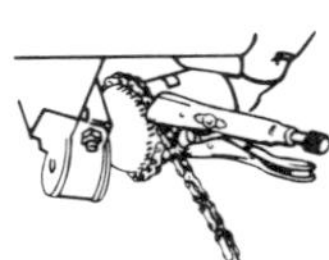
Use VISE-GRIP® Locking Chain Clamps to remove oil filter easily.

Removing flywheel from power mower is quick and easy with a VISE-GRIP® Locking Chain Clamp.

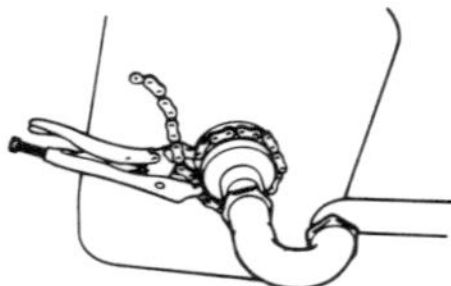
VISE-GRIP® Locking Chain Clamp is a powerful wrench for plumbing.

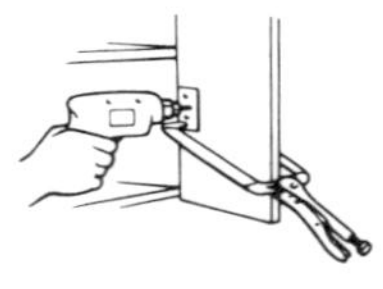
"Long Reach" VISE-GRIP® Locking "C" Clamps are ideal for carpentry work.

Use VISE-GRIP® Locking "C" Clamps for clamping angle iron.

Use VISE-GRIP® Locking "C" Clamps for awkward clamping jobs.

Use VISE-GRIP® Locking "C" Clamps for intricate work with vise.

Use VISE-GRIP® Locking Welding Clamp for holding bars.

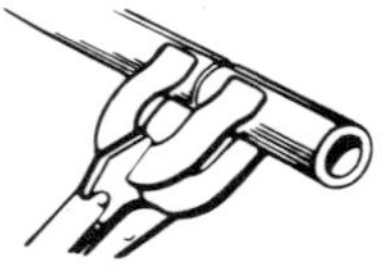
Use VISE-GRIP® Locking Welding Clamp for holding pipe.

Use VISE-GRIP® Locking Welding Clamp for sheet metal work.

Use VISE-GRIP® Locking Welding Clamp for riveting.

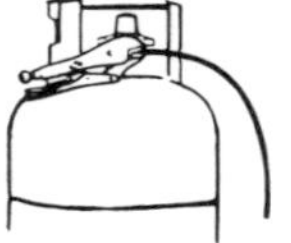
Use VISE-GRIP® Locking Pinch-off Tool to pinch-off butane gas line.

Use VISE-GRIP® Locking Pinch-Off Tool to pinch-off refrigerator tubing.



**7.10 Uses for Vise-Grip® Clamps**
**Courtesy: Petersen Manufacturing Co.**

Use VISE-GRIP® Locking Pliers as a speed wrench. Just lock to nut and give it a whirl.

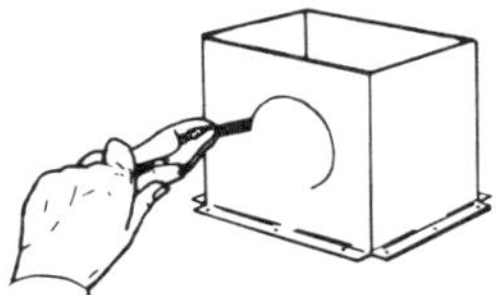

Use VISE-GRIP® Locking Pliers as an emergency saw blade handle.

VISE-GRIP® Locking Pliers adjust to pliers action for twisting wire. Grip will not slip.

VISE-GRIP® Locking Pliers make an ideal emergency handle in camp or kitchen

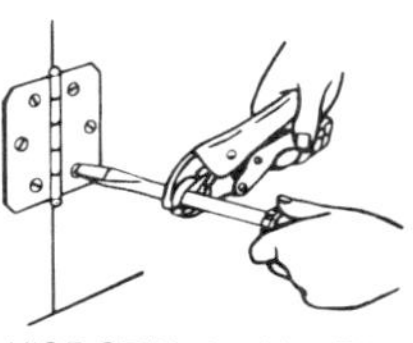

VISE-GRIP® Locking Pliers add leverage to any screwdriver.

Use VISE-GRIP® Locking Pliers to hold small pieces while grinding. Positively will not slip. Lessens danger of being injured.

VISE-GRIP® Locking Pliers pull cotter pins without straightening prongs.

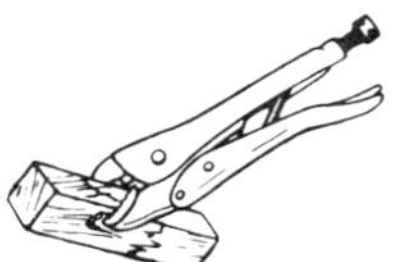

Use VISE-GRIP® Locking Pliers as a quick, powerful clamp for gluing and joining.

Only VISE-GRIP® Locking Pliers will hold without slipping on a job like this.

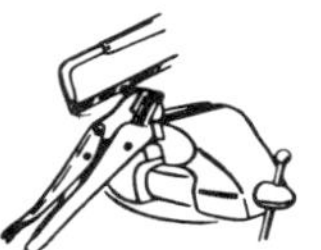

Use VISE-GRIP® Locking Pliers as a portable vise. Locks on, never slips, holds any shape.

Use VISE-GRIP® Locking Pliers as an emergency cable clamp if corroded battery bolt breaks.

Use VISE-GRIP® Locking Pliers to remove door hinge pins without damaging door or hinge pin.

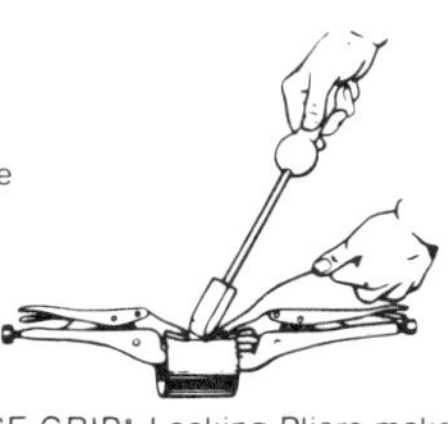

VISE-GRIP® Locking Pliers make an ideal clamp for holding sheet metal for soldering or riveting.

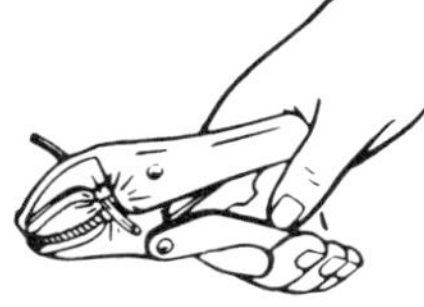

Use VISE-GRIP® as wire cutter —progressive bites will cut ¼" bolts.

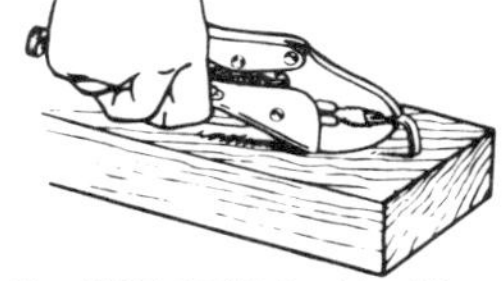

Use VISE-GRIP® Locking Pliers to pull out headless nails, even if nail is broken off flush with wood.

Use VISE-GRIP® Locking Pliers as a Portable toggle press for heavy forming, twisting, bending, and crimping.



**7.11 Uses for Vise-Grip® Clamps**

**Courtesy: Petersen Manufacturing Co.**

### Pliers: How to Select and Use Them

Pliers are used to cut objects as well as to hold them. They are not intended for use in tightening bolts; use wrenches for this purpose. (Figure 7.12)

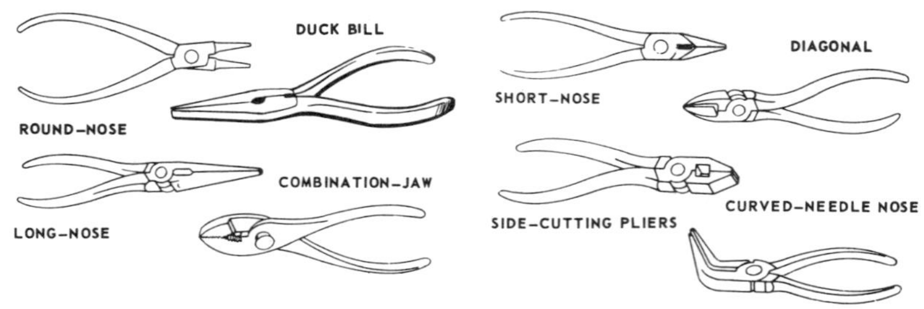


7.12 Pliers

**Combination pliers** have a slip joint which allows you to open their jaws while maintaining adequate pressure. To use the slip joint, open the pliers as wide as possible and push the pivot to the desired position. To make the joint smaller, perform the same operation. There is a side cutter at the junction of the jaws to cut soft nails and wires; hard objects will spring the jaws.

**Water pump pliers** and **channel-lock pliers** look very similar. Each has the ability to open very wide. The water pump pliers do this by using a slip joint which fits in a series of holes in the jaw; channel-lock pliers use a series of grooves on one head and ridges or ''lands'' on the other. While the water pump pliers are designed for use on water pump packing nuts, the channel lock pliers are for use in gripping oddly shaped objects.

**Diagonal pliers** are used to cut wire, cotter pins and small nails flush to the surface, if necessary. They are never used to grip objects because, obviously, they will cut them. **Side-cutting pliers** can be used for gripping objects although they are generally used for cutting small gauge wire. In addition, they can be used to strip insulation from electrical wire. Thus, they are best used in electrical work.

**Needle-nose pliers** and **duckbill pliers** have long and thin jaws which makes them useful in holding small objects, cutting and twisting wire, and doing other tasks which would be tedious without them. Usually, there is a provision for cutting wire at the joint of these pliers.

## SHOPBUILDER #7

Selections of holding tools (woodworking)—
(Choose according to your needs/Build your shop step-by-step)

BASIC TOOLS:

a. vacuum-base portable vise (2½″ jaws)

AMATEUR TOOLS: (Include tool lists above)

b. woodworking vise (7″ capacity—4″ x 7″ jaw)
c. C-clamps (2″, 4″, 6″)

ADVANCED AMATEUR TOOLS: (Include tool lists above)

d. C-clamps (1″, 3″, 5″, 7″, 8″)
e. sawhorses
f. wood screw clamps (2 clamps—size #1)

PROFESSIONAL TOOLS: (Include tool lists above)

g. Vise-Grip® C-clamp
h. wood screw clamps (4—size #2)
i. bar clamps

PROFESSIONAL CRAFTSMAN TOOLS: (Include tool lists above)

j. wood screw clamps (size #0)
k. band clamps

## SKILLBUILDER #7

Use these tests to determine the level of your skill:

ADVANCED AMATEUR: Using an appropriate size C-clamp, attach two blocks of wood together in 30 seconds.

PROFESSIONAL:
*Do the above plus* Using appropriate clamps, attach two pieces of scrap metal in

position so that they can be welded together at right angles to each other in 45 seconds.

**SKILLED CRAFTSMAN:**
*Do the above plus*

**Using the appropriate bar clamps, attach a 3′ long two-by-four to a 1″ plank at a 90 degree angle.**

# 8

# Glue and Other Adhesives

Chemistry has created a revolution in the way that projects are now fastened together in modern workshops. In some cases, plastic, metal and wooden objects are held together by adhesives more securely than by any other method.

## Part A: Woodworking and Plastic Work

### How to Select Glue

Glue is often stronger than the wood it holds together. It is a sticky substance made from animal skin and bones. The three basic types of glue are **bone glue, fish glue** and **hide glue**. All have uses in the workshop.

A very popular type of glue for use in joining wood parts in cabinet making is hide glue. The amber-colored liquid—about as thick as maple syrup—comes in ready-to-use form. It does not dry very fast and this makes it useful for jobs in which the careful positioning of parts is necessary. To use, be sure the surfaces are clean. Apply glue to both surfaces, using a brush if convenient. Clamp the parts in place, making sure that you do not apply too much pressure and force all the glue out of the joint. Let dry overnight in temperatures over 70 degrees Fahrenheit.

Many craftsmen, however, are turning from this old, and dependable glue to more modern, faster epoxies and resin glues.

The glue pot, once a common fixture in woodworking shops, is seen seldom today. Also, the use of bone glue, fish glue and hide glue takes too long for many contemporary craftsmen. Thus, they turn to synthetic glues—particularly epoxies—to hold their projects together.

Epoxy adhesives usually come in two tubes. When you mix a small amount from tube A with a small amount from tube B, you wind up with a powerful fast-setting bonding material. Epoxies often have tremendous strength; two drops will hold two tons of dead weight. Furthermore, you can bond metals and glass as well as wood. A very thin film usually works best, although you need to read and obey the instructions given with individual products. Drying time is extremely rapid—often 30 seconds is adequate.

Such high-powered glue can be dangerous, for it will fasten your fingers together! Use it sparingly and with great care so that you work with it in safety. Solvents are available so that you can unstick objects that are accidentally stuck together. Be sure and get the solvent when you purchase the epoxy.

For less demanding use, **polyvinyl resin glue**, or white glue which usually comes in a plastic squeeze bottle, will bond wood, paper, leather, fabrics and other porous materials together without staining. But there are other resin glues which are more expensive and stronger. **Aliphatic resin glue** is also excellent for use in woodworking; **resorcinol resin glue** should be selected for gluing wood that is subject to use in water; **polyester resin glue** is also used in such situations, particularly with fiberglass and wood boats; **acrylic resin glue** will fasten almost anything together. Even **cellulose nitrate cement** (commonly called airplane glue) can be used to fasten wood together securely.

All bonding work depends on selecting the correct type of glue or

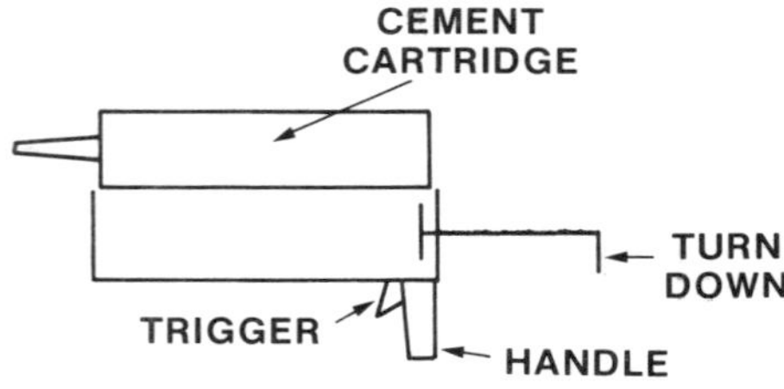


**8.1 A Caulking Gun**

cement and working with it according to instructions on a clean surface. (Figure 8.1)

### Contact Cement

**Contact cement** bonds on contact without clamps or presses. It remains flexible and water resistant.

Use contact cement to laminate plastic to cabinet tops; to install linoleum, asphalt tile and plastic tile; to bond paneling to a wall; to install cove base; to restore loose wood veneers; and for countless other uses in your woodshop. It can be used to bond wood, leather, cloth, glass, plastics, rubber, paper, felt and canvas—everything but metals.

Apply this thick fluid with a trowel or a tooth-edged applicator designed specifically for this purpose. Put a thin coat of contact cement on each surface to be attached together. The teeth of the applicator make a series of even thin beaded strips of cement. Wait 20 minutes for each piece to dry.

Align the pieces exactly. Once the two pieces are placed together and the cement makes contact, there is no way to get them apart again. Press the surfaces together and smooth.

For larger surfaces (over 3 sq.′), you need to use a slightly different procedure. Make sure that the surface is free from oil, wax, dirt and loose paint. Coat both surfaces, but lay some brown wrapping paper or wax paper over one surface until you align the other surface on it.

After the two surfaces are placed together perfectly, you can remove the protective paper so that the two objects are bonded together in that position—permanently. Use a rolling pin or similar roller over the entire surface to make sure that the surfaces are flat against each other.

### How to Use a Glue Gun

A **glue gun** is a tool that melts adhesives, lets you apply them in the exact location you wish, and then is removed instantly so the glue can cool and set quickly—usually within 30 seconds. (Figure 8.2)

To use, plug in the gun and wait 60 seconds for the tool to heat up. When the indicator light comes on, you can load the gun with the stick of glue. Pull back the ring knob, turning it 90 degrees. Pull the feed rod back as far as it will go. Insert the glue stick in the loading chamber on top of the gun. Push the loading rod forward until it pushes the glue stick into the melting chamber. Pull the ring knob back, turn it back to its original position so that it will push the feed knob and the glue stick forward. Touch the tip of the gun lightly to the project and melted glue will flow from the gun. Lift the gun and the glue flow will stop. (Figure 8.3)

**8.2 No Clamp Needed with a Glue Gun**
**Courtesy: The Swingline Co.**

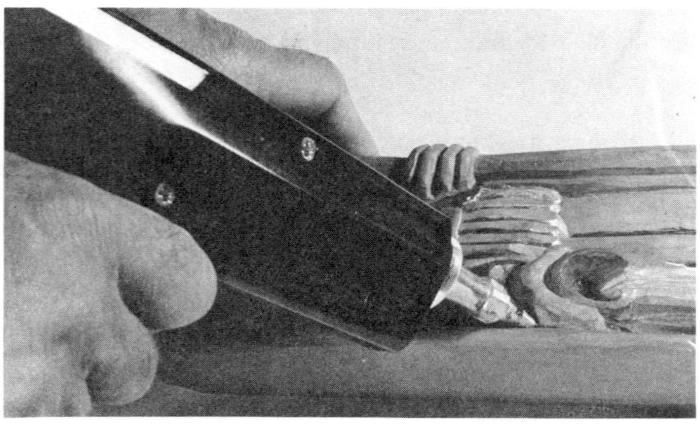

**8.3 A Glue Gun is Fine for Small Repairs**

There is no need to spread the glue as you might with a brush. Instead, make zig-zag strokes. Put the glue on one surface and connect the other surface with it. Do not try to put glue on both surfaces; it isn't needed.

You will find that you cannot put glue on a surface much longer than 12″ because the glue cools too rapidly. Thus, if you need to glue a surface of this length, use the glue (applied rapidly) on three or more zig-zag spots along its length. Even so, you may find that a different type of adhesive will give you better results.

Do not move the object for at least 3 minutes for best results, even though the glue cools to a firm bond in about 30 seconds. In the meantime, rest the gun on its stand so that you do not damage nearby surfaces with the heat from its tip.

Glue only objects that are not damaged by heat—this should be obvious. Be careful you do not burn yourself—temperatures reach 400 degrees Fahrenheit.

## Patching Damaged Work with Chemical Compounds

Wood can be repaired with chemical compounds. For small scratches on finished wood, heat shellac sticks of matching color and apply them to cover up the nick or gouge. Smooth the spot by rubbing it with a knife or spatula and you will have a difficult time seeing where the mar occurred.

For larger holes, use wood ground into dough form, like Plastic Wood®. Although one popular brand comes only in a light color that matches raw pine, other manufacturers produce formulas in ash, oak, walnut, cedar, mahogany, light oak and teak.

Usually, a cavity up to ½″ deep can be filled in one application. Deeper cavities require building up several layers of the material for best results. You can expect shrinkage to be about 1%, so allow a slightly raised surface.

After drying, which is usually less than an hour (and in the case of small holes, only 5 minutes), you will be able to sand, saw, nail or drill just as you would the original wood. The material holds screws and dowel pins; and it may be lacquered, stained, shellacked, varnished or painted.

In between the shellacking sticks and the deep cavity fillers is a putty that is used for minor surface scratches. It is a bit finer in texture than the large hole filler and can thus be sanded to a feather edge. Both materials are applied in the same way—with a thin-edged putty knife or spatula. Press firmly into place with a sliding motion and overfill slightly. Sand and finish when dry.

## Part B: Metalworking

Although most broken or damaged metal requires welding or brazing to mend it because of the stresses and strains involved, metallic objects which have limited stress and use can often be glued together.

### How to Glue Metal

Small metal ornamental objects are sometimes ruined if they are soldered, welded or brazed together. Too often, the patch shows. In such cases, use a liquid metal cement, an acrylic resin glue or an epoxy glue to fasten them permanently together in order for the break not to show.

In addition, you will find these powerful new glues just the ticket for making small metal sculpture. Use aluminum cement to repair spouting and even pots and pans. There are solder substitutes which do everything ordinary solder will do without heat—so that paint and other surfaces won't be damaged. Not only that, but the cold solder resists water, oil, gasoline and acids. It sets firm in minutes.

Use these miracle glues by coating the surface of the objects to be joined together. Do not use a lot of glue; a small amount is sufficient. Press the two objects firmly together, clamping them with a C-clamp or your Vise-Grip® or, in some cases, wrapping them with string or masking tape. Drying and setting time is usually less than an hour.

Further repairs to damaged metals can often be made with plastic body filler which bonds tightly to metal and can be shaped, sanded and painted to match the surrounding surface.

### SHOPBUILDER #8

**Selections of glue and adhesives—**
**(Choose according to your needs/Build your shop step-by-step)**

**BASIC:** (Plus clamps as listed in Chapter 7)
- a. white glue

**AMATEUR:** (Include items listed above)
- b. wood putty

**ADVANCED AMATEUR:** (Include items listed above)
- c. epoxy

**PROFESSIONAL:** (Include items listed above)
- d. hide glue (and other animal glues)
- e. resorcinal resin glue and/or aliphatic resin glue

**PROFESSIONAL CRAFTSMAN:** (Include items listed above)
- f. contact cement
- g. shellac sticks

## SKILLBUILDER #8

Use these tests to determine the level of your skill: GLUING MATERIALS

| | |
|---|---|
| ADVANCED AMATEUR: | Using white glue attach a ¼″ dowel in a ¼″ hole firmly and with no excess glue. |
| PROFESSIONAL:<br>*Do the above plus* | Using epoxy, glue five 1″ square pieces of tin to the edge of a piece of steel so that they resemble the teeth on a saw. |
| SKILLED CRAFTSMAN:<br>*Do the above plus* | Selecting an appropriate contact cement, attach a 1′ square piece of plastic to a 1′ square piece of plywood so that the edges are perfectly square. |

# 9

# Selecting and Using Multipurpose Tools

If you have limited space for your workshop, the ideal answer is to invest in tools which can be used for more than one purpose. By careful selection, you can wind up with a complete workshop to fit almost every need small enough to store in the back of your closet. Also, you can fit a large and complete multipurpose tool into a portion of your garage without crowding your car out into the rain and snow. All you need to do is to select carefully.

## Part A:

## Wood and Plastic Work

### Small Shop Tools Which Can Be Converted to Many Uses: Their Selection, Use and Maintenance

Although there are multipurpose hand tools like the hammer that contains a series of different sized screwdrivers in its handle and the saw which can also be used as a pair of pliers, most such devices are only gimmicks. They have very little real use. Furthermore, they are not precision tools. You will find that each advertised use is done better with a quality tool designed for that specific purpose. It's the old story of trying to do too much and not doing anything well.

However, you may fare better with multipurpose tools. The most expensive part of any power tool is, of course, the motor. By using the same motor to drive each device, you can get more tools for your hard-earned dollar.

The most common multipurpose power tool is the **electric hand drill**, which is used to saw wood, plastic and metal; to sand materials; to grind; to buff and polish articles; to mix paint and countless other uses. (Figure 9.1)

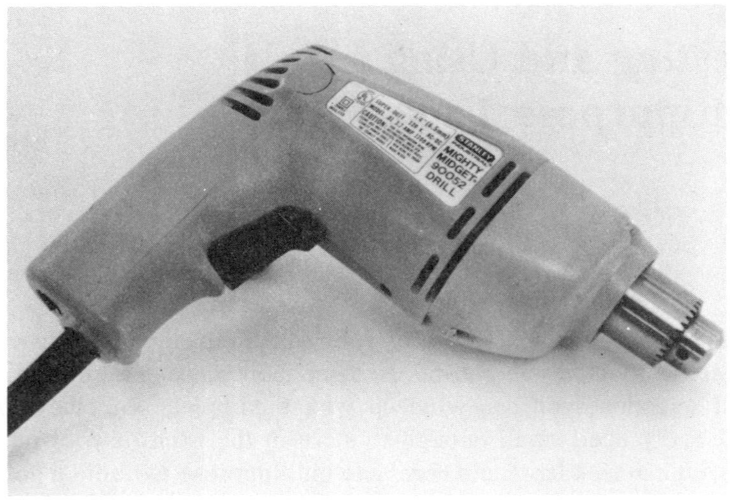


9.1 A Hand Power Drill
Courtesy: Stanley Tools

## How to Select Your Small Multipurpose Power Tool

| General Features | Yes or No? (Two *No* answers mean the tool is unacceptable) |
|---|---|
| Is there sufficient power available from your drill to run the tool safely and efficiently? | |

| | |
|---|---|
| Does the effectiveness of the tool depend upon variable drive speeds? Can your drill supply them? | |
| Is it easy to attach or disengage the accessory tool? | |
| Is the tool well-constructed? (Rustproofed? Lubricated for life?) Made by a well-known manufacturer? | |
| Are the controls clearly labeled? | |
| Does the tool seem safe? | |
| Is the tool complete or must you purchase additional items to make it work? | |
| Is its capability sufficient for your needs? Will it cut two-by-fours? Can it cut metals up to ⅛″? | |
| Are parts and supplies readily available? (Does it take odd-sized blades or strangely shaped sanding discs?) | |
| Is the tool capable of accurate work? (Are the markings or gauges poorly drawn or nonexistent?) | |

## How to Turn Your Hand Power Drill into a Complete Light-Duty Workshop

The following attachments and accessories are available to fit any make ¼″ hand power drill to saw, grind, plane, cut metal and pump liquids. Although these devices are not intended to replace quality tools designed for these specific purposes, you will find them useful in many situations.

### SAWING

Jigsaw attachment can be used as a scroll saw, crosscut saw, hacksaw and handsaw.

### PLANER

Alloy steel cutter planing attachment cuts across and with the grain making a 1¾″ cut.

### GRINDING

Grinding wheel and abrasive cloth discs can be attached to your drill to grind and polish tools, metals and much more.

### HEDGE TRIMMING ATTACHMENT

Attachment has a 12″ sickle bar type precision ground level gear with a side handle.

### SELF-PRIMING PUMP

Drain basements, appliances, water heaters, change oil and transfer chemicals with this attachment using a ¾″ garden hose thread to pump 200 gallons an hour 8′ to 10′ vertically.

### LEFT AND RIGHT ANGLE DRIVE

For boring in tight areas such as between studs; this attachment has a 2 to 1 speed ratio for slowing the drill down (for polishing, for example).

After using the chart to select an add-on tool, read its manufacturer's instructions carefully. Unfortunately, you may find them inadequate or nonexistent. If you are not sure how to use the tool, ask the salesman or store manager. If they don't know, you are best off buying the tool somewhere else where you can get this kind of information. At any rate, be sure that you understand how to use the accessory before you switch on your electric drill.

You will soon find that the major aggravation in using multipurpose tools is that you spend a lot of time switching from one use to another. Whatever mode you wish to operate the equipment in will require you to stop the machine and unplug it (for safety's sake). Then, you may find you will need one or more special tools to remove an accessory and replace it with another.

Furthermore, the prices of small power tools have become so competitive that they have dropped to the point where it is almost cheaper to buy a complete sabre saw, for example, than it used to be to buy the add-on unit. Thus, most add-on devices are ones that make use of your power drill for *unusual* functions such as pumping water or extending its use to reach hard-to-work in places by way of a flexible cable.

If you do decide to use such add-on devices, keep them in a dry place and attach any special keys or other fastening devices to them with a strand of electrician's tape. Generally, you will not find it necessary to lubricate them or to service them in any way. If they are dropped or damaged, it is almost always cheaper to throw them away rather than attempting to repair them.

If the idea of multipurpose tools intrigues you, you will be happier not wasting your money on gimmicks. Instead, invest in a quality multipurpose tool that serves as a complete first-rate workshop—like the equipment made by Shopsmith.

To be able to complete such projects as furniture, built-ins and additions to your home, you need a table saw, a drill press, a disc sander and a wood turning lathe. These are the four basic tools. Others, such as a jointer, a jigsaw, a bandsaw and a belt sander offer further versatility, but you can purchase them later as the need arises.

In general, prices depend upon the quality, features and capacity of the tool. Comparing the prices of power saws, for example is like comparing the prices of automobiles. You must consider depth of cut, table sizes and operating features in evaluating the prices of saws, just as you do the horsepower, weight and operating features in comparing car prices.

When comparing power tool prices, always compare *capacity, features* and *specifications* (such as motor size). Be sure you know what is included in the advertised price. You will often find that the combined cost of the table saw and drill press alone will be more than a complete, ready to plug in, multipurpose power tool.

In addition, most power tools are not delivered ready for use. Traditionally, most power tools come in a collection of crates, cartons and packages of parts. The job of assembling these power tools often takes longer than the first project or two that has been planned. Often, switches must be wired, motors mounted, and a multitude of parts bolted and assembled together before the owner can make even a practice cut.

Some power tools require that a bench be built or bought—others demand additional tables to support the work. Look for a power tool that is delivered tested and ready for use.

Power tool prices often do not include the motor and the bench. Prices of belts, pulleys, switches, cords and other items are often also excluded. In comparing prices, always be sure that you know which items are included in the advertised price.

Be sure that the multipurpose tool you buy can do all the basic operations (sawing, sanding, drilling and wood turning) without additional attachments or accessories.

Remember, of course, that accessories can provide an almost unlimited variety of operations for specialized woodworking jobs. These accessories range from molding cutters and mortising attachments to the jigsaw, jointer, belt sander and bandsaw. Make sure, therefore, that your multipurpose power tool has a wide enough selection of accessories to meet your future needs, and that they are designed so you can add them quickly and easily to your original unit. Do not forget to compare prices of accessories. For example, find out if the various tools that you are considering can accommodate a 12″ sanding disc and how much the discs themselves cost.

It is important, too, that your original power tool provide the wide range of speeds necessary for all the accessories you may want in the future. A one-speed saw, for example, cannot possibly provide the correct operating speed for all accessories. Also check whether the tool will take standard parts—for example, some tools can use only special bits and cutters.

Shopsmith, (as an example of a quality tool), has a 10″ saw, a 12″ disc sander, a 16½″ drill press, a horizontal boring machine and a 34″ lathe all in one compact unit. Thus, if you were thinking of purchasing this machine, you would fill in this information on the following comparison chart. When you finish with this chart, you have the basis for making a judgement on whether or not this tool fits your needs. (Figures 9.2, 9.3, 9.4, 9.5 and 9.6)

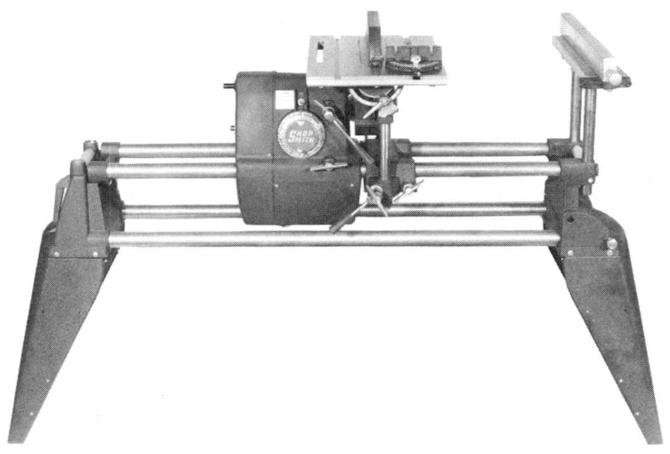

9.2 The Shopsmith
Courtesy: Shopsmith

9.3 The Shopsmith
Courtesy: Shopsmith

9.4 The Shopsmith
**Courtesy: Shopsmith**

9.5 The Shopsmith
**Courtesy: Shopsmith**

9.6 The Shopsmith
Courtesy: Shopsmith

## How to Select Your Multipurpose Tool

| General Features | Yes or No? (Two *No* answers mean the tool is unacceptable) |
|---|---|
| Motor included? (At least 1 hp) | |
| Stand or bench included? | |
| Are the bearings steel? Lubricated for life? | |
| Is it rustproofed? | |

| | |
|---|---|
| Is the speed control a dial or pulleys? (A dial is best) | |
| Are belts and pulleys enclosed? | |
| Is the on/off switch guarded? | |
| Are controls and handles labeled clearly? | |
| Is the tool delivered ready to plug in? | |
| Is everything included? No extras? | |
| Is there a provision for adding a jigsaw, belt sander, jointer, bandsaw and other tools? Easy to attach? | |
| Is there a provision for dual operation? (e.g. Both jigsaw and sander?) | |
| Are casters provided for? | |
| Is a minimum of floor space required? (12 sq.′ is more than adequate) | |
| Saw Features | |
| Is there sufficient power? (At least ½ hp) | |

| | |
|---|---|
| Is the speed variable? | |
| Is the blade of sufficient size?<br>(At least 8″) | |
| What is the depth of cut? (3″ is the minimum) | |
| What is the maximum distance from the blade to the fence? (36″ is fine; 48″ is excellent) | |
| What is the distance of the table front to the blade? (4″–5″ is adequate) | |
| How large is the table?<br>(It should be at least 8″ square)<br>Are extensions available? | |
| Does the table tilt? (Or the blade?)<br>(0–45 degrees?) | |
| Is the fence square and self-locking? | |
| Is there a miter gauge?<br>(It should range from 0–60 degrees) | |
| Sander Features | |
| Is there sufficient power?<br>(At least ½ hp) | |

| | |
|---|---|
| Is there a table? (A must) | |
| Is the table large enough? (8″ square is adequate) | |
| Is the sanding speed variable? (It should be) | |
| Is the sanding disc large enough for both your present and future needs? (6″–8″ is adequate—larger discs are better) | |
| Is there a forward disc feed? | |
| Is a miter gauge and a fence included for precision work? | |
| Drill Press Features | |
| Is there sufficient power? (Minimum ⅓ hp) | |
| Is the table large enough? (6″ square is adequate) | |
| Can the table or the motor be tilted—to assure precision boring to at least a 60 degree angle? | |

| | |
|---|---|
| Is the capacity large enough? (Can you drill to the center of a 12″ circle?) | |
| Is the distance of the chuck to the table adequate? (12″ is the minimum) | |
| Is the distance of the chuck to the floor adequate? (40″ is the minimum) | |
| Is the quill feed at least 3″? | |
| Lathe Features | |
| Is there sufficient power? (At least ¼ hp) | |
| Is the lathe speed variable? (It should range from 900 to 5200 rpm) | |
| Is there a precision tool rest? Does it slide parallel to your work? | |
| Is the distance between centers adequate for your work? (20″ is adequate; 36″ is fine) | |
| Adequate swing over ways? (At least 12″) | |

### How to Use Your Multipurpose Power Tool

Follow these instructions to use your multipurpose power tool (no matter what make) in each of its separate modes safely and efficiently. Except for procedures used in changing operation from one mode to another, these instructions are generally the same as for separate or single purpose tools.

*Table Saw*: Before turning the motor on, check to see that the blade is mounted correctly (teeth facing towards you) and that the arbor nut (which holds the blade on the arbor) is tight. Be sure that the upper and lower saw guards are in position.

Adjust the blade so that it will project ¼″ to ½″ above your work (hollow ground blades require ¾″ or more). A rule of thumb is that the deepest gullet of your blade should be slightly above the top of the wood that you are sawing. Set the rip fence manually to within ⅛″ of the required setting. Lock the fence and adjust the quill to make the exact adjustment. Then, lock the quill.

Use the miter gauge, positioned in either of the table slots, to hold the work square to the blade throughout the pass. Place your hands on the miter gauge and keep your body out of the line of cut. Use your left hand to keep the work pressed against the miter gauge and feed the work forward with your right. *Do not force the wood into the saw blade*. When the cut is complete, keep your hands in the same position and return the work and the miter gauge to the starting point. Switch the machine off and after the blade has stopped turning, remove the work. (Figure 9.7)

To make miter cuts with your table saw mode, adjust the miter gauge to the required angle. Grip the wood and the miter gauge firmly, because the wood will tend to creep as a result of the pull of the blade. Follow the same procedure as described above and make the pass slowly.

**Rip cuts** are made by passing the work between the saw blade and the rip fence without the use of the miter gauge. Feed the work through, keeping your left fingers hooked over the fence holding the work down and feeding it forward. The last 6″ or so are pushed through with a stick. Feed so that the overhang at the back of the table will tilt the board up where it can be gripped with the right hand and removed from the saw table. Cuts narrower than 3″ to 4″ must never be pushed through by hand; use a push stick. (Figure 9.8)

**Bevel ripping** is done by tilting the table to the desired angle and then locking it in. Advance the blade as the table is tilted; then advance

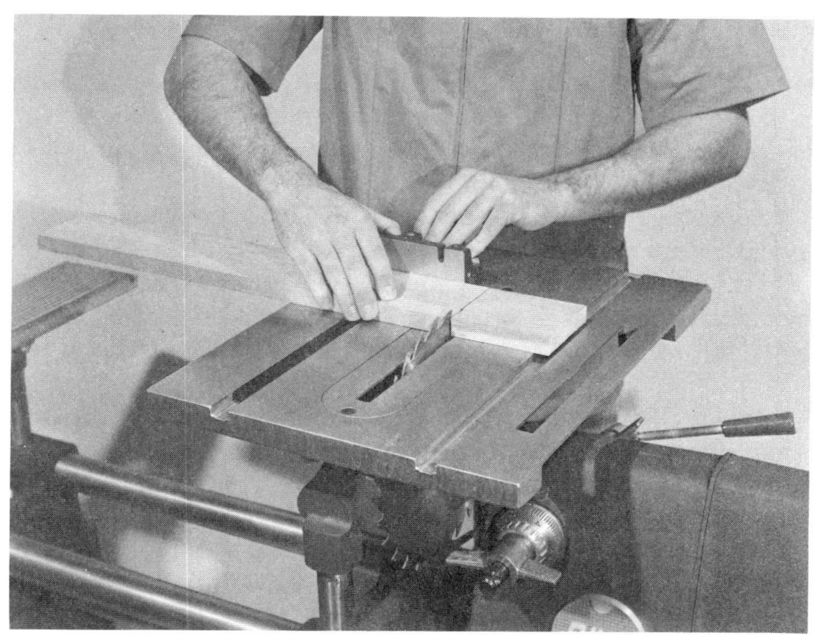

9.7 Using the Miter Gauge (Guards removed for photo)
Courtesy: Shopsmith

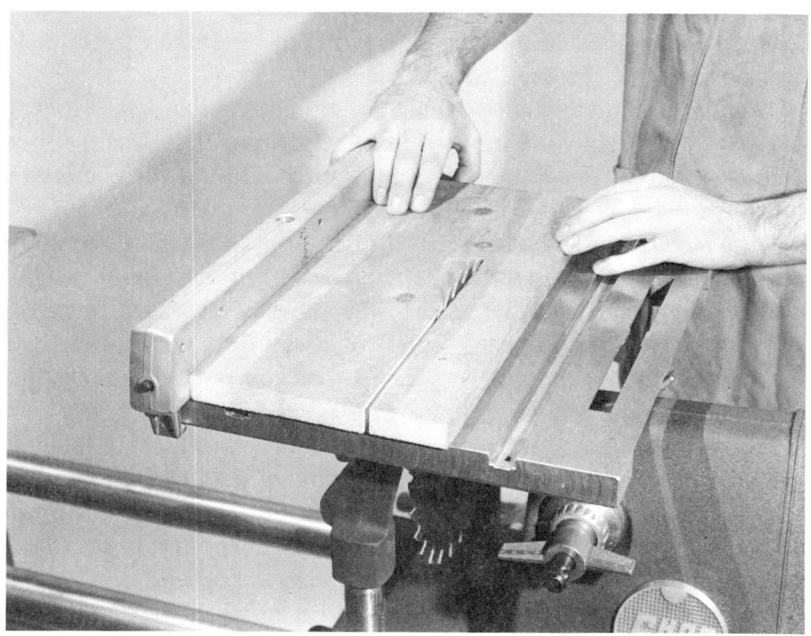

9.8 Maintaining Safety by Hooking Fingers over Fence (Guards removed for photo)
Courtesy: Shopsmith

the blade before lowering the table over it. Keep the blade centered in the slot in your saw table. **Compound angle cuts** and **cross beveling** also require similar table tilts. Always complete your adjustments of angle and blade *before* turning the motor on.

For cutting long pieces or wide widths, quality multipurpose tools have extension tables on which to rest the work. Place the wood in position and use a level to be sure that your cut will be accurate. With fine precision equipment, you can move the extension table close to the saw table, make any adjustments and then move the extension table away.

*Sander*: To change from the table saw mode to the sander mode is a simple operation in a top quality machine. Simply substitute a sanding disc for the saw and change the motor speed. Adjust the same table used for sawing to a height 1″ below the center line of the sanding disc and a distance of 1/16″ from the disc. For disc sanding with coarse paper, use 900 rpm; for medium paper, use 1200 to 1400 rpm; for fine paper, use 1600 to 2000 rpm. (Figure 9.9)

While inexpensive sanders use screws and plates to hold a disc of sandpaper, better quality machines use liquid adhesive to cement the paper to the disc. Let the adhesive dry for at least 20 minutes if you are attaching a new disc in this manner and then be certain to press the paper down firmly on the disc surface.

Sanding is always done on the down side of the disc. Hold the work flat on the table and move it into the turning disc. Use the miter gauge if possible. Feed smoothly and lightly. Do not force the work against the disc; instead, touch it lightly as many times as necessary.

For **bevels** and **cross miters**, tilt the table to the required angle, forming an open angle with the sanding disc. For **compound angles**, set the miter gauge and the table to the same angles used to cut the pieces on the saw, keeping the table 1/16″ away from the sanding disc. On work like this, you will be pleased that you have a multipurpose tool, because you can go directly from cutting compound angles to sanding them *without changing the position of the table!* Thus, your work will be easier and more accurate. (Figure 9.10)

Miter sanding is best done by sawing pieces 1/16″ oversize and then sanding them to the exact length. Set the miter gauge to the required angle and lock it in place. Turn the motor on and, pressing the work firmly against the miter gauge, feed it forward.

*Drill Press*: To convert your multipurpose tool from a sander to a drill press, replace the sanding disc with a drill chuck. If you wish to drill dowel holes for joining one edge to another, leave the drill in a

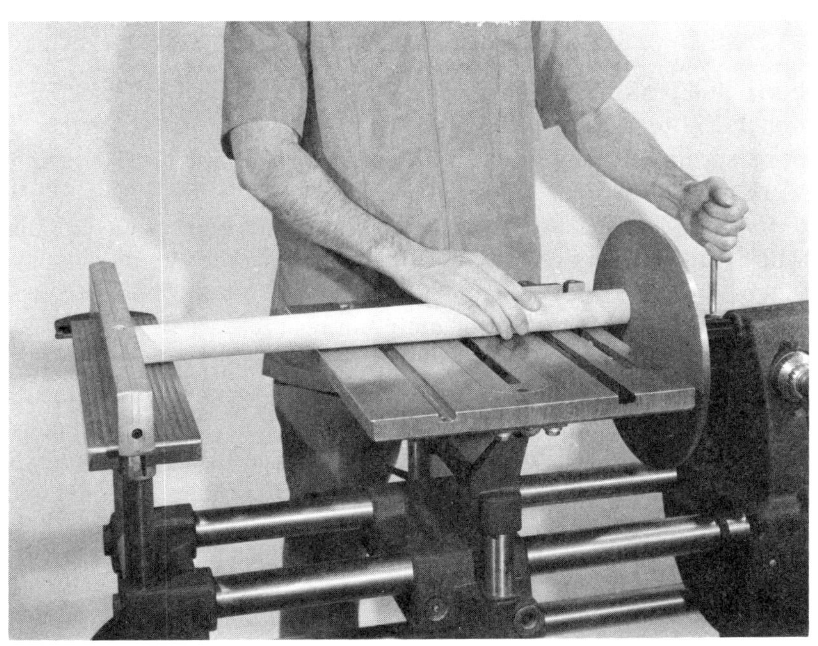

9.9 Use the Quill to Feed Sanding Disc
**Courtesy: Shopsmith**

9.10 Sand Accurately with the Miter Gauge
**Courtesy: Shopsmith**

horizontal position. If, however, you wish to use the drill as a conventional drill press, move the drill into a vertical position. Vertical drill press speed will range from 3000 rpm (for ¼″ work) to 700 rpm (for work over 1″ in size). (Figure 9.11)

Properly used as a horizontal boring machine, your equipment will facilitate many operations which are time-consuming, inconvenient or actually impossible on the vertical drill press. Change the speed to a slow 700 to 900 rpm for optimum results.

For example, you can drill **butt dowel joints** by locking the rip fence in place to act as a backstop to hold the work square to the drill. Lock the feed stop to control the depth of the hole. The only dimension line needed on the board edges is the distance between holes, which will save you a lot of time in measuring and marking. It is not necessary to center the holes between the edges if you place the same side of each board down on the table.

A quick way to mark the dimension lines for distance between holes is to place the boards together and butt one against the rip fence. Use the miter gauge to mark the lines across the edges of the boards.

Drilling **end holes** is easy—if you lock the miter gauge in place to act as a guide. **Jig drilling**, for example, as needed in drilling dowel holes in mitered pieces, can be done by locking the miter gauge at the correct angle and letting it serve as the jig. **Concentric drilling** (the type of holes needed in lamp bases, for example) may be done by mounting the tailstock and cup center used in the lathe mode to serve as an end stop. Lock the miter gauge in place to hold the work and drill. (Figure 9.12)

To use your multipurpose tool in the vertical position, move the motor to an upright position. The table must be turned at right angles to the motor and drill chuck. This is done by adjusting a table tilt lock so that the table moves 90 degrees. Lock the table in place about 15″ from the chuck. The correct height for the motor and chuck will vary according to your height.

Use sharp, top quality drill bits of an appropriate size. Lock them in the chuck with the chuck key. Remove the key before turning the motor on. Check to see that you have selected the correct rpm. John R. Folkerth, president of Shopsmith, recommends the following speeds for obtaining optimum results: However, note that these speeds overlap. You will get good results running a ½″ bit, for example, anywhere from 2200 to 3200 rpm.

- Drilling up to ¼″—3000 rpm to 3800 rpm
- Drilling ¼″ to ½″—2800 rpm to 3200 rpm

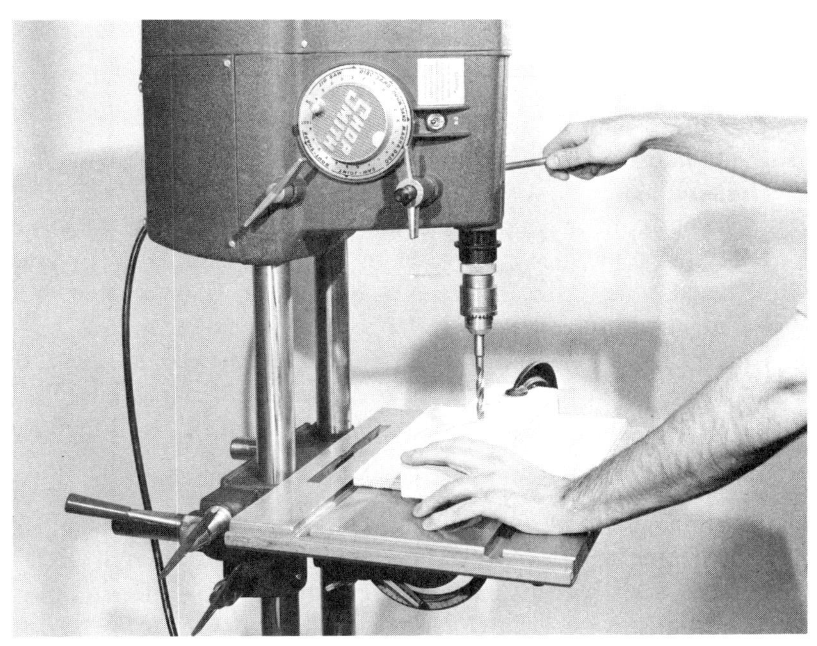

9.11 Avoid Slippage. Use Clamps
Courtesy: Shopsmith

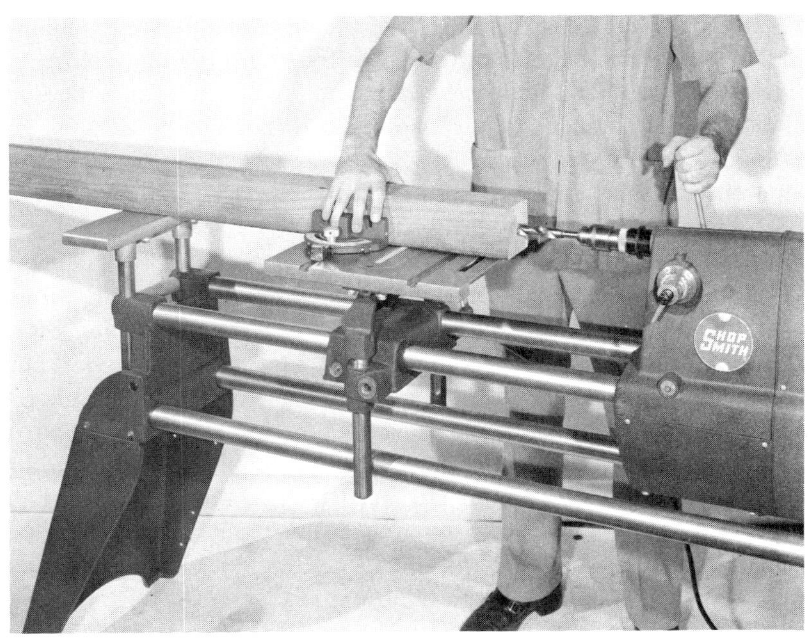


9.12 Drilling Horizontal Holes
Courtesy: Shopsmith

- Drilling ½″ to ¾″—2200 rpm to 2600 rpm
- Drilling ¾″ to 1″—1400 rpm to 2200 rpm
- Drilling over 1″—700 rpm to 800 rpm

Use a block of wood between the work and the table. Do not force the drill. Poor cutting action is usually the result of using the wrong speed or a dull drill. Clamp the work to the table, especially if you are drilling metal or large sized holes in wood. The drill can twist the work out of your hands thus making it dangerous.

*Control the depth of your drilling* by extending the quill until the drill bit point just touches the work. Then, turn the depth control dial to the desired depth setting and lock in place. The drill bit will then drill to exactly that depth.

Use your rip fence as a guide to maintain edge distance on a series of holes which are to be equal. To drill diametrical holes, tilt the table up to a 45 degree angle and set the rip fence so that the point of the drill is centered in the "V" that has been created. Use the rip fence and the miter gauge as jigs for drilling duplicate holes, after locating the position of the hole on one piece of work and setting the fence and miter gauge into position. Put other pieces of stock into the same position to drill duplicate holes.

Remove the table and use your vertical drill as a floor model drill press for such operations as drilling door locks. Mortising (making the hole that receives the tenon in mortise and tenon joints) may be done by using special attachments. Shaping of intricate edge designs and moldings may also be done with special accessories. Routing, a similar operation, can also be accomplished with the addition of a special router chuck. In all such operations, the drill press mode of the multipurpose tool is operated like any conventional high quality drill press.

*Lathe*: To operate your multipurpose equipment as a lathe, move the motor into a horizontal position and replace the drill chuck with a drive center. At the opposite end, attach the tailstock which will support the other end of your stock or spindle. Raise or lower this tailstock to achieve perfect horizontal alignment. Check to see that the points on the drive and cup centers are perfectly aligned. On Shopsmith equipment, this is done by bringing the headstock to the right end of the tubes. Extend the quill until the spur point almost touches the cup point. Look down on the points and if they are not in perfect vertical alignment, loosen the cup center mount screw and turn the cup center mount to bring the cup point in line with the drive point. Set the speed as shown below (Figure 9.13)

Take your stock which has been cut square and draw diagonal lines across each end to determine the center. Use an awl to form a hole at the center and seat the drive center at one end of the stock by tapping it in place with a mallet.

9.13 Turning Wood
Courtesy: Shopsmith

# Part B: Metalworking

## Selecting Multipurpose Tools for Your Metal Shop

Of course, you can also turn out first-rate work in your metal shop. You just need the right tools. In addition to top quality hand tools, you will need a high quality lathe, a top make drill press and excellent power cutting tools. With these items combined into a single multipurpose tool, you will be able to duplicate parts and make new and unique projects, all in a limited space.

Invest in metalworking multipurpose tools if you wish. However, there is no need to duplicate your woodworking equipment for your metal shop. With the recent developments in modern technology, you will be able to work successfully with what you have already invested in.

For example, you can turn non-ferrous metals on your lathe with carbide-tipped chisels at wood turning speeds. As you have seen in the chapter on using conventional lathes, a speed between 700 and 900 rpm is best for most metalworking tasks; but you can turn some objects safely and efficiently at speeds up to 3400 rpm.

Steel, aluminum and other metals can be cut with the circular saw as you have seen in previous chapters. Use an abrasive-coated wheel and wear your safety glasses. Run the wheel slowly, stand behind your work and avoid pressing the side of the cutting wheel with your project.

You can bore metal by using metal drills instead of wood drills. It's even possible to drill concentric holes in metal bars and rods. Clamp the work securely, making sure you've set the job up accurately. As a rule of thumb, the larger the drill, the slower the speed. For large holes (3″ and more), use a fly cutter at a slow speed. You can even sand metal if you select an appropriate abrasive disc and feed the work slowly.

Thus, the woodworking power tools that you now own can probably be used for metalworking. However, you must have a variable speed control; otherwise, they will be too dangerous and ineffective for most metalworking jobs.

If you intend to do almost all metalworking in your shop and very little woodworking, then investigate the possibility of purchasing multipurpose metalworking equipment which uses the same motor to drive a metalworking lathe, drill press and other tools by changing to different operating modes.

### How to Determine If You Need a Multipurpose Tool

Use the following checklist to determine which is the better choice for you in outfitting your metal shop.

1. Do you already have a large investment in separate tools—including power tools?

2. Do you dislike the idea of changing the tool from one operating mode to another?

3. Do you have enough room in your workshop area?

4. Do you intend to do limited metalworking?

If your answer is yes to these four key questions, you should stay with the use of separate tools and not invest in buying a large metalworking multipurpose tool.

On the other hand, if you do decide to choose new multipurpose equipment, try the guidelines for selection given earlier in this chapter.

### Making Sure Your Equipment Is Safe

Be certain that your selected multipurpose tool is not dangerous by checking that it is either double insulated or grounded with a three-prong plug in a properly connected outlet box. When you run the machine, make sure that you have placed the equipment securely in the

9.14 Choosing the Correct Speed
Courtesy: Shopsmith

mode in which you wish to operate it, and have removed all wrenches and other adjusting tools. Run the machine at the slowest speed possible for the particular operation you need—for the utmost safety. Disconnect the equipment when servicing or changing operating modes or accessories. Make certain that children and others unfamiliar with the equipment do not use it. (Figure 9.14)

## SHOPBUILDER # 9

### How to Service and Repair Your Multipurpose Tool

1. If the speed seems slow and erratic:
   a. check the motor speed indicator to see if it is set correctly
   b. check the house and line voltage
   c. check to see if the equipment is overloaded
   d. check if speed indicator or motor needs repair or replacement*
2. If the saw blade or sander is out of alignment:
   a. reattach and tighten
   b. check and straighten or replace spindle*
3. If the machine sounds too noisy:
   a. tighten the components used in the mode under use
   b. examine the workload to see if it is out of balance
   c. lubricate (if possible)
   d. check and replace bearings and housings (if available)*

   NOTE: For problems in operation in each mode (lathe, saw, sander, drill press), also refer to the repair and maintenance in the section on that specific tool (see index). Lubricate with #10 machine oil every 10 hours of operating time.

---

*means this operation is very expensive

## SKILLBUILDER #9

**Use these tests to determine the level of your skill: USING MULTIPURPOSE TOOLS**

| | |
|---|---|
| ADVANCED AMATEUR: | Operate in any three modes, one right after the other—changing the configuration of the tool as appropriate in 5 minutes. |
| PROFESSIONAL:<br>*Do the above plus* | Use the multipurpose tool to cut and sand a block of pine 1⅝″ x 2 1/16″ x 6 5/32″ in 10 minutes.<br>Turn a spindle 6″ long (of pine) and then bore a hole in its center. (No time limit)<br>Cut a 2⅜″ circle in sheet metal. |
| SKILLED CRAFTSMAN:<br>*Do the above plus* | Turn a tapered shaft 12″ long (tapering from 2¾″ diameter to 1⅝″ diameter) and bore a hole lengthwise through it. Finish to a satin smooth surface.<br>Drill a concentric hole in 6″ long 1″ metal stock. |

# 10

# Sprayers and Other Painting Tools

To give your project a good finish is not as complicated as you may think. By selecting the type of finish that is most suitable and then applying it, using the step-by-step methods described below, you will have your friends admiring your handiwork.

## Part A: Woodworking and Plastic Work

### Selecting and Using the Proper Painting Tool

Painting is done with brushes, rollers and spray devices. Brushes range in size from tiny ones with only a few bristles to monsters measuring 8″ across. For both interior and exterior use with latex or oil base paints, the best all-around brush is a polyester-nylon brush bonded in epoxy. Probably the most useful width is a 2″ brush. Furthermore, in a top quality brush, you should expect the bristles to be tipped and shaped. Cheap brushes are almost useless; the bristles tend to come out very easily and get stuck in your work. (Figure 10.1)

Thus, instead of buying cheap bristle brushes, if you must get a brush that is inexpensive, purchase one of the disposable foam rubber ones that work well yet need never be cleaned. For short jobs, it may be cheaper to use a brush of this sort and throw it away after use than to buy a cheap bristle brush and have it mess up your work; or to buy an expensive brush and cleaners of all sorts and then never use them again.

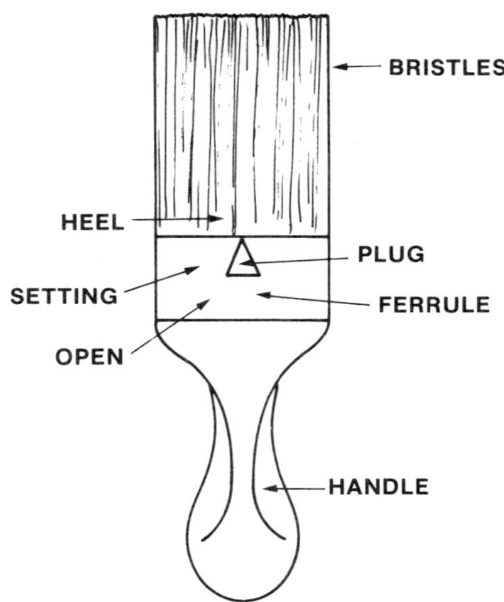


10.1 A Paint Brush

To keep quality brushes in good condition, observe several basic rules:

1. Never keep your brushes in water, it will destroy them. Wash latex paint out of your brushes with soap and water, or oil based paints with special commercial solvents and water (or turpentine or paint thinner). Then dry them and shape the brushes before storing.
2. Never dip the brushes into paint deeper than one-third the length of their bristles. Wash the paint out of the bristles before it clogs up in their base and causes dripping.
3. Keep brushes used for latex paints separate from the brushes used for oil based paints and never mix them—even if you have cleaned them thoroughly.
4. Don't let the paint dry out in the brushes during a work break. Either clean or wrap them in aluminum foil or cellophane to keep them airtight.

In addition, be sure that you use the brush correctly. Dip it into the paint and then wipe or slap the brush lightly against the rim; do not scrape the brush against the paint can. Brush, don't scrub the paint into the surface.

Make long and even strokes with a steady and firm pressure. Lift the brush at the end of the stroke. Don't carry so much paint on your brush that you can hear it slapping. Always work from the unpainted area into the wet area (which you painted on the last stroke). Then go over both areas with quick, light strokes.

Wood projects can be stained, shellacked, varnished, or painted. Most craftsmen prefer shellac or varnish to paint because it reveals the natural beauty of the wood.

**Stains** are used to bring out the natural grain or to change the color of the wood. They are applied with a brush or a sponge and the excess is wiped off. Stains range from water stains (which raise the grain and require sanding), chemical stains (usually applied to give the appearance of age) and oil stains (the easiest to apply and which bring out the grain of the wood). After application, dry thoroughly (12 to 24 hours), sand when necessary and apply a finish.

**Shellac** is a popular finish for light-colored woods like pine, but it can be used on other woods as well. Avoid using it on table tops for it is easily damaged by heat or water. It is simple to apply. Brush, following the grain, smoothing it out with one final light stroke. Shellac should be thin and brushed on the surface, allowed to dry thoroughly (which usually takes only 2 to 3 hours), sandpapered and followed by additional coats. The final coat should be lightly sandpapered and waxed.

**Varnish** is much more difficult to apply. The key is to avoid carrying too much varnish on the brush. After dipping the brush into the can (avoid shaking or stirring which causes the formation of bubbles), strike the brush on a wire stretched across the rim of the can, or work the varnish into the brush by stroking it back and forth on paper. Then, brush the varnish in a thin coat onto a small area about the size of your hand. Use as few strokes as possible. Smooth the surface using a light stroke with the tip of the bristles. Dry thoroughly for a day or two and follow with additional coats.

The key to correct painting is in the acronym SPA. Remember that quality painting requires *selection, preparation* and *application*. You must select the correct paint for the job, considering the type of surface, color and special problems (nonchalking paints are best for trim on brick houses). You must prepare the surface by sanding, using knot sealers, washing the oil and dirt off, filling cracks, using primer and performing other additional techniques called for by the paint in use. Finally, you must apply the paint correctly, following the manufacturer's instructions as to temperature (usually between 40 and 90 degrees), atmosphere (windy, dusty or rainy weather will cause paint to fail), time of day (usually late morning to late afternoon is best), the number of coats (one or two for old surfaces, three coats for new surfaces) and the drying time (particularly between coats). If you follow the SPA procedure, you'll be guaranteed that your paint job will last!

For exterior painting, start painting at the highest point and work down on one side. Then, begin at the top on the next side. Many craftsmen paint only one side of the house a year, keeping the work down as well as the cost. In four years' time, you will have painted the house probably more thoroughly than if you had painted the whole house at once. Manufacturers of top quality paints maintain the exactness of the colors so that you won't be able to tell the difference.

On windows, paint the wood separating the glass first, then the frame, trim, sill, and apron. Take the shutters and storm sash off, and paint them after placing them on sawhorses or other supports. Paint the unpainted area into the wet portion of the painted area and then smooth the surface with a few light strokes.

Using a roller is faster than using a brush. Rollers work well on masonry and other rough surfaces; brushes work better on wood. In addition, if you use the roller on large open surfaces and the brush on corners and other small areas, you will really speed up your work. (Figure 10.2)

**10.2 A Roller**

Dynel fiber makes the best roller cover. It stays springy and alive and will not mat down. It is especially good for use with latex paints.

Use the following chart to make your selection of the length of nap you need:

| To paint the following surface, | with this paint, | use this roller |
|---|---|---|
| PLASTER, WALLBOARD, WOOD (smooth surfaces) | latex, oil, alkyd, enamel, one-coat latex, semi-gloss latex, flat or thixotropic latex | ¼″ short nap |
| PLASTER, ACOUSTICAL TILE, DRYWALL, WOOD (rougher surface) | latex, oil, alkyd | ⅜″ medium nap |
| MASONRY, WOOD (rough surface) | latex, oil, alkyd | ¾″ long nap |

Select a 7″ or a 9″ roller. A tapered roller makes it easy to paint up close to woodwork; trim rollers and corner rollers also make painting simpler.

Fill up your tray one third of the way and roll the roller into the paint and out of it several times. Start painting the walls from the top. In a 3′ square space, roll out a "W" and then go back and forth filling in the area between the strokes. Always work from the unpainted into the painted area.

Find out whether your upward stroke or your downward stroke gives the smoothest finish; it varies from roller to roller. Use that stroke for your final professional finish.

Clean-up is easy if you select the correct solvent and do the job right away. If the paint hardens on the rollers, you will have a difficult job. When you quit for lunch, wrap your rollers in plastic wrap so they will be moist when you return. To simplify cleaning your tray, wrap it in plastic. Then, all you need to do is to remove and discard the plastic. Unless you tear the plastic liner, you won't even have to wash the pan.

For latex paints, use water; soap isn't necessary. For alkyd or oil base paints, enamels and varnish, use mineral spirits or turpentine. Remove the cover from the roller frame to make cleaning easier.

Hang the roller up—do not stand it on end. Store it in a safe and dry place.

### What to Do About Paint Failures

Not every surface you paint will be smooth; many will have been painted a number of times, and some will have been painted improperly. To do the job right, you will often have to remove the inadequate coatings. Use a propane torch and a putty knife to scrape the paint off; a commercial paint remover and a putty knife to scrape it off; or sandpaper and a scraper to cut it off. To avoid future problems, analyze the reason for the failure and correct it.

#### How to Correct Paint Failure

1. If the paint has blistered and peeled (caused by moisture in the wood beneath the paint):
   a. remove loose paint
   b. repair leaks and make vents
   c. use a blister resistant paint
2. If the paint has cross-grain cracking (caused by painting too frequently or not allowing previous coats to dry adequately):
   a. paint less often
   b. strip paint to bare wood and repaint allowing adequate time between coats
3. If the paint chalks excessively (caused by poor quality paint or too thin a coat):
   a. use non-chalking paint
   b. wash surface with mineral spirits
   c. repaint with quality paint
4. If the paint mildews (caused by continuous warm and damp conditions):
   a. wash the surface with trisodium-phosphate solution (Soilax)
   b. use mildew resistant paint
5. If the paint peels between coats (caused by oil or dirt or incompatible types of paint):
   a. remove paint and repaint

### Power Spray Equipment and How to Use It

Spray painting is used whenever you need a finish that is free of brush or roller marks. Most frequently, this is the sort of finish that you will need on metal objects, not wood.

For covering a limited area, use spray cans. Paint is very expensive in these cans because you are also paying for the propellant and the container; but the ease in use and the small amount of paint required may make it worthwhile for you.

For heavy-duty use, use a sprayer and compressor combination to cover really large areas quickly and thoroughly. Small outfits ranging up to ¾ hp are adequate for small jobs; better outfits ranging from ¾ to 1 hp will do the job much more easily; large outfits from 1½ to 3 hp and more are generally used in commercial applications and for running two or more sprayers at the same time.

To understand how to select the right sprayer-compressor for the type of work you expect to do, you need to examine the PSI and SCFM ratings. The PSI (pounds per square inch) rating is the measurement of the air pressure that is delivered to the nozzle of the spray gun. In general, the higher the PSI rating, the thicker the paint that can be sprayed. Most small outfits, for example, operate with a rating of 15 to 50 PSI. Professional quality sprayers have a rating of 40 to 85 PSI.

SCFM, or the standard cubic feet per minute rating, measures the amount of air flowing through the hose and the spray gun. In general, the higher the rating, the finer the finish because the more the density of the paint is broken up. Professional quality sprayers usually deliver from 7.5 to 14 SCFM, while small sprayers designed for simple painting jobs often use only 2 to 4 SCFM. To be sure, you must match the ratings between compressor (the pump that puts the air under pressure) to the spray gun (the device that squirts the paint in a fine mist). (Figure 10.3)

In addition, you will find that you sometimes have to choose between bleeders and non-bleeders. It isn't as bad as it sounds. A bleeder is used with a continuously running compressor; the air flows through the gun constantly but the paint flows only when a trigger is pressed. A non-bleeder is used with a tank-type compressor, and the paint and air both flow only when the trigger is pulled.

To operate, fill the gun cup with paint mixed to the correct consistency—usually as it comes from the can. But in the case of lacquers, varnish and shellac, thin them about 50–50—with lacquer thinner (for lacquer), turpentine (for varnish) and alcohol (for shellac).

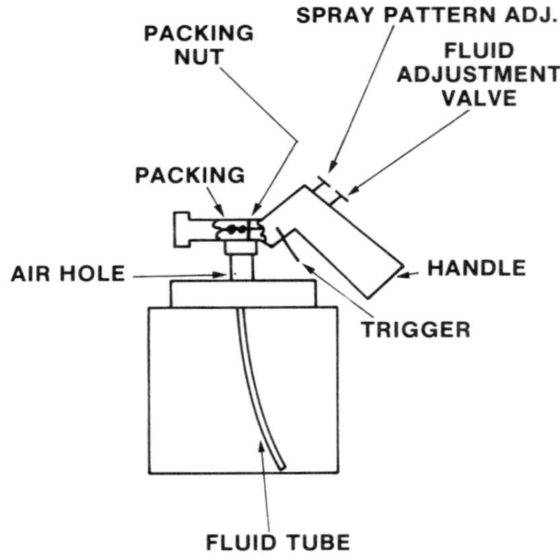


**10.3 A Spray Gun**

Since the paint flow is regulated by the adjusting screw turn it almost closed and then open it gradually. Keep the gun 6″ to 8″ from the surface maintaining a 90 degree angle. Move from left to right with smooth and even strokes. Don't stop at the end of a stroke, but move downward and back the opposite direction in one even motion. Overlap your strokes.

Some painters use an alternate method of hitting the trigger just before your gun is aimed at the edge of the work and release it just after the other edge is reached. You can use vertical strokes instead of

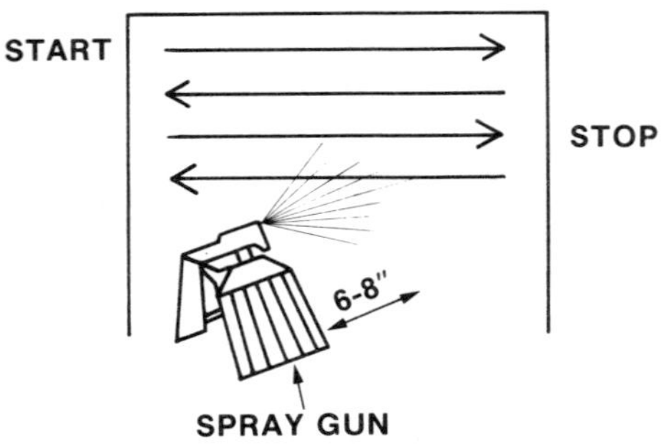


**10.4 A Spray Pattern**

horizontal ones with this method and achieve excellent results. In addition, by using this method and vertical strokes you will find it easy to paint round or cylindrical objects without having the paint run.

Do not spray directly into a corner; spray one side and then the other side—making them meet instead of overlap. Avoid spraying work lying flat. If you have no alternative, start with the side nearest you and work away from you. To avoid getting paint on surfaces you do not wish to cover, use masking tape—before you start. (Figure 10.4)

### How to Service and Repair Your Spray Gun

1. If paint leaks from the spray gun:
   a. remove and clean the tip
   b. tighten the loose fluid tube
   c. loosen fluid-needle packing nut
   d. tighten packing nut
2. If the gun does not spray:
   a. check and correct all switches and connectors
   b. add paint (or thin to correct proportion)
   c. check connections and pressure (adjust)
   d. clean nozzle
   e. clean clogged air cap
3. If the spray gun sputters:
   a. tighten fluid tube connection
   b. tighten nozzle
   c. replace packing around fluid needle
4. If there are streaks:
   a. keep gun at 90 degree angle to the surface
   b. keep strokes parallel
   c. make your strokes slower
   d. clean clogged air cap and nozzle
5. If the gun over-sprays:
   a. decrease the air pressure
   b. move closer (6″–8″ away)
   c. check paint consistency
6. If paint has the texture and look of an orange:

   a. increase air pressure
   b. thin paint to proper consistency
   c. move closer to the surface (6″–8″ away)
   d. move slower in your stroke
7. If paint runs or sags:
   a. increase distance from work (6″–8″ away)
   b. move faster in your stroke
   c. check the paint for the right consistency
   d. keep the spray gun at a 90 degree angle to the surface
8. If the paint is uneven:
   a. move the gun evenly throughout the stroke
   b. clean the nozzle

Clean your sprayer immediately after you are finished using it. Remove the paint and rinse the gun cup with solvent. Clean the inside of the lid and the tube with a cloth and solvent. Put solvent into the cup and attach it to the gun. Run the unit, spraying the solvent into a cloth or on newspaper. Some painters hold the cloth directly over the nozzle and pull the trigger several times. Then, remove the cup and operate the gun without it to clear the tubes.

### How to Use Your Propane Torch

In addition to loosening and removing asphalt tile, thawing frozen pipes and loosening rusted nuts and bolts, your propane torch is excellent for removing paint (Figure 10.5)

First, attach the correct head (soldering and needlepoint heads are available)—you want to use the wide-mouthed tool that makes the flame fan out. Check to see if the valve is closed. Thread the fuel cylinder by turning to the right until it is seated. Do not use a wrench to tighten.

Open the valve a full turn and light with a spark. Many new models use a slightly different principle for lighting. Open the valve ¼ turn for 5 seconds and then close it. Light a match and open the valve slowly until the torch is lit or open one full turn, and light with a spark lighter.

Adjust the flame from 1″ to 1½″ and let it burn for 10 seconds. You will find that the torch operates best when almost vertical. At times when you are using it in a horizontal position, you'll find the flame will shoot out in a wide sheet—as if the propane were suddenly flowing out. There is no need to be alarmed. However, if you need to do work using the torch in a horizontal position, buy a flexible tube with a blowtorch head. This attachment allows you to keep the propane bottle in a stationary position while you use the head in any position. Check the joints and couplings several times to see they are firm while you are using the torch.

If you smell gas, test with soapy water to see if bubbles appear. Never use a lighted match. The torch is safe, but handle it carefully and never operate it unless you have a fire extinguisher nearby. The danger is not from the torch itself but from the possibility of igniting nearby objects.

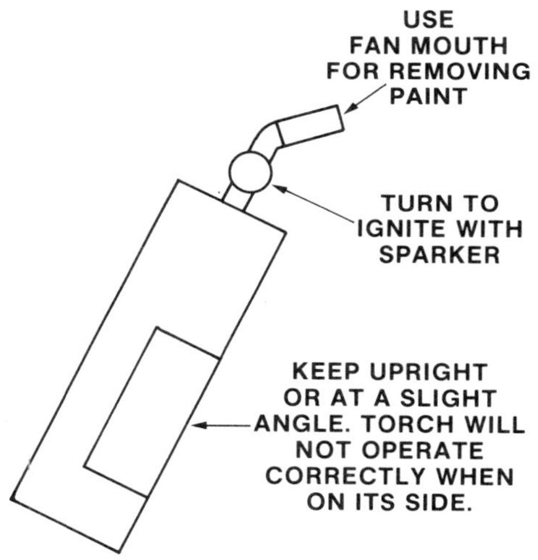


10.5 A Propane Torch

### Selecting the Right Ladder

To paint ceilings, you can use an extension on your roller (a long pole), but you will find many occasions in which a ladder is a must. Stepladders run from 4′ to 10′ in 2′ increments. The steps are generally 3″ wide and are riveted and braced for sturdiness. Ladders of 5′, 6′ and 8′ should have two rigid side braces and three horizontal bars, while the 10′ size requires six braces and five horizontal bars. (Figure 10.6)

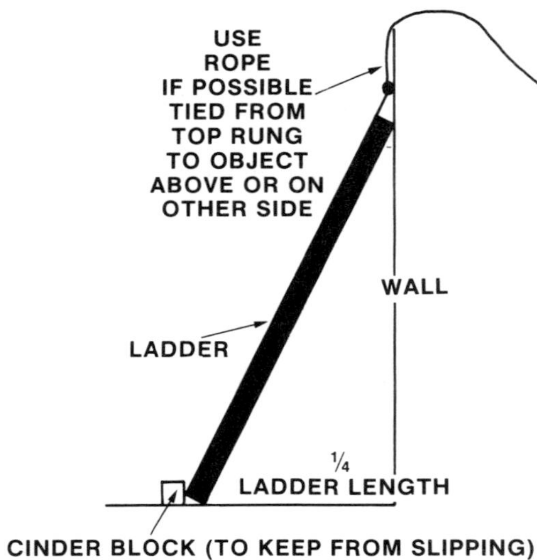


**10.6 Using a Ladder**

Buy aluminum stepladders; they are much stronger and longer-lasting than wooden ones. If you have an old wooden stepladder, test it from time to time to see if it needs work to make it sturdier. Never paint a ladder; you want to see cracks in the wood if and when they develop.

You will find stepladders generally useful for most small jobs inside the home. Outside, you must have extension ladders. Insist that the one you buy is made of aluminum for light weight and has an easy-to-work extension mechanism. Usually, you hold the ladder top away from the wall and pull on a rope which is connected to two pulleys, in order to pull the top of the ladder to the height you wish. It then locks into place. It is lowered by pulling upwards slightly until the locked portion is loosened.

Two sections should extend the ladder an average of 13′ from its original size. Ladders run from 16′ to 32′. They have smaller rungs than a stepladder (usually 1⅝″).

The rules for working on an extension ladder are simple, if you can remember to bring an "S"-shaped hook to hang your paint can from the rung in front of you. To be safe, never adjust the ladder while you are standing on it, never stand on the top three rungs, and never, ever, step back to admire your work.

If you are using an aluminum extension ladder, remember that they can be blown over in the wind if no one is on them—so it is wise to secure them with rope. Also, be careful when moving them so as not to hit overhead wires—metal ladders conduct electricity.

# Part B: Metalworking

Most of the time you can paint metal after a minimum of preparation. You seldom need to remove all of the old paint—only those parts which are scaling or chipping. However, you may need to remove rust or grease so that the paint will adhere. Then, you can spray or brush the new coat of paint on the surface. Some surfaces do require additional work, as will be discussed.

## Preparing Metal Surfaces for Painting

Clean and prepare metal surfaces mechanically or chemically. Mechanical cleaning is done by sanding, wire brushing, scraping and burning. These jobs can be done by hand or with a machine. Although it is unlikely that you would need to sandblast a metal surface, you can rent a sandblaster (which works much like a paint sprayer) and the additional protective clothing and masks. No matter which method you use to remove old paint and rusting, wear safety glasses, a respiration mask and gloves.

Chemical cleaning is most often used to remove grease and wax from the surface. Gasoline, mineral spirits and commercial cleaners are all useful. On rare occasions, you will use a paint remover to take off the old paint. However, it is usually better to leave as much old paint on the surface as you can to maintain a better bond. So, if the old paint is adhering to the metal, leave as much on as possible and paint over it.

New galvanized surfaces should not be painted for six months, although you can wash them with vinegar and use a special primer available at most paint stores. Tin can be painted if you first wash it with turpentine. With other metals, remove grease, rust and prime.

**How to Select the Correct Paint for Metal Surfaces**

| METAL | PAINT |
|---|---|
| Copper | Spar varnish |
| Galvanized Iron | Aluminum paint (after primer)<br>Enamel (after primer)<br>Spar varnish |
| Iron | Aluminum paint (after primer)<br>Enamel (after primer) |
| Aluminum | Aluminum paint<br>Enamel (after primer) |
| Steel | Aluminum paint (after primer)<br>Enamel (after primer) |

On metal surfaces, prime both new metal and old metal from which paint has been removed (you do not need to prime over the old paint that still adheres to the metal). Allow the primer to dry adequately before applying one to two coats of paint.

## SHOPBUILDER #10

**Selections of painting tools—**
**(Choose according to your needs/Build your shop step-by-step)**

BASIC TOOLS:

a. paint (or shellac, varnish, or lacquer)
b. brush (2″ nylon-polyester)

AMATEUR TOOLS: (Include tool lists above)

c. 7″ roller (Dynel fiber)
d. paint tray
e. paint tray grid

ADVANCED AMATEUR TOOLS: (Include tool lists above)

f. putty
g. patching plaster
h. stepladder (6′)
i. sandpaper (assorted)
j. propane blowtorch
k. putty knife, scrapers (1″–2″)
l. spray cans of paint

PROFESSIONAL TOOLS (Include tool lists above)

m. roller extension pole
n. wire brush, scrapers, putty knives (1½″, 3″, 4″, 4½″, 5″)
o. drop cloth
p. turpentine/mineral spirits/solvents
q. brushes (½″ to 4″ nylon-polyester)
r. varnish brushes, camel's-hair brushes
s. paint remover (liquid)
t. ladders (30′ extension ladders)
u. protective face masks
v. sprayer and compressor—3 hp to deliver 8.5 SCFM at 40 PSI (with 25′ hose)

PROFESSIONAL CRAFTSMAN TOOLS: (Include tool lists above)

w. fiber-hair dusting brush
x. brushes (1″, 1½″, 2″, 2½″, 3″, 4″, 5″, 6″) nylon set in epoxy
y. caulking gun and caulk
z. scaffolding

## SKILLBUILDER #10

**Use these tests to determine the level of your skill: PAINTING AND FINISHING MATERIAL**

| | |
|---|---|
| **ADVANCED AMATEUR:** | *Part 1*: Paint a 2′ x 3′ surface by hand so that it is evenly coated and almost no brush marks show, in 2 minutes. *Part 2*: Spray paint a similar surface so that it is evenly covered with no dripping or running, in 1 minute. |
| **PROFESSIONAL:** *Do the above plus* | Varnish a piece of plywood (3′ x 2′) so that no brush marks show in 3 minutes.<br>Use a 9″ roller to cover the 8′ x 12′ wall of a room with latex (or other wall paint) in 15 minutes, so that no marks show and the paint is distributed evenly.<br>Spray paint an ordinary tin can so that no drip marks show (outside only). |
| **SKILLED CRAFTSMAN:** *Do the above plus* | Paint a 2′ x 4′ window so that no paint appears on the glass or on the wall, in 20 minutes.<br>Spray paint a small toy car in a color lighter than it is, without getting the tires wet. |

# 11

# Building an Efficient Workshop

A well-designed and carefully organized shop is fun to work in. Also, your projects will be completed more rapidly if you have everything at your fingertips and don't have to struggle in makeshift quarters.

## Part A: Woodworking and Plastic Work

### Basic Steps in Selecting Tools to Fit Your Needs

Use the checklists that are given throughout this book to help you select the best possible tools for your use. Start with the basic tools and then obtain the others as your needs and interests change. Allot yourself a specific budget for investing in tools and stick to it. Resist buying gimmicks and seldom-used tools just because they are offered at a low price. In the long haul, you will never resent paying for a top quality tool.

To get the most use out of your tools, you need to use them in an efficient location. Furthermore, you need to have places for your tools so that you never have to search for them and waste time doing so. Thus, you need to plan your workshop as you begin to select your tools.

At first, of course, you can keep all your tools in a tool box. Make or buy one of the type that carpenters carry on the job for your wood tools, and get a machinist's tool box for your metalworking tools. One popular and practical way to keep your tools together is to purchase the inexpensive, high impact plastic tool carriers that are designed for specific tools. For example, when you get a portable sander, get a sander box which has room for extra sandpaper discs or belts, plastic wood, scrapers and other tools that you would need to use whenever you are sanding. The power drill box has provisions for drill bits (which can be inserted into holes marked for size), compartments for countersink drill bits, measuring tools and even for a small supply of screws, nuts and bolts. The power sabre saw box has a compartment for carrying blades, small marking and measuring tools, and similar objects in addition to a place for the saw itself. By using these carriers, you will be able to carry exactly what you need to the job and not have to waste time searching for misplaced objects. (Figure 11.1)

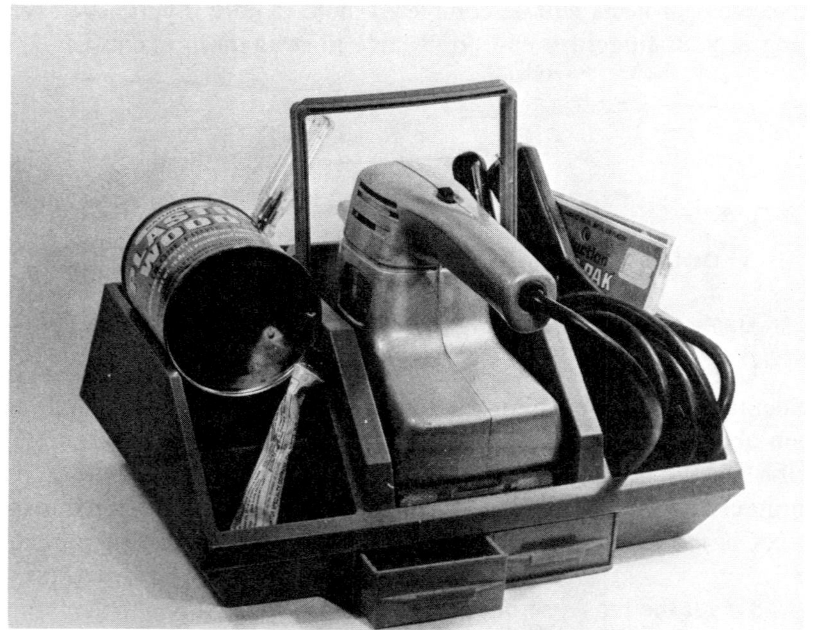

11.1 A Tool Carrier

Top quality power tools often have cases as optional accessories. These differ from tool carriers in that they completely encase the power tool. Some cases can even be locked to keep unauthorized persons from tampering with your power equipment. These cases also have room for a limited amount of additional equipment, including extra blades and parts. The only other important difference between these custom cases and the carriers (besides cost) is that the carriers are all roughly the same size and shape, which makes them easier to store. (Figures 11.2A, 11.2B and 11.2C)

All-steel tool and utility boxes are best for storing metalworking tools. However, there are several that are designed for carrying woodworking tools. A fine quality one has a protective bottom of wood to keep sharp-edge tools from dulling, blocks to carry handsaws, and a

**11.2A Parts Holders**
**Courtesy: The Hirsh Co.**

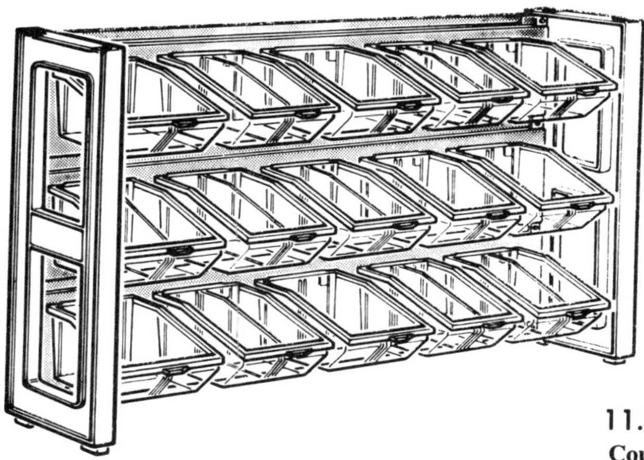

**11.2B Parts Holders**
**Courtesy: The Hirsh Co.**

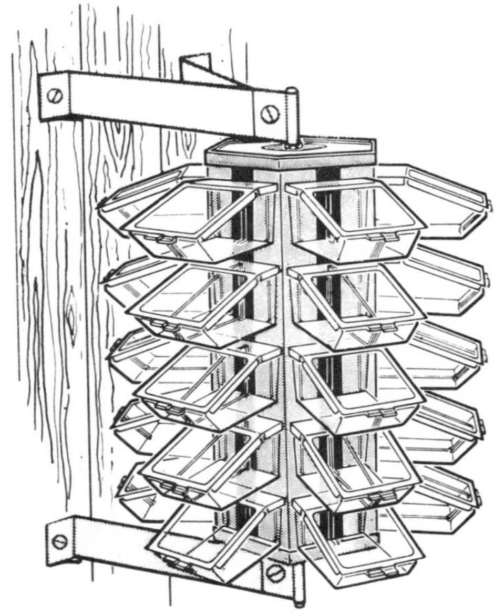

**11.2C Parts Holders**
**Courtesy: The Hirsh Co.**

knockout slot to permit carrying a large square. Boxes like this are usually 30″ to 36″ long, 8″ to 10″ wide and 10″ to 12″ tall.

Steel boxes for metalworking tools usually have one or two lift-out trays for separating small tools. Fine quality machinist's tool boxes have compartments and drawers that are felt-lined to protect the precision instruments carried in them.

A good-sized machinist's tool box will have seven or eight drawers and a top till all felt-lined; and will be about 24″ long, 8″ wide and 13″ high. It should have a built-in lock to keep your valuable metalworking tools safe from prying hands.

A mechanic's tool box usually has cantilevered trays which come into view as the top of the box is opened. These unlined trays are useful for carrying small tools as well as frequently used parts. Make sure that the quality box you buy has drawers that ride on bushings, or something other than the raw rivets which hold the box together. Also, look for a box with a large, easy-to-hold grip that is securely fastened. The most popular size is 18″ long, 10″ wide and 12″ high.

For full-fledged mechanical work, you might invest in a large tool chest with a cabinet—both on wheels. Some offer as much as 12,000 cubic inches of storage space. A fine quality tool chest and cabinet will have eight to ten drawers each, all of which can be locked for security. It is a good idea to mark the contents of the drawers on them to save time in finding the items you need.

You will find that these cabinets measure 40″ high by 18″ wide by 27″ long and the chests measure a slightly smaller 18″ high by 26″ long by 12″ wide so that they will fit on top of the cabinets. Look for large casters (at least 4″) to make moving the cabinet and chest easy. If you have no need to move your tools about, you can use the drawers in a fine quality workbench for the same type of protective storage.

However, there are roll-about workbenches available which are only 30″ wide, making them small enough to store in a closet when not in use. Tools can be stored in the limited drawer space and on hooks on the perforated hardboard (pegboard) mounted at the rear. However,

**11.3 A Roll-Away Workbench**
**Courtesy: The Hirsh Co.**

mounting tools on peg board is not successful if the workbench is moved a lot—the tools may fall and become damaged. (Figure 11.3)

If you decide on a workbench of this type— which is particularly good for apartment dwellers, especially because it can be converted to a regular bench if you purchase a home—select one with a sound and sturdy frame. The work surface is limited (20″ by 30″) but adequate. Make certain that the wheels can be locked into place. Finally, before purchase, measure your closet to be sure that it will fit inside.

The more conventional workbench is a heavy iron or wooden one that is often bolted into place. For most work, it is necessary that the bench be absolutely immobile. Also, it is necessary that the top be as level as possible—free from warping or distortion. It is for this reason that many commercially made workbenches use industrial grade particle board.

Although it used to be popular to construct your own workbench—usually as one of your first projects if you were starting wood

**11.4 An L-Shaped Workbench**
**Courtesy: The Hirsh Co.**

and metalworking—this is not so popular today. There are numerous manufacturers who turn out workbenches far superior to those homemade ones once so common. (Figure 11.4)

For example, metal base benches (which are designed so that they can be level with a screwdriver) have a variety of configurations available, so that you can design your own to fit your needs and assemble it from standard components. Select a model with no drawers, five or ten drawers, one or more shelves, and doors—anything you desire—and assemble it in an afternoon. You will be ready to make projects on it that night.

For general, all-around use, insist on a 2′ by 5′ top at least 1″ thick, to withstand hammering and pounding. In addition, you should expect a crossbraced steel frame for great stability. Usually, such units are 32″ high for a comfortable working level. You may want the bench higher or lower, but you will find it almost impossible to get one that varies more than an inch from this measurement. Thus, you will have to adjust it by using a stool to seat you at the most comfortable height. You will find that sitting is easier than standing at your work.

If you enjoy woodworking, you'll love making projects on a woodworking bench designed for the professional wood shaper. Recently, Scandinavian designed benches have become popular. The reason for this is that they are versatile. There is a side vise in addition to an end vise and clamping bars on the top. The extra long length (78½″) will let you glue projects like grandfather's clocks on the top surface. You can plane or chisel with ease because the side vise has its own built-in stop to keep the wood from moving. (Figure 11.5)

To locate your workshop, select a spot easily accessible from outside (to make it easy to carry in materials), with adequate electrical outlets, water and drainage (to save on costly installation of these utilities), and away from bedrooms—if possible—to cut down on complaints about noise.

Install your workbench against the wall wherever possible. Place your power equipment in the open so that you will be able to work with large pieces of wood. Check to see that you have adequate lighting—for the entire shop and for each individual power tool. Generally, an average sized workshop will require ten electrical outlets; you can limit this number drastically if you use a multipurpose power tool for sawing, drilling, sanding and turning wood stock. (Figures 11.6, 11.7, 11.8 and 11.9)

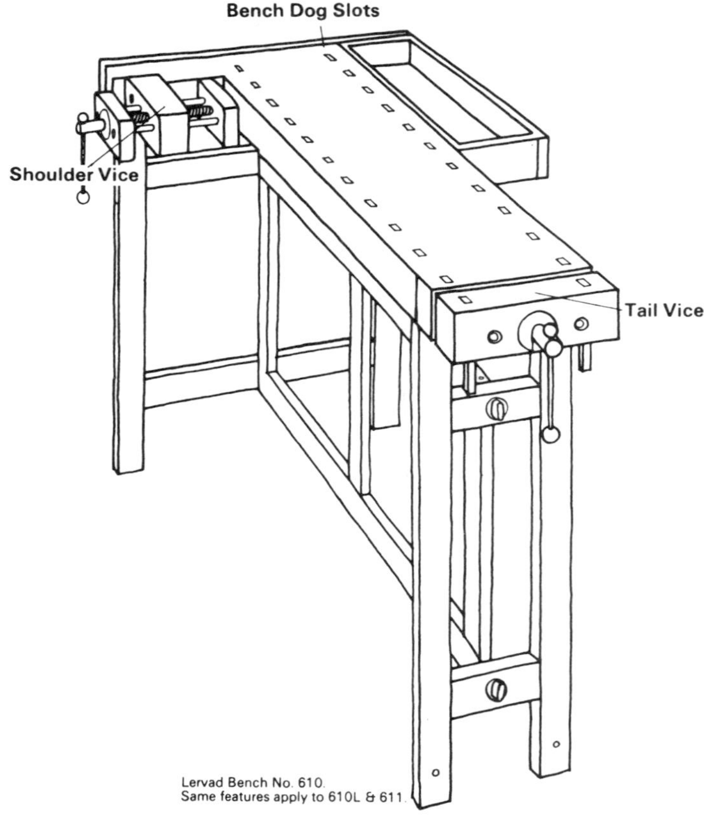


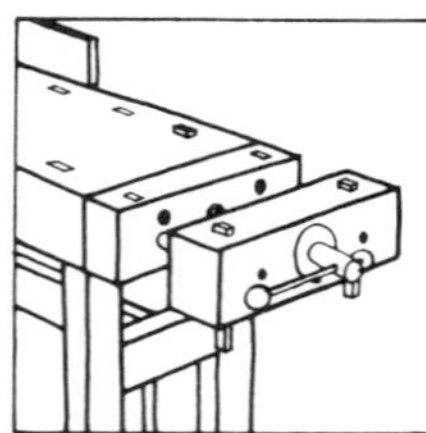

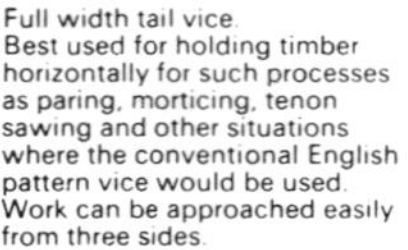
Full width tail vice.
Best used for holding timber horizontally for such processes as paring, morticing, tenon sawing and other situations where the conventional English pattern vice would be used. Work can be approached easily from three sides.

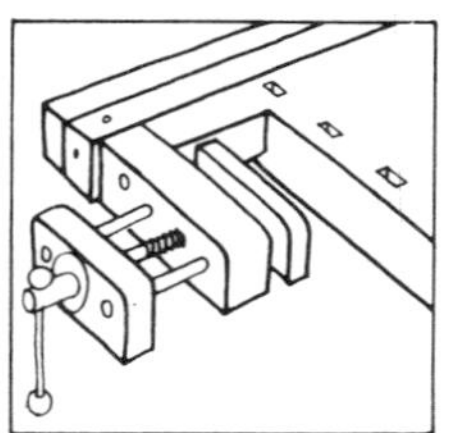

Shoulder vice.
Has its jaw space unimpeded by spindles so that even the largest timbers can be held vertically. Delicate pieces are gripped as perfectly as large ones and the wood is supported on three sides. Generally used for operations where the wood is held vertically (e.g. dovetail cutting, end grain planing, carving etc.).

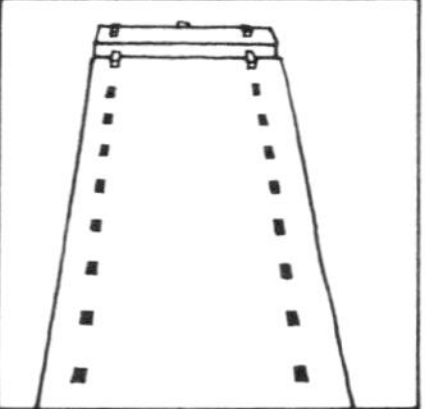

Double row of bench dog slots.
A feature exclusive to Lervad. Working in conjunction with the full width tail vice the dogs provide a four-point hold perfect for surface operations, such as face planing, drilling, rebating, fret and coping sawing etc. Also as cramps for setting up and gluing and for sawing large boards. Easily accessible from three sides making frequent re-positioning of work unnecessary.

## 11.5 A Woodworker's Bench

**Courtesy: Leichtung, Inc.**

Draw several arrangements on paper to see what tool should go where. Plan not only for adequate space around each tool but try to keep tools close to each other on the basis of their use. That is, keep the sander near the bandsaw because you'll use one right after using the other. Therefore, there is no need to walk all the way across the shop to reach it.

For accurate planning, some craftsmen have drawn full-sized outlines of their heavy power equipment on the floor to see how much room they have in getting around it. Try this useful trick and you may

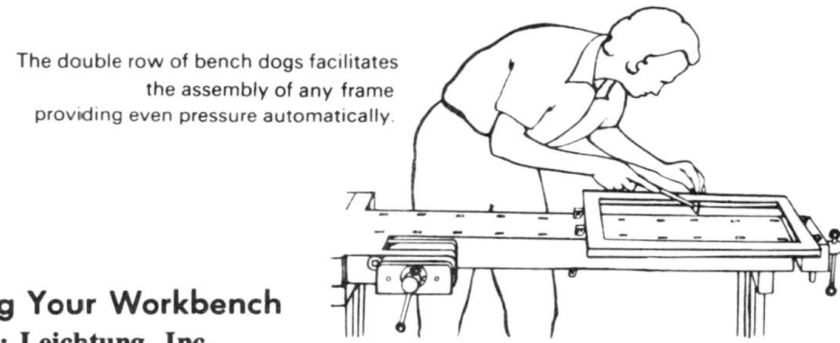

The double row of bench dogs facilitates the assembly of any frame providing even pressure automatically.

**11.6 Using Your Workbench**
**Courtesy: Leichtung, Inc.**

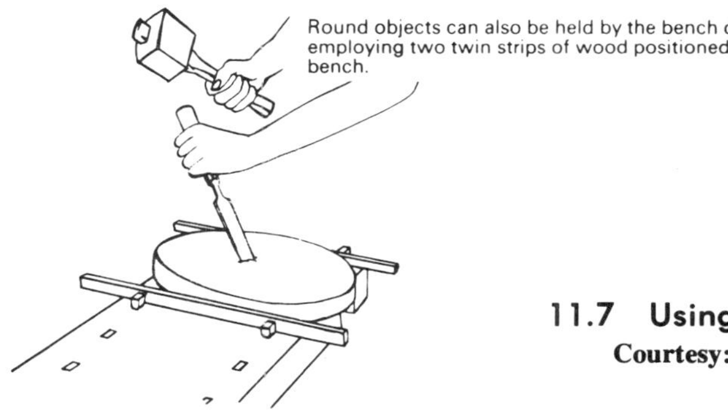

Round objects can also be held by the bench dogs by employing two twin strips of wood positioned across the bench.

**11.7 Using Your Workbench**
**Courtesy: Leichtung, Inc.**

The bench dogs will hold triangular or other odd shapes. Position small waste pieces of wood between the work and the dogs to prevent marking of the work when you tighten up.

**11.8 Using Your Workbench**
**Courtesy: Leichtung, Inc.**

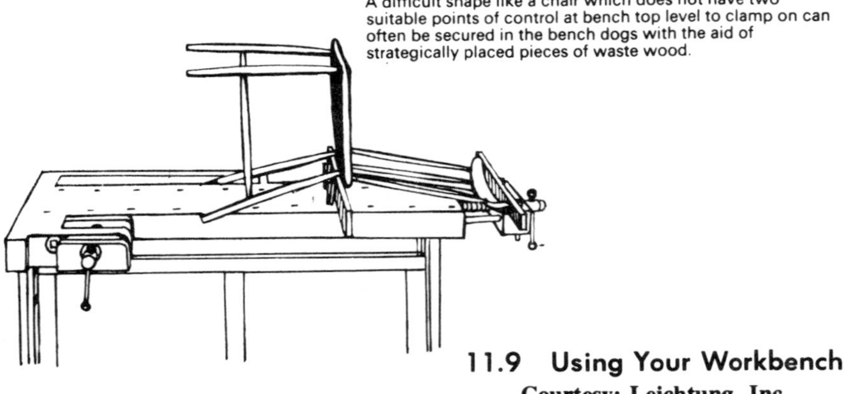


**11.9 Using Your Workbench**
**Courtesy: Leichtung, Inc.**

save yourself a lot of work moving heavy objects back and forth. Allow half again as much room as you think you will need; you'll be astonished at how quickly you will outgrow tiny quarters.

In addition, plan ahead. Do not be afraid to leave space for that jigsaw you hope to buy sometime in the far distant future. Then, when the time comes, you'll be able to fit it into your plan without sacrificing anything else. (Figures 11.10, 11.11, 11.12, 11.13 and 11.14)

Cut down the problem of loud noise from your shop in two ways. Mount your tools on rubber pads or grommets to absorb some of the vibration and use soundproofing tiles on your walls and ceilings. This will cut down on noises of motors and similar power equipment—what may be called continuous sound problems. You will not be able to do much with intermittent sound problems, like hammering. However, if your family complains, these two methods of damping out loud continuous vibration noise may help.

Dirt and bad smells coming from the shop can also be a matter of annoyance to others in the household. If you use your workshop vacuum cleaner regularly and caulk around openings, you can cut down the amount of dust filtering into the house. To eliminate the smells of paints and other chemicals, and other odors which come from using processes like vulcanizing, use a small electronic air filter which ionizes the air. It does a better job than spray deodorants which disguise the odor with a more pleasing but stronger fragrance.

An even more important problem is in keeping your workshop safe. Use locks to keep youngsters out of cabinets containing dangerous chemicals and away from operating power tools. Maintain a special place for inflammable chemicals. Make sure that you have at least one fire extinguisher in the shop; more, if possible. Install a smoke/fire detector. Plan beforehand what to do in case of a fire or other emergency.

11.10 Using a Multipurpose Shop Tool
Courtesy: Shopsmith

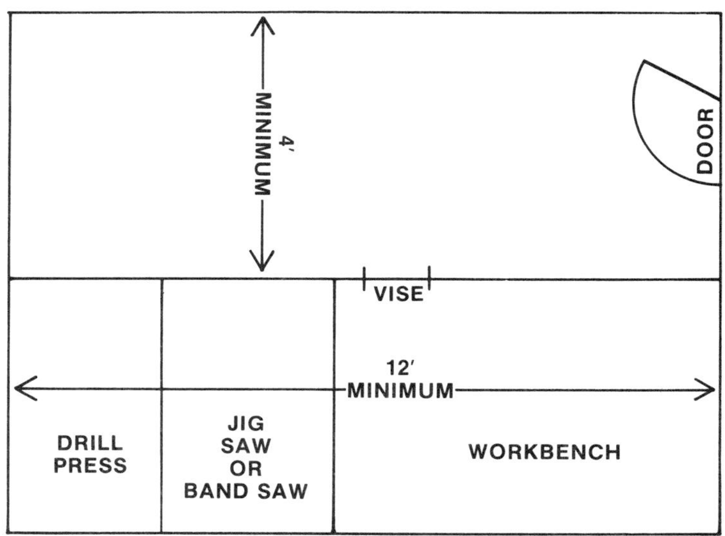


11.11 A Simple Workshop: Plans

Furthermore, learn the rudiments of first aid and keep a small first aid kit in the shop. The kit need only contain peroxide, bandaids, tweezers (for removing splinters), a small amount of gauze, and tape. Make it your goal never to have to use the contents of the box. However, have it ready just in case.

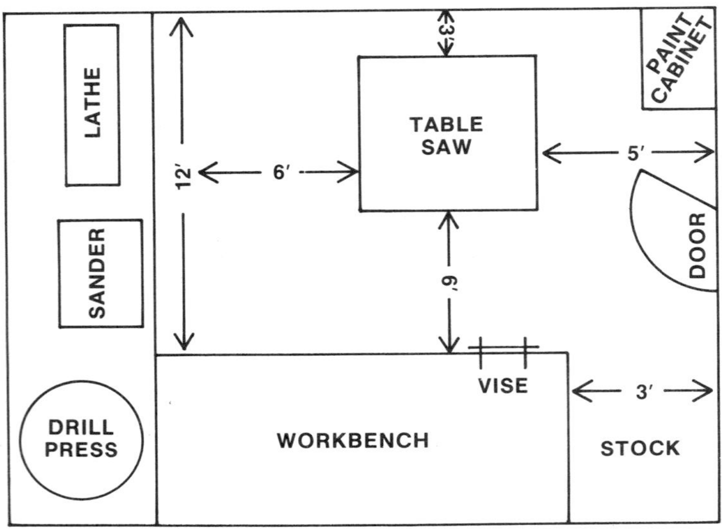


11.12 An L-Shaped Workshop: Plans

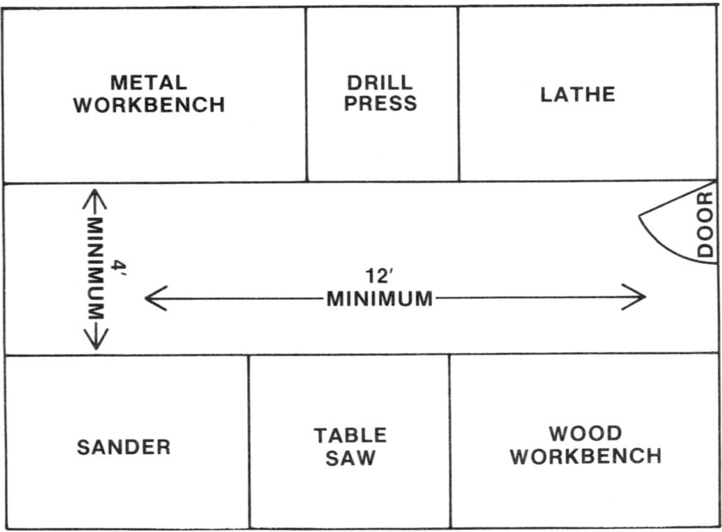


11.13 Combined Metal/Woodshop: Plans

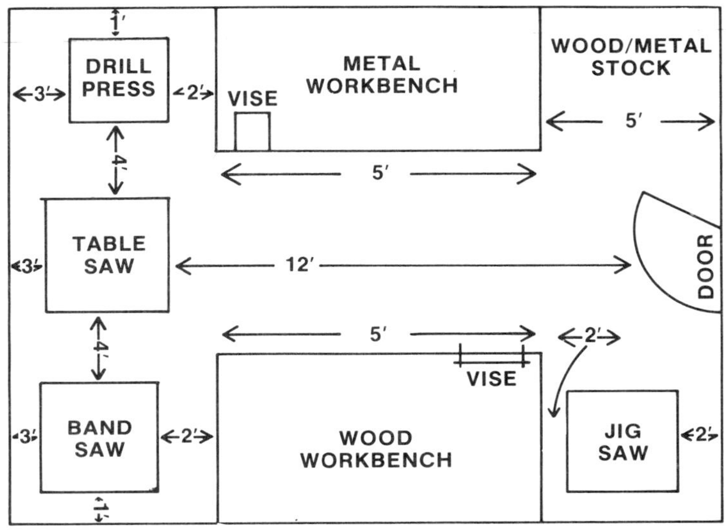


**11.14 A Large Workshop: Plans**

Build your workshop in a series of stages. First, you need some kind of a cutting tool—preferably a table saw. Later, you will want to add other types of power saws: a jigsaw, a bandsaw and perhaps replace your table saw with a radial saw. If you do this in stages, as most craftsmen do, you will be happy only if you buy first rate equipment. Otherwise, the bandsaw that you buy as you become more experienced will be of so much better quality than your table saw, that you will resent working on the older equipment and find it difficult to turn out good work on it.

Remember, however, that it is almost impossible to keep up with the latest equipment. There is no need to discard that good saw just because the newest model out has some new gew-gaw on it. Instead, you may be able to get the new gimmick as an after market, add-on option. Maybe you will find that you can do just as well without it.

## Part B: Metalworking

Although you can use your woodshop for metalworking, if you intend to do a lot of work with tin, steel and iron, you will be happier to have a separate shop or at least a separate work area.

## Setting Up a Metal Shop

Generally, a separate workbench is required for metalworking. It should be one that can be hammered upon; therefore, it must be very sturdy. It need not have a finished top of the sort needed in a woodshop. However, it should be roughly the same size as your woodshop workbench. Ideally, it will have drawers and a shelf or two for storing metalworking tools and unfinished projects. (Figure 11.15)

A good vise is also a necessity. Select a blacksmith's vise which has a leg extending to the floor and is thus designed to absorb hammer blows. In addition, you might find a pipe vise useful, particularly if you think you might do some plumbing work around your home. Bolt all vises down; do not let them sit on your bench.

Most metalworking tools are best stored in drawers, although it is possible to hang them from pegs on a pegboard if absolutely necessary.

Finally, select a spot that is safe. If you intend to do any work with a torch, be sure that you have asbestos lining on your workbench and that you have fire extinguishers nearby. Be sure that there is adequate lighting over both your woodworking bench and your metalworking bench.

**11.15 Storage Space**

# 12

# Making Your Workshop Safe

Select the tools for your workshop with an eye on their safety. In addition, protect yourself as you work by using items that will prevent injury.

## Looking for Safe Tools

Make sure that the tools you buy are designed for safety. Electrical tools must be double insulated or otherwise protected from shock hazard. Furthermore, these tools should have adequate guards and safety features such as electrical switches placed in locations where they cannot accidentally be turned on.

Saws must have guards over the blades. Grinding tools must have transparent shields over them to protect your eyes. Sanding tools should have bags to collect dust; at the least they must have an ejection chute which throws the dust away from you. In short, when you buy any tool—look for the safety features. (Figures 12.1 and 12.2)

Furthermore, you must use the tool with common sense. Follow these general safety rules:

1. Read the manual or instructions before you use the tool. Look for any comments about the tool's hazards.

2. Plan your work so that you won't use the tool in a dangerous manner (clamp your work down, for example) or in a hazardous location (don't work with electrical tools on a damp floor).

3. Never operate the tool without the guards and similar protective devices in position.

12.1 Operate Only with Safety Guards in Place
Courtesy: Shopsmith

12.2 Move Wood with Push Sticks
Courtesy: Shopsmith

4. Avoid wearing clothing and jewelry that can catch in the tool. Keep long hair secure with head coverings.

5. Disconnect the tool from the power supply whenever you are changing parts or adjusting it.

Keep your shop workbench and other areas uncluttered and clean. Avoid accidents caused by knocking over objects or slipping on dirty floors.

For rough tough cleaning that your workshop demands, you need a vacuum cleaner. It's true that you should have a good push broom, a dustpan and a small brush for many jobs, but you also need some way of cleaning without raising dust. A common household vacuum cleaner is not adequate. You need a tool designed specifically for the workshop.

Many fine quality vacuums now on the market will pick up both stubborn dirt and liquids. Such a machine should have an automatic cutoff switch for when the equipment is full of liquid. Of course, you can pick up water with almost any vacuum cleaner if you are able to shut it off before the liquid reaches the motor. Generally, it isn't worth the risk; use equipment designed for the purpose, instead.

Select a vacuum cleaner with sufficient power (at least 1 hp) and sufficient capacity (8 gallon minimum—which will hold 4/5 of a bushel of dirt or 5 gallons of liquid), and make sure that it is mounted on wheels. It is best to buy a well-known make; parts and replacement filter bags may be hard to find if you buy an off brand.

Get in the habit of cleaning your workshop as soon as you finish with an operation. Don't let the dust hang in the air; instead of brushing your workbench off and sweeping the floor around your jigsaw, use your vacuum to pick up the sawdust.

Clean the vacuum frequently and you will find that it is much more efficient. If you change the replaceable vacuum filter bags on a regular basis—once a month is usually enough—you will find that it is easy to keep the machine in good shape. Almost all cleaners have factory sealed lubrication and no maintenance is necessary or possible.

### Eyeshields

Avoid injury to your eyes by wearing eyeshields while performing any task in your workshop. If you already wear eyeglasses, you still need extra protection.

The simplest shields are merely large plastic eyeglasses with earpieces bent to fit your head. Some models have plastic earpieces which can be heated to shape them permanently. Be sure if you use these glasses that you attach a rubber throng to each end to keep them on; otherwise, you may feel them slipping off while you are busy using both hands—thus putting your eyes in danger. (Figure 12.2)

**12.3 Protect Eyes with Safety Glasses**
**Courtesy: Omark Industries**

Avoid the type of safety glasses that give you no protection around the edges. Quality safety eyeshields are usually made of soft pliable vinyl that gives ample clearance even over big frame prescription glasses. Perforations at the sides allow free flow of air so that you are comfortable even in warm temperatures. The plastic lenses should be at least .050″ thick for ample protection.

Safety spectacles—once popular—are not as comfortable as modern welder's goggles, or all-purpose goggles which are made of soft vinyl (which is very light and comfortable). Both types have an adjustable rubber headband to keep the glasses on no matter what position you are in. The major difference between these and other safety glasses is that the lenses are replaceable. You can insert specially colored glass lenses (unbreakable, of course) to protect your eyes from the intense glare of the welding flame.

In addition to selecting the correct pair of safety glasses suitable for the kinds of work you do in your shop, get a pair that will fit snugly with respirators and masks to keep the dust and fumes out of your lungs.

Some craftsmen, however, prefer face shields. These large, heavy-duty acetate shields mounted in aluminum frames are either 6″ or 8″ long and thus protect your entire face. Quality shields have replaceable acetate shields in colors that will help protect your eyes from the glare of welding and brazing operations. Also, they are equipped with friction pivots so the shield can be moved quickly out of the way. Sweatbands are a necessity with shields of this type.

### Dust Masks: How to Select and Use Them

Respirators or dust masks are necessary to protect your lungs from fine sawdust and other types of dust, paint spray, grindings from metal and similar airborne objects.

A fine quality unit has replaceable filters and a cotton face-piece—necessary because it absorbs perspiration and stops facial irritations. Gauze filters are available on other models. Some simpler models are sterilized by boiling, and weigh as little as 1 ounce. Generally, the types of masks used by physicians and surgeons are unsuitable because they do not trap the type of airborne dust and particles encountered in the workshop.

Unfortunately, many amateur craftsman do not realize the possible dangers that can result from breathing in particles of paint, carbon, wood dust and other foreign matter, and think that a respirator is a needless luxury. However, you would be wise to use these devices whenever you are spray painting latex base paint, lacquers and epoxies. Also, you will find that the device protects you from solvent vapors, cement dust and sawdust.

A few craftsmen are even beginning to understand the problems of noise pollution and the use of hearing protectors is becoming more common. These "earmuffs" have foam ear cushions and protect you from harmful effects of noise. Hearing protectors for moderate noise levels (up to 110 decibels) are adequate for the amount of noise encountered in the home shop—slightly below the noise of the table saw, for example. Other types are available for handling the noise encountered in manufacturing and industry. Play it safe, protect your hearing and you won't be sorry.

### Avoiding Injury Through Lifting

Protect yourself from harm in your workshop by knowing how to lift and by using mechanical devices to make the task easier.

First, whenever you lift, don't bend and use your back. Instead, stoop or squat and lift with your legs by rising as you lift. You'll find that this makes it less likely for you to be injured.

However, you can use winches and hoists to make the job even easier. One popular winch-hoist combination weighs only 6½ pounds but can lift up to 2000 pounds. An electric winch—that runs on 12 volts DC—will move objects up to 2800 pounds up a 20% grade. In addition, of course, you can use rope and pulleys to rig your own block and tackle.

Also use the principle of the lever to raise objects with less strain. Don't exert yourself more than you must.

### Protecting Your Hands

Use gloves (leather or cotton for ordinary work; rubber coated for work with chemicals; insulated for very hot or cold jobs) or the new chemical "invisible glove" that coats your hands with a unique combination of vegetable oils and anti-drying agents. One coat of this spray will protect your hands against stains, paint, oil, grease and chemicals.

### Selecting and Using the Right Fire Extinguisher

Always be prepared to fight a fire in your workshop even though the chances are you will be lucky enough and never have to do so. However, be sure to install a smoke/fire detector in your workshop.

No work area is complete without an extinguisher which fights two kinds of fires: Type B and Type C. Type B fires are caused by flammable liquids such as gasoline, oil, paint and grease. Type C fires are caused by malfunctioning, energized electrical appliances such as motors and switches. Thus, you need a dry chemical fire extinguisher with a visual gauge to tell you that it is in operating condition when you check it monthly. Most simple extinguishers are operated by squeezing the handle to release harmless dry powder that smothers fires instantly. Do not throw water on this type of fire—you will only cause it to spread! Although one extinguisher is usually sufficient, you will have more peace of mind if you keep two on hand.

Two extinguishers should be more than enough to put out any fire that might occur. However, if you use the extinguisher, be sure to replace it within the hour. The extra extinguisher gives you protection in the meantime.

If the fire blazes out of control, get help. Experts say that the first 3 minutes are crucial, and a fire must be extinguished in that time or it can be dangerous. Plan your escape route before an accident happens. Leave the house, getting everyone else out and phone from your neighbor's. If the fire is electrical, shut off the electricity—if possible.

For prevention, do not let oily rags accumulate. Keep piles of waste at a minimum. Keep your paint and other flammables in a metal cabinet which you can lock.

### Checking Electrical Currents to See If They Are Safe

Almost all power tools operate on 120 volts alternating current. All tools have their amperage listed—usually on the manufacturer's nameplate. Check it to avoid overloading your household circuits. For example, if your wiring system is designed to carry 15 amps per circuit (as many older homes are), and you plug in two tools—one rated at 7.5 amps and the other at 10 amps—you will blow out the fuse. In fact, usually a ½ hp motor is all that a 15 amp circuit can carry. Therefore, be sure that you have adequate electrical wiring to carry the load. Most workshops need three circuits: one for lighting and two for power tools.

Be sure that your electrical tools are double insulated to avoid shock, or that they are grounded with a three-prong plug used in a grounded wall socket. To check if your wall socket is properly grounded, use a voltmeter. Connect one lead to the hot side of the socket and the other lead to the screw holding the plate on. If you get a reading, you know the wall socket is grounded; if you get no reading, the socket is not grounded. You can also use a neon circuit tester in the same way. If it lights, the socket is grounded.

Inexpensive adapters with a pigtail or bracket that is connected to the middle screw in the wall socket, are acceptable for occasional use. Never remove the green gounding wire from the adapter plug. For a permanent workshop, have grounded sockets installed by a competent electrician.

For periodic checks on your household line, use your voltmeter to test whether or not the line voltage is adequate. Insert the two leads into the socket and read the voltage on the face of the meter. Use your neon circuit tester's leads inserted into the wall socket to tell you if the socket is live or not—safely.

Be careful in using extension cords. Lengthy cords cause a drop in voltage which can make a tool lose half its power, thus making it inefficient and, in some cases, dangerous. For tools rated ½ hp—7.4 amps; ¾ hp—10.4 amps; and 1 hp—13 amps; use the following table for selecting the correct extension cord:

**Use This Chart to Select**
**Safe Extension Cords for Motors**

| | | WIRE GAUGE | | |
|---|---|---|---|---|
| | | #18 | #16 | #14 |
| ½ hp motor rated at 7.4 amps | 25′ | OK | OK | OK |
| | 50′ | NO | OK | OK |
| | 100′ | NO | marginal | OK |
| ¾ hp motor rated at 10.4 amps | 25′ | NO | OK | OK |
| | 50′ | NO | NO | OK |
| | 100′ | NO | NO | NO |
| 1 hp motor rated at 13 amps | 25′ | NO | marginal | OK |
| | 50′ | NO | NO | marginal |
| | 100′ | NO | NO | NO |

### Avoiding Flood Damage

If your workshop is flooded, cut off all electricity so that you won't be shorted out. Move the tools to a higher level, if possible, drying them off at once and coating them with oil. Use rust remover to keep your tools in prime condition. Don't wait too long to clean them or you may find the task impossible.

Even more important may be returning your shop to normal. To avoid shock hazards, be sure that the floor and equipment are dried out completely before you attempt operation. Use a propane heater (electrical heaters have the same shock hazards as your electrical tools.)

# Appendix: Practical Projects

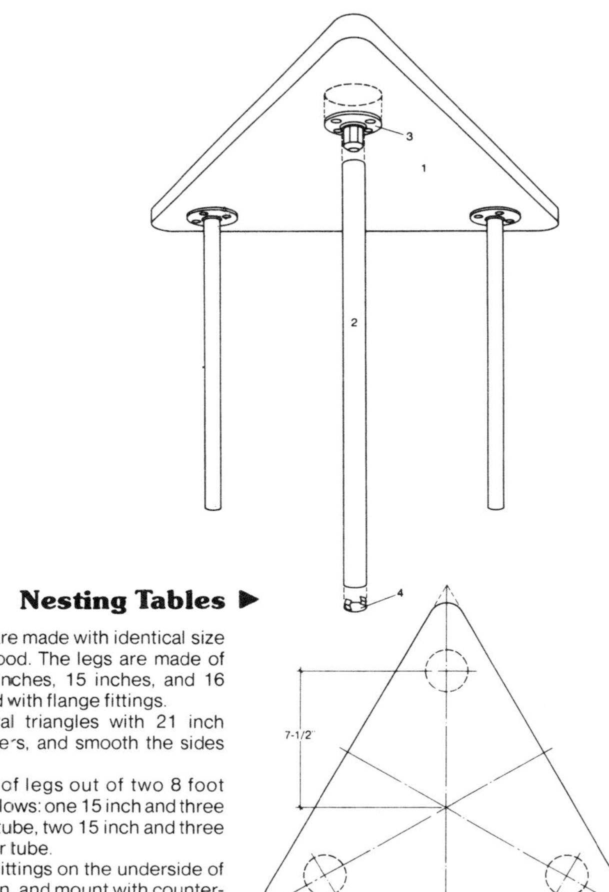


## Nesting Tables ▶

These three tables are made with identical size tops of 3/4 inch plywood. The legs are made of 3/4 inch tubing—14 inches, 15 inches, and 16 inches long—mounted with flange fittings.

Cut three equilateral triangles with 21 inch sides, round the corners, and smooth the sides and tops.

Cut the three sets of legs out of two 8 foot lengths of tubing as follows: one 15 inch and three 16 inch legs from one tube, two 15 inch and three 14 inch legs from other tube.

Position the flange fittings on the underside of the table tops, as shown, and mount with countersunk wood screws. Attach tubing to flanges and cover with end caps. Finish tops with stain or paint.

**Nesting Tables**
**Courtesy: Reynolds Metals Company**

# Modular Wall System

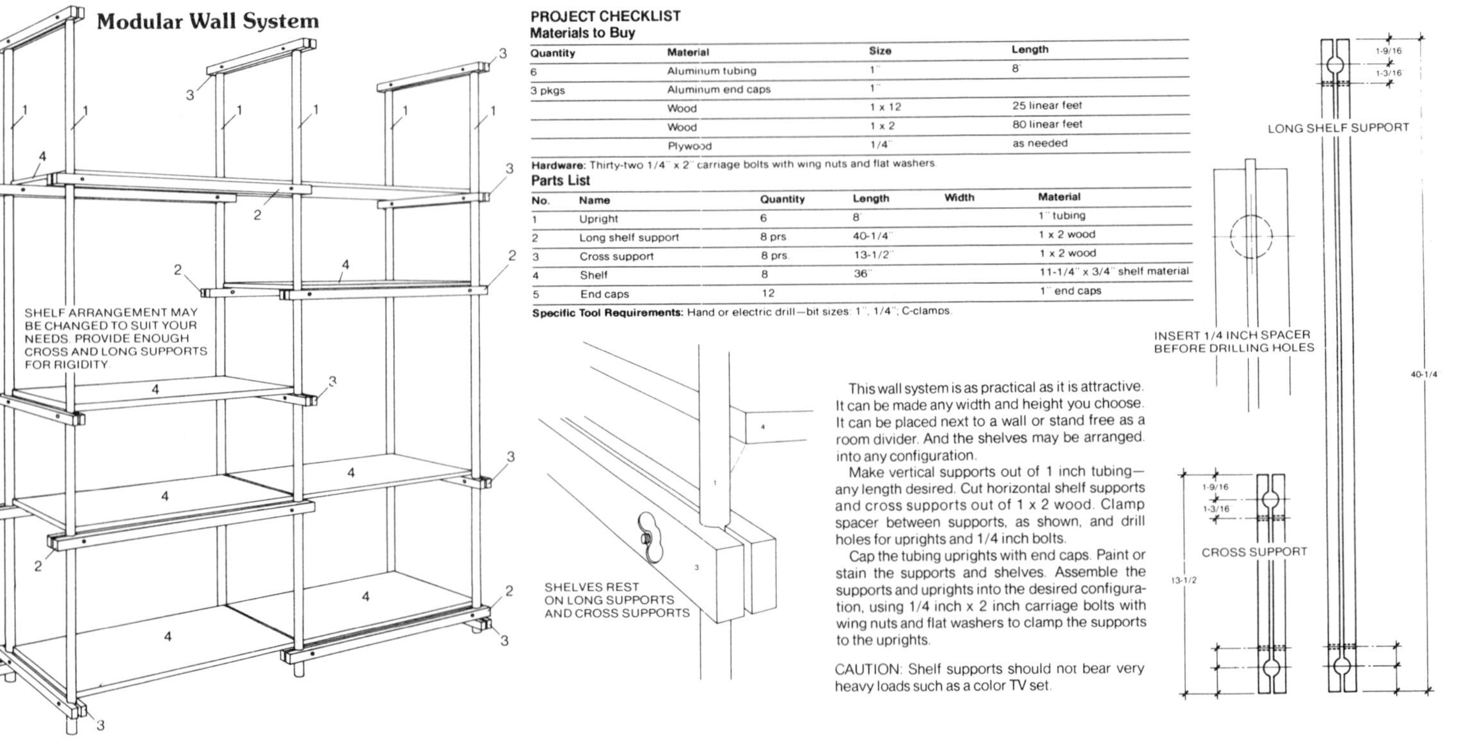


**PROJECT CHECKLIST**
**Materials to Buy**

| Quantity | Material | Size | Length |
|---|---|---|---|
| 6 | Aluminum tubing | 1" | 8' |
| 3 pkgs | Aluminum end caps | 1" | |
| | Wood | 1 x 12 | 25 linear feet |
| | Wood | 1 x 2 | 80 linear feet |
| | Plywood | 1/4" | as needed |

**Hardware:** Thirty-two 1/4" x 2" carriage bolts with wing nuts and flat washers.

**Parts List**

| No. | Name | Quantity | Length | Width | Material |
|---|---|---|---|---|---|
| 1 | Upright | 6 | 8' | | 1" tubing |
| 2 | Long shelf support | 8 prs. | 40-1/4" | | 1 x 2 wood |
| 3 | Cross support | 8 prs. | 13-1/2" | | 1 x 2 wood |
| 4 | Shelf | 8 | 36" | | 11-1/4" x 3/4" shelf material |
| 5 | End caps | 12 | | | 1" end caps |

**Specific Tool Requirements:** Hand or electric drill—bit sizes: 1", 1/4"; C-clamps.

This wall system is as practical as it is attractive. It can be made any width and height you choose. It can be placed next to a wall or stand free as a room divider. And the shelves may be arranged into any configuration.

Make vertical supports out of 1 inch tubing—any length desired. Cut horizontal shelf supports and cross supports out of 1 x 2 wood. Clamp spacer between supports, as shown, and drill holes for uprights and 1/4 inch bolts.

Cap the tubing uprights with end caps. Paint or stain the supports and shelves. Assemble the supports and uprights into the desired configuration, using 1/4 inch x 2 inch carriage bolts with wing nuts and flat washers to clamp the supports to the uprights.

CAUTION: Shelf supports should not bear very heavy loads such as a color TV set.

**Modular Wall System**
**Courtesy: Reynolds Metals Company**

# Boat Ladder

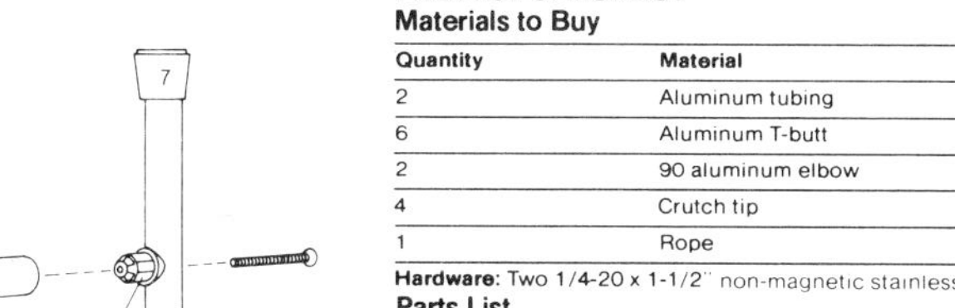


Cut the lengths for the side rails (1), rungs (2), and short legs (4) as specified. After making cuts, remove any burr and slightly chamfer inside the tube ends with a pocket knife.

Using a T-butt connector with the bolt removed as a drilling guide, drill 1/4 inch holes through the side rails (1) at the locations where the top two rungs (2) and the short legs (4) are connected. To insure that your ladder will fit squarely against the freeboard, care should be taken to drill the short leg holes at a 90-degree angle to the rung holes.

Fasten the T-butt connectors (6) to the side rails. Placing the fitting in a vice, tap the T-butt bolt lightly with a hammer to dimple the tubing. Slip the rungs and short legs onto the connectors and tighten.

Slip the elbow fittings (5) into the bottom rung (3) and tighten. Connect the bottom rung to the side rails and drill 1/4 inch holes for 1/4-20 x 1-1/2 inch bolts. These holes should be drilled approximately 1/2 inch from the bottom of the side rails. Bolt the bottom rung securely into place.

Add the crutch tips (7) to the exposed ends of the side railings and short legs.

PROJECT CHECKLIST

**Materials to Buy**

| Quantity | Material | Size | Length |
|---|---|---|---|
| 2 | Aluminum tubing | 1-1/4" | 6' |
| 6 | Aluminum T-butt | 1-1/4" | |
| 2 | 90 aluminum elbow | 1-1/4" | |
| 4 | Crutch tip | 1-1/4" | |
| 1 | Rope | 3/8" | as needed |

**Hardware:** Two 1/4-20 x 1-1/2" non-magnetic stainless steel bolts with nuts and lock washers.

**Parts List**

| No. | Name | Quantity | Length | Width | Material |
|---|---|---|---|---|---|
| 1 | Side rail | 2 | 30" | | 1/4" tubing |
| 2 | Top rung | 2 | 10-5/8" | | 1-1/4" tubing |
| 3 | Bottom rung | 1 | 10-1/4" | | 1-1/4" tubing |
| 4 | Short leg | 2 | 3" | | 1-1/4" tubing |
| 5 | Elbow fitting | 2 | | | 90 elbow |
| 6 | T-butt connector | 6 | | | T-butt |
| 7 | Crutch tip | 4 | | | crutch tip |
| 8 | Rope | 2 | as needed | | 3/8" rope |

**Specific Tool Requirements:** Hand or electric drill—bit size 1/4"; Vice (optional).

**Boat Ladder**

**Courtesy: Reynolds Metals Company**

## Wall Cabinet

Our wall-mounted cabinet is simple to build and can be put to use anywhere in the home or office. Top, bottom, sides, back, and compartment dividers are made of 3/4 inch shelving wood. For the sliding doors, any material of 1/8 inch, 1/4 inch, or 1/2 inch thickness can be used. We used 1/4 inch hardboard. You may follow dimensions shown or alter to suit your needs.

Cut wood pieces to size. For our cabinet, we used 1 x 12 material for outside pieces and 1 x 8 material for the divider shelves. Assemble with glue and finishing nails. Use simple butt joints, as shown, for easy construction.

Cut the sliding door track to fit between the cabinet ends, top and bottom, and install with a few screws to check door fit and alignment. Remove track. Paint or stain cabinet and doors.

Re-attach track with screws every 6 to 8 inches. Track sets come complete with screws. Mount unit to wall with 2-1/2 inch screws into studs.

When mounting to other materials, use appropriate fasteners.

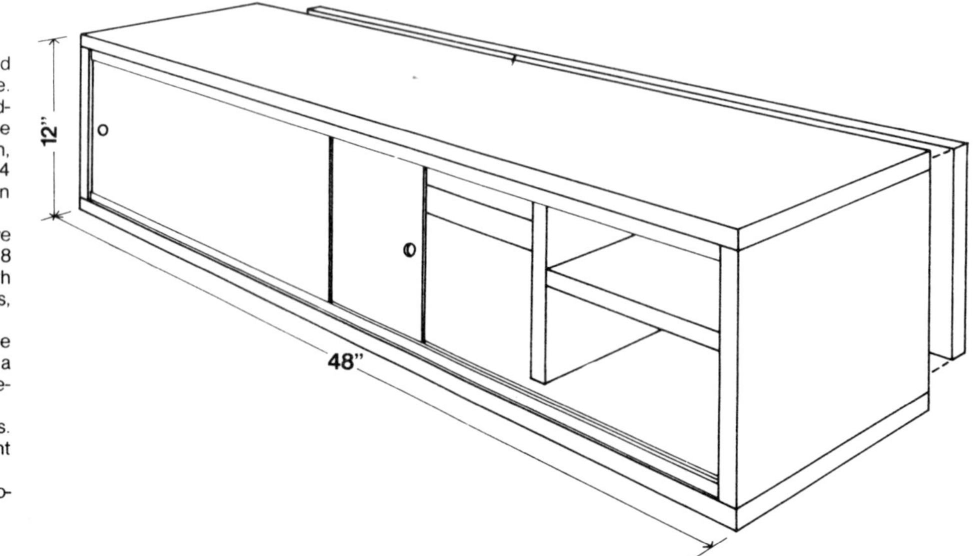


**Wall Cabinet**
**Courtesy: Reynolds Metals Company**

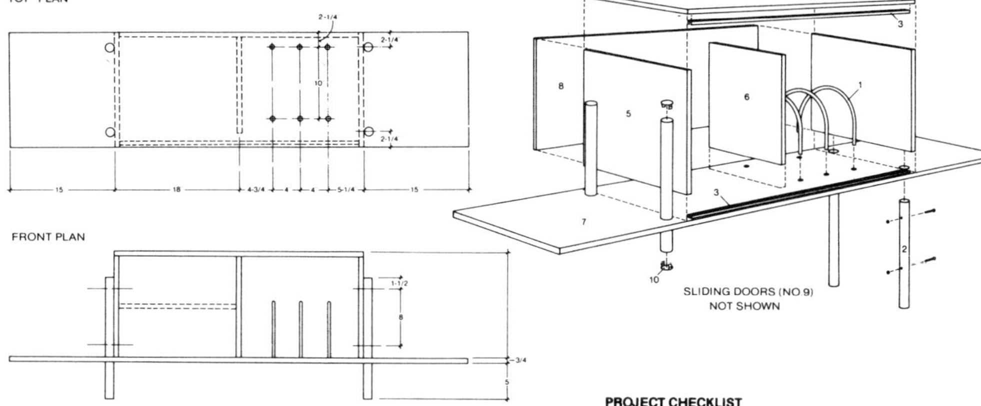


## Stereo Component Cabinet

This stereo component cabinet is designed to give you maximum flexibility in component placement and record storage. Sliding doors conceal sections for components and records, and the cantilevered base holds speaker enclosures. Dimensions can be adjusted to fit the size of your components or the available room space.

Cut all parts as shown in the exploded view drawing to the specified or desired dimensions. Drill 3/8 inch holes in the base (7) where the record dividers (1) are inserted. Drill 1-1/4 inch leg holes in the base at the locations shown in the top plan.

Assemble the cabinet (parts 4, 5, 6, and 8) with white glue and three #8 x 1-3/4 inch flathead wood screws per joint. If desired, add the optional component shelf in the left hand compartment at this time.

Install the sliding door track (3) 1/4 inch back from the front edge of the cabinet. Make sure the top and bottom tracks are properly aligned.

Drill 3/16 inch bolt holes in the legs (2). Insert the legs through the leg holes in the base and, using the bolt holes as a drilling guide, drill through the side panels. (5). Bolt the legs into place with #10-24 x 2-1/2 inch roundhead machine screws and flat washers. Cap the legs top and bottom with end caps (10).

**PROJECT CHECKLIST**
**Materials to Buy**

| Quantity | Material | Size | Length |
|---|---|---|---|
| 1 | Aluminum rod | 3/8" | 6' |
| 1 | Aluminum tubing | 1-1/4" | 6' |
| 1 set | Aluminum door track | 1/4" | 4' |
| 2 pkgs. | End caps | 1-1/4" | |
| 1 | 3/4" plywood | 48" x 66" | |
| 1 | 1/4" hardboard | 18" x 28" | |
| 2 | Door pulls | | |

**Hardware:** Eighteen #8 x 1-3/4" flathead wood screws; eight #10-24 x 2-1/2" roundhead machine screws with nuts and flat washers.

**Parts List**

| No. | Name | Quantity | Length | Width | Material |
|---|---|---|---|---|---|
| 1 | Record divider | 3 | 24" | | 3/8" rod |
| 2 | Leg | 4 | 17" | | 1-1/4" tubing |
| 3 | Door track | 1 set | 34-1/2" | | 1/4" door track |
| 4 | Top | 1 | 36" | 15-3/4" | 3/4" plywood |
| 5 | Side panel | 2 | 14-1/4" (height) | 15-3/4" | 3/4" plywood |
| 6 | Center divider | 1 | 14-1/4" (height) | 13" | 3/4" plywood |
| 7 | Base | 1 | 66" | 15-3/4" | 3/4" plywood |
| 8 | Rear panel | 1 | 14-1/4" (height) | 34-1/2" | 3/4" plywood |
| 9 | Sliding door | 2 | 13-7/8" (height) | 17-7/8" | 1/4" hardboard |
| 10 | End caps | 8 | | | 1-1/4" end caps |

**Specific Tool Requirements:** Hand or electric drill—bit sizes: 3/8", 3/16", and 1-1/4"

Form the record dividers into a "hoop" shape by bending rod around a 10 inch diameter round form. Avoid overbending the rods. Position the dividers in the base holes.

Insert door pulls in sliding doors (9) and position doors on track. Remove legs from the cabinet and finish the interior and exterior of the cabinet and base. Reassemble the legs.

**Stereo Component Cabinet**
**Courtesy: Reynolds Metals Company**

## Divided Record Holder

Here is a simple way to create a divided record holder that sits on a stereo console, cabinet, or shelf. The base can be made of plywood or solid wood with wooden knob feet available from a lumber yard or hardware store. The dividers are made of 3/8 inch aluminum rod formed into a "hoop" shape.

Although our record holder is planned as a separate unit, the aluminum rod divider idea can be built into an existing shelf system, bookcase, or cabinet. Use the construction directions for forming and installing the dividers given below.

To make the divided record holder, cut the wooden base to the desired dimensions. Drill holes in each corner of the base to insert the threaded wood dowels that screw into the knob feet (base hole size on dowel diameter).

Holes for each end of the dividers are drilled about 9 inches apart and are 3/8 inch in diameter. We spaced the hoops 4-3/4 inches apart, but you can vary the spacing or add more dividers for a longer record holder. When installing dividers in a shelf, where the appearance of the bottom of the shelf is important, do not drill the divider end holes clear through the shelf, but make them deep enough to hold the dividers securely.

Cut the divider rods 24 inches long—four lengths come out of an 8 foot rod. Bend each divider rod by hand around a 9 inch diameter circular form—for example, a wooden circle mounted on a flat surface. Make the bend from the center of the rod outward. Be careful not to overbend the rods. The natural spring at the ends of the hoop must hold it in place once it is positioned in the base. Set the dividers in the base holes. Stain or paint the base as desired.

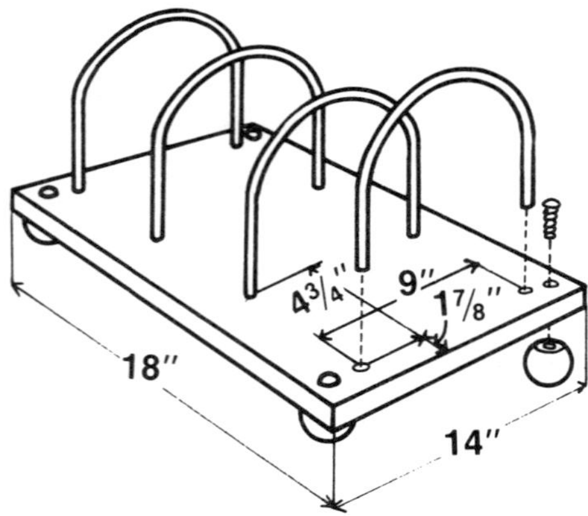


**Divided Record Holder**
**Courtesy: Reynolds Metals Company**

# Magazine Rack

This modern magazine rack is as fun to make as it is attractive. The basic idea is an aluminum frame that holds fabric in a W shape, but the design possibilities are endless.

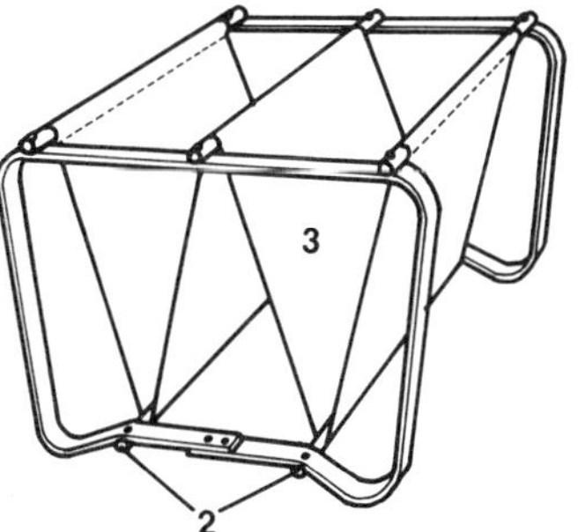


To duplicate our design for the side frames (1), begin with two 6 foot lengths of bar. Find the center of each bar and mark the bend points as shown in the illustration. Make the two top bends by shaping the bar around 2 inch diameter wood forms. (See Forming with Bending Jig, opposite side.) After making the two top bends to the desired angle, make the two lower bends with the same 2 inch form. Next bend the bar ends in the opposite direction until the two ends overlap, as shown. Allow about 1-1/2 inches of overlap, then trim and smooth the ends. Fasten the overlapped ends with two pop rivets. Make sure that the two side frames have profiles which are as identical as possible.

Cut five 17-1/2 inch lengths of aluminum rod for the cross pieces (2). File "flats" in both ends of each cross piece—3/4 inch in from the ends and about 1/16 inch deep—so that the rods have a flat surface to attach to the bar frames.

Starting with the top center cross piece, position each cross piece at its attachment points on the side frames and drill one fastening hole in each end with a 9/64 inch bit. Keep in mind, when attaching the cross pieces later on, that the top pieces are screwed *on top* of the frame and bottom cross pieces *underneath* the frame.

For the webbing, we recommend using a durable fabric such as cotton duck or vinyl. Our design requires about 60 inches of length. Cut the fabric 17 inches wide and make 3/4 inch hems on both sides. To create a snug fit, stitch a loop on one end, insert one of the cross pieces, and attach the cross piece to a top end of the side frames. Use #6-32 x 3/4 inch plated machine screws for all cross piece attachments.

Now attach the other top and bottom cross pieces and stretch the webbing around them in the W pattern. Tack the second end loop with straight pins around the final cross piece. Disassemble the two end cross pieces, remove the fabric, and complete the stitching. Then reassemble with the webbing looped around both end cross pieces.

**PROJECT CHECKLIST**
**Materials to Buy**

| Quantity | Material | Size | Length |
|---|---|---|---|
| 1 | Aluminum rod | 3/8" | 8' |
| 2 | Aluminum bar | 1/8" x 3/4" | 6' |
| 1 | Fabric or other material | as needed | |

**Hardware:** Ten #6-32 x 3/4" R.H. machine screws and nuts; four 1/8" pop rivets.

**Parts List**

| No. | Name | Quantity | Length | Width | Material |
|---|---|---|---|---|---|
| 1 | Frame member | 2 | approx. 58" | | 3/4" x 1/8" bar |
| 2 | Cross piece | 5 | 17-1/2" | | 3/8" rod |
| 3 | Webbing | 1 | approx. 60" | 17" | fabric, leather or other yard goods |

**Specific Tool Requirements:** Hand or electric drill—bit size 1/8"; Pop riveter.

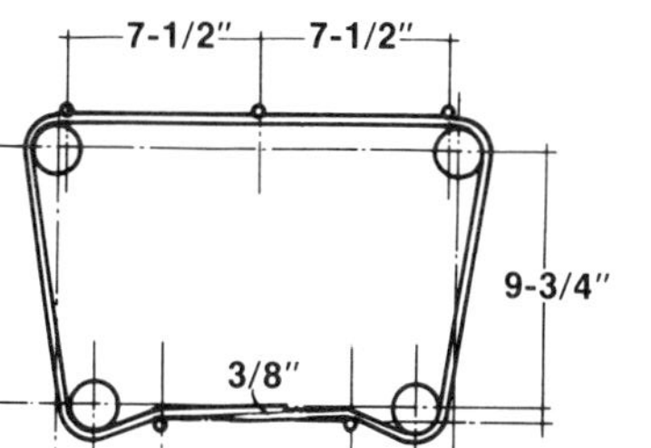


## Magazine Rack
**Courtesy: Reynolds Metals Company**

**PROJECT CHECKLIST**
**Materials to Buy**

| Quantity | Material | Size | Length |
|---|---|---|---|
| 2 | Aluminum angle | 1" x 1" x 1/8" | 8' |
| 3 | Aluminum angle | 1" x 1" x 1/8" | 6' |
| 1 | Aluminum tubing | 1" square | 6' |

**Hardware:** Sixteen #10-24 x 1/2" machine screws with nuts; seven aluminum pop rivets—1/8" dia.; two #10-24 x 1-1/4" machine screws with nuts.

**Parts List**

| No. | Name | Quantity | Length | Width | Material |
|---|---|---|---|---|---|
| 1 | Side member | 4 | 18" | | 1" angle |
| 2 | Upright | 4 | 14-3/4" | | 1" angle |
| 3 | Cross member | 4 | 48" | | 1" angle |
| 4 | Center divider | 1 | 48-1/8" | | 1" square tubing |
| 5 | Center brace | 1 | 56-1/4" | | 1" angle |

**Specific Tool Requirements:** Hand or electric drill—bit size: 3/16"; Coping saw; Pop riveter.

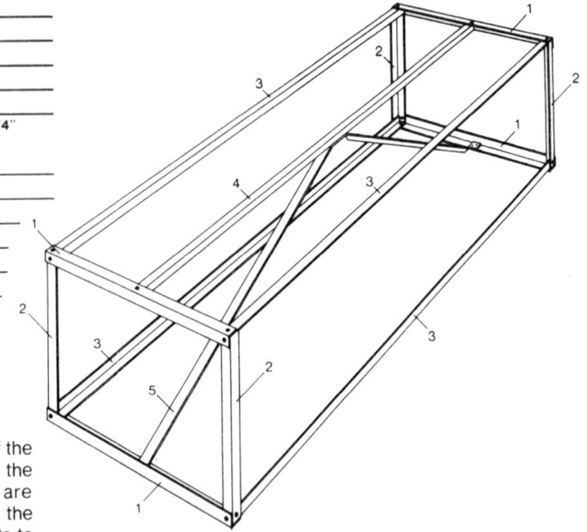

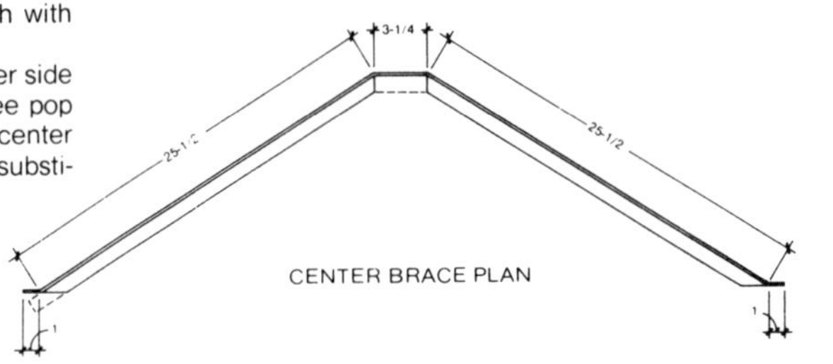

# Patio Planter

This aluminum-frame patio planter holds potted plants for outdoor display. It is designed to hold two rows of 8 inch pots so they will be safe from damage and can be moved in or out of the sun. It is made of 1 inch x 1/8 inch aluminum angle and 1 inch square tubing.

Cut side members (1), uprights (2), and the center brace (5) from 6 foot sections of aluminum angle. Cut cross members (3) from 8 foot angle sections. Cut and bend the center brace (5) as shown in the detail drawing.

Drill 3/16 inch screw holes through the side members and uprights where they join together at the corners. Attach these parts with #10-24 x 1/2 inch machine screws. With the same size drill bit and screws, attach the cross members. Be sure that the two screw holes at each corner are slightly offset so that the two screws do not interfere with each other.

Drill 3/16 inch screw holes at the center of the top side members and through the ends of the center divider (4) where these two parts are joined. Before drilling these holes, clamp the pieces in position and insert several clay pots to make sure the spacing is correct. Make any necessary adjustments in the positioning of the center divider, then drill the holes and attach with #10-24 x 1-1/4 inch machine screws.

Attach the center brace ends to the lower side members with pop rivets. Attach with three pop rivets where the center brace meets the center divider. (Pan head metal screws may be substituted for pop rivets.)

AFTER ASSEMBLY, ROUND OFF CORNERS WITH FILE TO REMOVE SHARP POINTS.

CENTER BRACE PLAN

**Patio Planter**
**Courtesy: Reynolds Metals Company**

# Index

## D



## E



## F

## T